Before THE Wind

3184
3005
45

Before THE Wind

A New Zealand Yachting Anthology

Compiled by Loris Chilwell

A. H. & A. W. REED
Wellington – Sydney – London

First published 1979

A. H. & A. W. REED LTD.
65-67 Taranaki Street, Wellington
53 Myoora Road, Terrey Hills, Sydney 2084
11 Southampton Row, London, WC1B 5HA
also
16-18 Beresford Street, Auckland
85 Thackeray Street, Christchurch 2

ISBN 0 589 01106 5

Typeset by Printset Processes (Christchurch) Ltd
Printed by Kyodo-Shing Loong Printing Industries Pte, Ltd, Singapore.

Contents

Acknowledgements

IT would have been impossible to assemble this book without the help of many kind people who have given generously of their time and facilities. Among these my special thanks go to John Malitte for advice and help throughout; to E. H. (Ted) Oldfield for the use of his yachting library; to all those members of the editorial, fileroom and photographic department staff of the *New Zealand Herald* who have helped me use their records so extensively; to Neil MacKinnon for lending his collection of yachting photographs; to Neil Robinson of Hodder and Stoughton for his co-operation.

Thanks also to the staffs of the Royal New Zealand Yacht Squadron, the Royal Akarana Yacht Club, the Banks Peninsula Cruising Club and to Mr D. G. Hogg, vice-commodore of the Royal Port Nicholson Yacht Club; also to staff members of the *Auckland Star,* the Auckland Institute and Museum, the Auckland Central Library and to Mrs "Trish" Davies of Hood (N.Z.) Ltd, Auckland.

Without the support of the publishers, authors and photographers who have allowed reproduction of their work and of the contributors of fresh material, there would have been no book. Acknowledgement of the source is made beneath each title or caption, and to each one of these so named goes my sincere thanks. Among these should be mentioned Mrs Dalice Manning for permission to use a story by her late father, P. A. Eaddy, from his book *Neath Swaying Spars.*

Although every effort has been made to contact the authors, publishers or beneficiaries of books now out of print, in the case of *The Venturesome Voyages of Captain Voss* enquiries have been unsuccessful.

Publisher's Note

WE live in a metric age, and strictly speaking most of the measurements in this book should be converted to metrics. But this has not always been appropriate, because while metrics may well be the formal language of the land the old imperial measurements linger on in the spoken word. To have metricated some spoken phrases in this book would have robbed them of their flavour.

In addition, some yachting terms simply cannot be converted to metrics. A "nautical" or "sea" mile, for example, is the length of one minute of latitude – it bears no real relation to the imperial land mile and should not, therefore, be converted to kilometres. A knot is the speed of one sea mile an hour and also cannot be changed.

Boat measurements have, however, been converted from feet to metres, with the exception that some traditional terms such as "eighteen-footer" have been allowed to remain. Sail areas and rating formulas have "gone metric".

Finally, some of the material in this book has been previously published elsewhere. Where measurements have been metricated in these cases the old imperial figure has been retained in brackets. The latter has also been sometimes retained when it has been part of reported speech. The author expresses her disagreement with the policy of metrication in this book.

Prologue

THE history of New Zealand as an inhabited land is owed to the sea, for our forebears all came that way — at first by canoe or sailing ship, later by steamer. Only some of the newest New Zealanders owe their presence to the air age, and no one lives more than half a day's travel from the ocean.

Among the crews working the white sails along the coasts, on the harbours and inlets which indent our long coastline, many are farmers, as much at home on the sea as on the land. Sailing boats are everywhere, scattered and hidden among the bays and estuaries, filling the marinas and boat harbours, at anchor in quiet havens or sailing the seven seas.

Down the decades New Zealanders have sailed their boats in ever increasing numbers, and many a good tale of adventure at sea has never got past the ears of a few cronies in a warm cabin over a couple of beers. Here are told tales of gales sailed through, calms endured, gear broken and repairs improvised, anchorages thankfully gained after misfortunes, races lost and won.

For those with the sea in their blood there is no music to compare to the sounds of sails, wind and sea on a good passage; no painting as wonderful as the scenes viewed under way or at anchor: no satisfaction as great as sailing in a good ship with good company; no stories as fascinating as the experiences of others who traverse the seas under sail.

To this band we dedicate this book.

Loris Chilwell

Why go sailing?

by IAN TRELEAVEN

From the *History of the Banks Peninsula Yacht Club* (Pegasus Press)

IMAGINE yourself one dark night on board a 30 ft (9 m) keeler banging to windward in a steep sea somewhere off Long Lookout on the north coast of Banks Peninsula.

You are standing your watch on deck as you fight your way to the east on a passage to Akaroa. You crouch there, wet and weary, thinking only of your approaching turn in the sack and why the lights of Little Akaloa fail to drop astern. Trickles of salt water meander between your oilies and down your back and under your armpits. The only solace is the warmth of your feet still dry in your sea boots.

Then the skipper, that unfeeling bastard, pokes his head up the companionway and decides that it is time to change to a smaller jib. You crawl for'ard, one hand for yourself and one for the ship, and with the watch below, painfully win the battle with the flogging sails. Back to the cockpit you struggle, now wet to the skin, your sea boots full and your eyes stinging with salt water. There is a queer feeling in your stomach.

"Now she feels better," says the skipper. You think: "Balls, what in hell am I doing out here?" But you have joined an elite band of sailors who each answer this question in a different way. The comfort of the cabin is only relative. Try sleeping on a beer barrel which is being kicked by a horse; the noise and the motion are just the same. Your bunk is no haven of rest as you brace yourself against each lurch and plunge, marvelling all the time that the screaming of the wind in the rigging and the crashing of the seas on the hull do not spell doom for this cockleshell. Then the damned fool cook decides it is time for a brew and the cabin fills with the stench of incomplete combustion from the primus. Once again your liver comes up to meet your lungs.

But this is ocean sailing and probably the most uncomfortable and slowest way to travel. The only pleasure is the feeling of achievement at the end of a successful passage, and the peace of a sheltered anchorage at the end of the battle. More and more people are finding this pleasure on the sea. Most sports in this automated world are contests between man and man, but sailing, like mountaineering, is a contest between man and the elements. It evokes a primal urge to meet the challenge of nature and to triumph.

And that is what sailing is all about. Or some of it anyhow. For the rest ask any yachtsman. He may not be able to put it in words, but he will know.

This is a wonderful sport, for once you are out on the ocean you are alone with the elements and all men are equal. It is probably the most democratic sport in the world, and in New Zealand people from all walks of life are enthusiastic yachtsmen. In 1921 Lord Jellicoe, then Governor-General, skippered his 14-footer (4.3 m) *Iron Duke* in the Sanders Cup contest. Brigadier Sir Bernard Fergusson was afloat whenever possible. So from governors-general, through all professions, trades and other occupations you find all men united in their common love of the sea.

Contrary to common opinion, yachting is not necessarily a rich man's sport. The New Zealander, with his natural ability to turn his hand to anything, quite often turns to boatbuilding, and in every fleet there is a large number of amateur-built yachts – real proof of the enthusiast's determination to sail his own ship.

Captain Voss's amazing canoe

by CAPTAIN VOSS

From *The Venturesome Voyages of Captain Voss* (first published in Yokohama in 1913, later by Martin Hopkinson Ltd.)

In this book the worthy captain tells of three voyages in tiny vessels, the second made in Tilikum, *an 11.5 m Canadian-Indian canoe hollowed out of one red cedar log. He sailed her round the world with a series of mates and eventually visited New Zealand, arriving in Invercargill in February 1903 and leaving from Auckland in August. He visited as many ports as possible and made a host of friends wherever he went. Captain Voss described his fitting out of the canoe thus:*

RED cedar is very durable, but soft and easily split. I was therefore obliged to take great precautions in strengthening her so that she would be able to withstand the rolling and tumbling about in hard sailing, or probably in the heavy gales she would most likely encounter during our trip. To put the little vessel in seaworthy condition, I bent, 24 in (610 mm) apart, 1 in (25 mm) square oak frames inside the hull from one end to the other, fastened with galvanised iron nails, and, as the canoe was not quite deep enough for my purpose, I built up her sides 7 in (180 mm).

Inside of the vessel I fastened "two-by-four" (50 × 100 mm) floor timbers, over which I placed a kelson of similar measurement, and fastened the same with bolts to a "three-by-eight" (75 × 200 mm) keel. On the bottom of the keel I fastened 300 lb (136 kg) of lead. She was then decked over and I built a 5 by 8 ft (1.5 by 2.4 m) cabin in her and a cockpit for steering, after which I rigged her with three small masts and four small fore and aft sails, spreading in all 230 sq. ft (21.3 sq. m) of canvas. The masts were stayed with small wire and all running gear led to the cockpit, from where the man at the helm could set or take in her sails.

In this strange craft, in which the greatest beam measurement was 1.6 m, the captain overcame every kind of trial the sea can provide, even losing his mate overboard in huge seas on a passage from Fiji to Australia. We rejoin him on the west coast of New Zealand.

We left Wanganui for New Plymouth, distant 100 miles. Cook Strait truly resembles its great namesake; like Captain Cook it is not to be trifled with. When it blows there, it blows hard and, owing to shallows and currents, a very bad sea is experienced.

Sailing from Wanganui with a moderate westerly breeze, accompanied by a hazy sky, we directed our course to the south-west. This served our purpose by enabling us to obtain sea room to meet a possible gale.

We were no more than about 20 miles off the land when the wind hauled into the south-west with fast increasing force. However, in order to clear the lee shore still further, we held our course until the wind compelled us to take in the sails and heave-to under sea anchor. To be only 20 miles off a lee shore in a heavy gale is rather risky, and we had gained little more. So to lessen the drift of our boat, we rigged a second sea anchor. For this purpose we employed our bunk boards, some old canvas and ropes, and one of our ordinary anchors. We discovered that with two sea anchors the drift did not exceed three-quarters of a mile an hour, and we therefore felt assured that the gale would have to blow quite a long time before *Tilikum* would strike the rocks. Having a riding sail over the stern besides, and after putting a light on deck, we both sat down in the cabin and, over a comfortable smoke, talked about our experiences on the Wanganui bar a few days previously.

Meanwhile the gale raged, and it proved to be the worst I experienced throughout my cruise in *Tilikum.* It was accompanied by large, hollow-breaking seas, and our little vessel had to do all she could and tried strenuously to rise to the top of the high combers. She rolled and pitched and, with heavy spray flying over her, sluggishly worked her way over the seas. It was the first gale my mate experienced in the *Tilikum,* and he complained of the continuous rolling and pitching, saying that it made him sick.

Before many hours had passed we were wishing for a change in the weather, but the wind did not moderate, and was later accompanied by heavy rain squalls. As we drifted more and more to landward, I commenced to feel a little uneasy; for I knew that if the gale lasted all day we would be smashed to pieces before nightfall. But a good shipmaster never reflects on danger until he be right near it. I stuck to this principle, and refrained from expressing my thoughts about the weather and the lee shore to my companion, but waited patiently for the change, which eventually came with unexpected suddenness. It was before daybreak, when the wind rapidly hauled into the south-east and the seas soon lost their dangerous breaking caps, when I steered *Tilikum* to the westward. At seven o'clock the weather cleared up, our approximate position being then 10 miles off the land and 40 miles from Cape Egmont.

As a reminder of the previous night's gale, a large swell was still settling through from the south-west; but otherwise the wind and weather were all that one could wish, and helped my mate's stomach to recover its equilibrium. Early in the afternoon, we rounded Cape Egmont and shaped our course for New Plymouth, which was then not more than 25 miles distant. However, the wind lightening during the night, we failed to make port until the following morning.

New Plymouth is a nice little town of about 5000 inhabitants and, owing to the splendid farming country surrounding it, is named by the

Maoris Taranaki, i.e., the garden of New Zealand. One great drawback to the city is the fact that there is no harbour.

When they discovered that we had come a long way in a canoe, the Maoris honoured us with a welcome in Maori style. In crowds they flocked to town from neighbouring districts to inspect our little vessel, and a song was given us in native language, followed by quite a long speech delivered by the chief. The natives then inspected the *Tilikum* inside and out and, having satisfied themselves that she was a real canoe, gave us three cheers before they departed.

Overseas in *Arethusa*

by RONALD CARTER

From *Little Ships* (A. H. & A. W. Reed)

The name of Hereward Pickmere of Whangarei has long been cherished among cruising yachtsmen in Northland waters for his excellent, detailed charts of coastline and anchorages. In 1975 it became even better known when his daughter published posthumously an atlas of his charts, which had been unobtainable for many years.

In September 1931 he took his yacht Arethusa *to Fiji, where he was engaged on government work. He lived on her and cruised in Fiji waters for four years, sailing her home in November 1935.*

THE auxiliary cutter *Arethusa* was built in Northcote, Auckland, and launched in 1917. She measured 33 ft 4 in (10.1 m) overall, 31 ft 4 in (9.5 m) on the waterline, 11 ft 7 in (2.5 m) in beam and 4 ft 6 in (1.3 m) in draft. A single-skin vessel, she was constructed on the carvel principle, having kauri planking 1 in (25 mm) thick, pohutukawa sawn frames, a plumb stem and a slightly raked elliptical American tuck stern. She carried a long bowsprit and a big gaff cutter rig. Her power plant was a 15 h.p. Kelvin sleeve engine, which gave her a speed of six knots in calm water.

"My ideas are, in many cases, unorthodox, and quite a number of yachtsmen will heartily disagree with them," Pickmere said. "However, I usually managed to get where I was going in a reasonably short time; always kept my ship in good order and appearance; dodged coral reefs or managed to get off them unaided for quite a number of years, and am still alive."

His logs of the journeys to and from Suva are of more than usual interest as logs go, because of the comments accompanying the entries and down-to-earth advice to any who might follow him.

Arethusa left Auckland for Suva at 2 p.m. on September 17 1931, and apart from a couple of loose ventilator cowls lost overboard there was little to comment upon during the first few days.

"September 21: Trouble with tail shaft. Uncoupled shaft, removed thrust housing and repaired damaged main thrust bearing. Note: accessibility of motor and shaft, proper tools and spare parts for ordinary repairs very important. Do not build machinery in where one cannot get at it comfortably and safely during an emergency.

"September 23: Wind north-west increased to gale force, heavy head sea. Close-hauled on port tack under full cruising canvas; 820 sq ft (40 sq m). Sea rising fast and motion of yacht easier. Note: mountainous

Right: **Captain Voss's amazing sailing canoe.** *Tilikum* **photographed during her New Zealand tour in 1903.** *Auckland Public Library Photograph Collection*

Above: **Hereward Pickmere's cutter** *Arethusa*, **back in Auckland in December 1935 after the events described in his log.** *Auckland Star*

Right: **A sad farewell. Erling and Julie Tambs and their children Tony and Tui on the day of** *Teddy's* **departure from Auckland.** *Auckland Institute and Museum from The Weekly News*

Above: Teddy **in happier days, sailing down Auckland Harbour under her newly fitted leg o'mutton mainsail at the end of 1931.** *The Weekly News*

Below left: **Johnny Wray's** *Ngataki* **racing past North Head, Auckland, in 1934. The events described in "Through the Hurricane's Eye" were two years away.** *New Zealand Herald*

Below right: Sheila II **photographed after her arrival, battered and worn, on the coast of West Australia during Adrian Hayter's long solo voyage home to New Zealand from England. Hayter's voyage began in August 1950 and ended at Westport in May 1956.** *West Australian Newspapers*

seas preferable to short chop, and faster time made in biggest seas, especially when sheets are eased. *Arethusa* does not like short choppy head sea, on account of her bluff bow, but manages very well in really big seas. High freeboard and broad beam gives her plenty of reserve buoyancy. Broad tuck stern, 9 ft (2.7 m) wide, found to be decided advantage in heavy following seas. Have never known a sea to come over aft, even when running through breakers or crossing a reef or bar.

"September 26: Fresh south-east breeze, speed six knots, log reading 1060 miles. 4.15 p.m. sighted Tuvana Reef from rigging, distant about 4 miles. Changed course to north-west for Matuku Island, distant 132 miles. Note: from here northwards, the wind was mostly east-north-east light to fresh, showing the advisability of making good easting before reaching trade wind zone.

"September 27: 6 p.m. anchored off Matuku Island reef. Two canoes with five natives aboard came out to visit us. 8 p.m. away again, under full sail.

"September 28: 6 a.m. fresh east-north-east wind; changed to first mainsail; now under 1000 sq ft (92 sq m). Broad lead on starboard tack. 10 a.m. passed Naselei lighthouse; gybed over and altered course to south-west. 12 p.m. off Makuluva Island, log taken in. Note: when in proximity to reefs in the tropics there is considerable risk of losing the log rotor, owing to barracouta, sharks and fish of the tuna species. For this reason I never used a log if it could be avoided. Did lose one rotor at night near Vomo Island. After saluting HMS *Canberra,* flagship of the Royal Australian Navy, brought up and anchored in the harbour of Suva.

"Total distance run, from Queen's Wharf, Auckland, to Suva: 1352 miles. Log read 1330 (2141), but was streamed outside Rangitoto Island in the Hauraki Gulf, and taken in off Makuluvu Island. Total time taken on passage: 10 days, 23 hours. Sailing time: 10 days, 21 hours. Average speed: 5.2 knots.

"Remarks on hull design and construction: buoyancy gained by high freeboard and broad beam most useful at sea. Overhangs are useless and detrimental in open-sea work. I consider *Arethusa's* tuck stern and underwater hull form aft to be the most seaworthy yet designed. Bow not too high, but may be better in head sea if lengthened a metre or so and rather finer above the waterline. Bluff bow is disadvantage in short head sea, although not too wet, and it is a distinct advantage off the wind owing to its buoyancy. *Arethusa* has a deadwood hull, keel being 20 in (500 mm) deep amidships, below garboard. I consider this unpopular method of construction to be much superior to the moulded-down garboards, as it is very much stronger; affords good protection to hull proper when grounding; does not leak; permits greater depth of outside ballast without excessive draft. Moulded garboards result in a deep inaccessible well inside, where leaks are most likely to occur, and are most difficult to find and stop.

"Arethusa's windward sailing is impaired by having to drag a

20 by 15 in (500 by 381 mm) propellor in a large deadwood aperture, which is more detrimental than the propellor drag, as it interferes with the slip-stream past the rudder.

"Her draft is 4 ft 6 in (1.3 m). This was found to be quite enough. Yachts on long commissions in tropics, where patent slips are not available, except in Suva, must occasionally go up for inspection on a beach. As rise and fall in tide is rarely more than 4 ft 6 in (1.3 m) and, in many places, only 3 ft or less, it is obvious that a shoal draft vessel of less than 6 ft (1.8 m) draft is desirable. *Arethusa* was slipped in Suva only once a year, usually at the end of March, when she received one coat of topside paint and two coats of anti-fouling. I usually beached her about September for another coat of anti-fouling paint, and that was all the protection she ever had against the teredo worms. I never had the slightest trouble with teredo, excepting in the hardwood false keel. A new hardwood keel was riddled after only one year, and was replaced by kauri pine, which was not attacked.

"Ballast: two tons on keel. I prefer iron keel to lead, as it is so much stronger and more rigid, and does not get chewed about on coral. *Arethusa's* keel ballast is cast iron, 11 ft (3.3 m) long, 15 in (380 mm) deep, and 8 in (200 mm) wide, and is set amidships, immediately below the keel, the spaces at the ends being filled with kauri pine deadwood, rising well up at the forefoot, and slightly aft to the heel of the rudder stock. The iron is protected by a mixture of red and white leads and zinc, and then copper-painted. I have no use for copper sheathing on a ship's bottom."

After describing *Arethusa's* strong construction and sail wardrobe in full, Pickmere continues.

"It will be observed that *Arethusa* appears to be grossly over-canvassed compared with other sea-going vessels, but I consider it to be a great advantage to be able to carry sufficient sail to be able to take advantage of fair weather, especially in the tropics. Most seagoing vessels, both large and small, have been wrecked in the tropics in broad daylight in flat calm weather through their inability to stem a 'set'.

"*Arethusa's* long boom – 31 ft (9.4 m) [10 ft – 3 m – of which is outboard] – seems to worry many people, but I have not yet experienced the difficulties which are said to arise at sea owing to excessive overhang in the main boom. Changing sails at sea is simplified by having a steel wire outhaul rope through a sheave at the end of the boom and bowsed taut by means of a double purpose tackle.

"It is most important to have sufficient lift in the foot of the mainsail, and it is sometimes necessary to top the boom when running in a high sea. *Arethusa's* spars and rigging are considered by some to be far too light. It is sufficient when I say that she has weathered a good many storms, but as yet she has not lost any spars. I have carried away backstays, bowsprit shrouds, preventers, and topmast shrouds, but only through "cracking on" in heavy seas.

"Dinghy: I always carry the dinghy across the tuck, on short bumpkins; I was informed about eight years ago that this was a dangerous practice; that it was sure to get smashed up in a heavy following sea. I still prefer to carry it in this position, especially in a heavy following sea, and have never had any worry from doing so. It is usually loaded with dunnage and spare gear when I am at sea. This method of carrying the dinghy would not be practicable with a narrow or overhanging stern, lacking the reserve buoyancy of *Arethusa.*

"Choosing an ocean cruiser. Given a choice of vessels, I should choose a craft of *Arethusa's* type: straight stem, a little finer perhaps, but not much; American tuck stern, identical with *Arethusa's*; cutter rig, capable of carrying large sail areas; long bowsprit and boom, with provision for jib-headed sails, besides the gaff rig. Not more than 5 ft (1.5 m) draft, nor less than 30 ft (9 m) on the waterline, high freeboard and broad beam.

"Open cockpit very safe for the watch on deck and has not yet shipped any dangerously heavy water. It also permits of considerable protection from the weather for the crew, and is very handy for breaking out or stowing sails and other gear without having to do it all on deck.

"A light lifeline, even 12 in (300 mm) high, above the sheer rails, is most useful. I should much prefer to undertake an ocean voyage in the *Arethusa* than any of the small cruising yachts I have yet seen, and prefer her rig to that of the Bermudian, yawl or ketch."

During *Arethusa's* homeward journey in November 1935 Pickmere encountered two storms, during the first of which the port preventer and backstay carried away. The sails were furled and *Arethusa* lay to a drogue and two oil bags while repairs were made. The second storm came up as they sailed down the coast from Cape Brett, so they took shelter in Little Omaha Cove for the night and continued the following day under close-reefed mainsail. It was during this last leg of his journey that Pickmere observed: "Yacht labouring under excessive sail, but unable to work crew forward to shorten down. Ship now fast becoming unmanageable. Eventually we managed to furl mainsail and continued under staysail."

His comments on this passage were characteristically full of good advice for those who would follow him.

"Sails. We would have progressed better had we carried the jib-headed trysail all the way, as the time saved by using the large mainsail was lost through breaking of rigging and gear. Had the preventer and backstay not carried away, we should not have been obliged to heave-to for repairs. Neither these or the peak halyard would have parted with the trysail set, whereas the gaff sail with its 23 ft (7 m) gaff places undue strain on the rigging, even when close-reefed, unless the sea is calm.

"Landfall. The reasons we made for the North Cape instead of following the shortest route were: (a) In the event of foul winds, to anchor inshore and await a favourable slant; (b) To take advantage of calmer water in the event of severe westerlies; (c) To run for shelter, or make harbour in the event of running short of fuel or provisions, due to calms; also to report our arrival should the radio fail, or we become overdue.

"Motor. Without the help of the motor during the long calms, we should have been caught out in the open sea during the second gale. This would not have mattered excepting that the passage would have occupied at least three days more, and there may have been some anxiety as to our safety in view of the bad weather.

"From my observations on this passage, with two gales, separated by a considerable period of calms and light and variable winds, I consider that a sea-going yacht should be equipped with a suitable motor and sufficient fuel, and that only jib-headed sails, or very short gaff mainsails be used. Also that a small vessel is just as safe, and infinitely more comfortable, hove-to under close-reefed storm sails, or reaching, rather than lying to a drogue, with or without oil streamed.

"*Arethusa* was heavily laden on both passages, but on the return trip had the disadvantage of heavy cargo stowed high up and throughout her entire length, instead of amidships, which is more suitable.

"The homeward passage occupied 13 days, six hours sailing time, the distance logged being 1411 miles at an average speed of 4.5 knots."

Farewell to *Teddy*

by ERLING TAMBS

From *The Cruise Of The* Teddy (Jonathan Cape)

In August 1928 Erling Tambs and his bride Julie set forth from Oslo, Norway, at the beginning of their married life, in their 38-year-old cutter Teddy, *a former pilot boat on the Norwegian coast. Together they cruised the oceans, gaining a dog called Spare Provisions and producing two children along the way. In New Zealand their second child, Tui, was born, and* Teddy's *journey ended here in 1932.*

In Little Ships *Ronald Carter describes the* Teddy: *"She was originally a Norwegian pilot cutter, designed by the notable naval architect the late Colin Archer, and measured 40 ft (12.2 m) overall, 13 ft (4 m) in the beam and 6 ft 6 in (2 m) in draft. She was an immensely powerful craft, of very heavy construction and although over 40 years old was still in good trim."*

THE farewells were over.

We had cast off the last mooring-rope and shaken the last friendly hand. Slowly, very slowly we glided away from the boat-steps. A navy pinnace offered to tow us past the harbour wharves. When, after belaying the tow-rope, I again turned my gaze towards the landing-stage, I saw that the crowd on the wharf was thinning out. Perhaps a score of friends still kept on waving: Mick-Jim-Nurse-Brownie-Cobs-Gibbie-Fred . . .

I suddenly felt a pang of regret, as I realised that I should probably never see again those lovable people who had favoured us with the rare and precious gift of friendship. Yet, I could not stay. I am not made to live in a well-ordered community for long. I am a wanderer:

It's like a book, I think, this bloomin' world,
Which you can read and care for just so long,
But presently you feel that you will die
Unless you get the page you're reading done,
An' turn another – likely not so good;
But what you're after is to turn 'em all.

Kipling

More than 13 months had elapsed since we first entered the harbour. Many times since then had we sailed in and out – on the trans-Tasman race, on our cruise to Tonga; many times. On the whole they had been 13 happy months.

Now *Teddy* cut her furrow through the waters of the Waitemata for the last time. To starboard arose the well-known cone of Rangitoto, visible from seaward at a great distance. To port, the sunny splendour of Cheltenham Beach glided by. We tried to pick out the trees sheltering the little house which had been our home for four months. Bathing maidens waved their towels in farewell.

Rangitoto Beacon sped by. Three hours later we sailed through the tide-rip in Whangaparaoa passage, and as dusk settled upon the surroundings it began to blow from the eastward. *Teddy* rolled heavily.

The cabin was flooded with farewell presents; in the galley, paper bags and packages of stores tumbled about. They should have been emptied into boxes and tins and properly stowed before we went to sea. In the bustle of farewells we had found no time for such details. Truly, we were hardly ready for sea. Also we were tired. We decided to run into Mansion House Bay at Kawau for the night.

Kawau is a beautiful little island some 30 miles from Auckland and a favourite goal for weekend excursions. There is a little pier in Mansion House Bay, alongside of which I could moor the boat without going to the trouble of anchoring. This latter was an essential consideration, seeing that the anchor was securely lashed in the forepeak and the chain stowed away in the stern.

When, about 10 at night, we made *Teddy* fast to the pier, it was pitch dark. Kawau had gone to sleep.

Rising the next morning, we found that the easterly had developed into a hard gale from the north-east. We were in no particular hurry to get to Brisbane, our next destination, so, instead of roughing it outside, we remained in the sheltered comfort of Mansion House Bay.

For three days the gale lasted, but by Wednesday morning, 9 March, it had exhausted itself and we departed. Leaving the shelter of the cove, we found a disappointingly light breeze of southerly wind blowing outside. The tides were at their maximum, running strongly northward and setting us backwards almost as fast as we could beat to windward against the light wind.

However, after several hours of sailing, we contrived to weather the reefs and thence lay south of Kawau, heading well to windward of the southern point of Challenger Island, a little rocky islet which is separated from the south-east end of Kawau by a narrow channel.

The gale had left a heavy swell, which broke thunderously over the rocky ledges of the point.

The breeze seemed to freshen a little as we were approaching these rocks, but the tide was setting strongly to leeward, so that when we were within 100 yards of the point, it was obvious that we could not weather it. The point then lay east of us, and *Teddy* headed south-east. I therefore put the helm down in order to go about.

Strange! She would not obey the helm.

The wind had suddenly died out.

However, *Teddy* was still moving ahead; she surely had sufficient headway to respond to the rudder, and there was no sea. Here, on the western side of the point, the water was almost smooth. Smooth indeed, abominably smooth! Glassy, like the polished surface of a river, where it hastens towards a precipice.

I tried again – drove the tiller hard to leeward, again and again. No response! Consternation seized me; the current had *Teddy* in her power!

With accelerating speed we were driven towards the point, on the other side of which the swell rose into gigantic breakers, which, hurling themselves against the rugged obstacles with thundering fury, sent rumbling waterfalls of foam over the rocky ledges. Sunken rocks off the point showed their frothy fangs, 30, 20 yards away. Oh, how I hated them, those rocks, those breakers, those snarling fangs, threatening, sneering, evil, inevitable . . .

I rushed forward and ran out the heavy sweep, tore and pulled and rowed with impotent rage. My wife cast off the halyards. The sails came clattering down.

Like a mill-race the current swept round the point.

Then the sweep broke.

I grabbed the spinnaker-boom in a foolish attempt to stop a weight of 25 tons driven onward at five knots speed. A desperate man will do stupid things.

Now, we were close against it. We felt the lift of the surge. Cold breaths of moisture-laden atmosphere chilled us. My heart shrunk within me: *Teddy's* end was near.

We struck the first time. I felt how the rocks crunched beneath our keel. *Teddy* heeled over, hard, then, righting herself, was lifted again and carried onward, past the point, right into the breakers . . .

I shouted to my wife to fetch little Tui from out of her bunk in the cabin. The same instant *Teddy* was seized by an enormous wave, lifted high, and with one big sweep, thrown sideways against the rugged rocks. Then everything seemed to happen at the same time. Planks crushed, spars splintered. Rumbling – crashing – shrieking – rushing waters – and above it all the thundering roar of ten thousand unfettered demons of the waves.

Sometimes buried in foam so that we lost our breath, sometimes clinging to an almost perpendicular deck, when the sea was on the return, we needed all the presence of mind that we could muster. The mainboom had come adrift. One of the topping lifts had jammed in a block-sheave aloft, keeping the heavy spar suspended just over the cabin coamings and leaving it to sweep wildly from side to side, hardly 20 in (500 mm) above the deck, whenever the boat rolled. The boom was like a huge club swung with deadly intent by a cunning giant hand. To dodge its shattering blows, we were continually forced to flatten out on the foam-swept deck.

Tony in his canvas harness, tied by a short rope to the rail, was in immediate danger. I succeeded in undoing his rope and then, in that fraction of a second when the main boom hung still, while gathering momentum for another sweeping assault, I ventured to leap onto the rugged face of the rock. It was a desperate chance. For one terribly long moment I hung by one hand, with the other attempting to support Tony, whose grip around my neck was gradually loosening, while the rush of returning water seemed to load insufferable tons of weight on to us. The next moment I found a foothold and climbed on to the ledge, where I left Tony with strict orders to grab a hold and hang on. Then I returned to the boat.

Again and again the receding surf would drag the doomed boat away from the cliff, brutally tearing her trembling timbers over an uneven rocky bottom, bumping her, ripping her with jagged teeth and leaving her heeling to seaward with the lower part of a precipitous deck submerged in surging foam and the main-boom end swinging insanely about in the milky whirlpool. Then the next wave would pick her up and dash her against the rocks with the full force of her own weight. Oh, how I suffered!

I had taken Tui from Julie and told the latter to jump ashore as a chance offered. With my wife ashore to receive the baby, our chances of saving her would be all the better, I judged.

My wife slipped, or jumped short, or was washed overboard, none of us knows exactly how it happened. I only knew that I saw Julie disappear in the seething foam between the boat and the rocks. I saw my wife being whirled about in the churning, roaring surf amid countless jagged spikes protruding from the rocks. At intervals I saw her head, a foot or an arm above the seething waters, now close to the cliff, now away out. I saw her clinging to the rocks in a desperate attempt to climb up even while the next breaker came thundering in. I pointed seaward, shouting for her to try to swim clear of the surf. Then the breaker was upon her. I could do nothing until I had saved Tui. There was no place on the boat where I could leave the baby even for 10 seconds without committing her to certain death. As it was, I had sufficient reason to fear that Tui would drown in my arms before I could bring her ashore. But it is hard to see one's best friend fighting a desperate battle for life without being able to give her assistance.

However, Julie had not been battered to death against the rocks. She came to the surface again and grabbed hold of the mainsheet, but before I could tend her a helping hand, the boom ran out, jerking tight the sheet and hurling my wife away.

Somehow I contrived to bring Tui ashore. Hurriedly I handed her to Tony, instructing him to look after her and not to leave her, no matter what happened. I then hastened to the rescue of my Julie.

But in the meantime she had achieved the seemingly impossible feat of swimming clear of the surging breakers. With infinite relief I saw her making for a large piece of floating timber on the sheltered side of the point, meantime using the broken sweep for a support. A motor-launch

I had not previously noticed had put out a dinghy to her assistance. She called out to me in a voice which showed that she was very much alive. Well, she had certainly proved her mettle.

Tony, too, had behaved like a hero. Without a word he had taken to his duties like a man, sitting on the rocks where I had left him in charge of Tui. He never budged, even when the breakers washed over them occasionally. In all my misery I could not help feeling proud of him.

Spare Provisions had also been washed overboard. I had seen the poor dog fighting in the surf, but could do nothing for her. However, she had saved herself; limping and bleeding, she joined our little group of castaways.

The fishing-launch brought us back to Kawau. When the family had been put up at the Mansion House, I returned to the wreck to see if anything could be salvaged. It proved impossible; the seas were continually sweeping over the hull, which was waterlogged and badly strained. Her flag, the proud ensign of the Royal Norwegian Yacht Club, awarded her for her merits, was still flying, half-mast, where it had jammed in the rush of events. "As if *Teddy* bemoaned her own end!" said one of the fishermen. I felt differently. To me it seemed as if my noble boat mourned not only her own funeral but the end of a beautiful dream and the misfortune of the master who loved her.

I turned away. I had seen her dear and pretty lines for the last time.

When I returned on the following morning *Teddy* – my kingdom – had vanished.

Through the hurricane's eye

by JOHNNY WRAY

From *South Sea Vagabonds* (A. H. & A. W. Reed)

In 1931, out of a job and out of money, Johnny Wray started building Ngataki *from kauri logs salvaged from coastal beaches near Auckland. He designed her himself along the lines of Erling Tambs's* Teddy, *substituting square bilges and a square stern as they were easier to build. His book tells of all the difficulties he surmounted in building and launching the boat and his subsequent voyages. We join him in March 1936, when* Ngataki *met a tropical cyclone while being sailed to Norfolk Island. His crew were Eddie Ansell and Don Alexander.*

WE had broached-to and it was quite clear that we had carried on too long. This was a bit too much for a joke. We would have to heave-to, even though it was a fair wind.

The staysail, now viciously kicking and thrashing, was lowered and lashed down and the mainsail was hauled hard inboard, as we hove-to. *Ngataki* came nearly head-to-wind and began to ride the waves easily, but she had a lot of water in her – 6 in (150 mm) above the floor – and she was not too buoyant.

Eddie was down below pumping. Keeping a weather eye open to windward for breaking seas, I attempted to relash the dinghy, which had broken adrift on deck. I was naked now, so was Don. It was no good wearing any clothes on deck under these conditions.

The wind gradually increased to full hurricane force and the mainsail was lowered, for no canvas, however strong, could have stood up to it. The seas were rapidly mounting higher and higher. Away to windward I saw a gigantic breaker advancing. From a slightly different direction another huge sea was coming towards us, and it began to look as though those two hills of water would just about meet where our little ship lay. "Look out Don," I yelled. I sprang into the rigging and climbed up the shrouds. I got high above the deck, but there was no getting away from THAT sea.

I have a dim recollection of an enormous wall of white, seething water bearing down on us, a violent, sickening crash, and the next instant I was under water. There was a deafening, roaring noise in my ears, and all the forces of the world were pulling me away from the shroud to which I clung.

The wire was torn from my grasp and I was in green water, somewhere below the surface. I swam to the surface and there, a few yards away, I saw the keel of my *Ngataki* sticking up in the air. A bit of the topside was also showing, but it seemed she was sinking fast. We were 100 miles off land; there was no hope of swimming THAT far through shark-infested waters.

This, then, was the end.

For something better to do, I swam over to poor *Ngataki* and climbed up the topside. A moment later I saw Don climbing on the stern. We looked at each other and grinned weakly. Then, wonder of wonders, the boat began to rotate and the mast appeared. It began to rise out of the water as the gallant *Ngataki* slowly righted herself.

It was the proudest moment of my life seeing my ship right herself; even relief at being saved from a watery grave gave place to pride at that moment. I actually grinned; "How's that?" I yelled to Don. "Wonderful!" he shouted. It was. That the ballast did not break loose and burst through the cabin-floor can be attributed only to a merciful Providence. Then Eddie's head popped out of the half-open hatch. He had been down below the whole time. Sitting on the cabin ceiling in the dark, Eddie had decided he was on his way to the bottom of the sea. Now he was intensely surprised and relieved to find the ship was still above water.

But she was only just floating. Water had poured through the partially closed main hatch and there was nearly 3 ft of water in the cabin. In calm water the *Ngataki* had 12 in (300 mm) of freeboard, but now the decks were awash. We would have to work like maniacs if we were to keep the ship afloat. Our decks were swept clean. Our leeward bulwarks had been torn off and, together with lifebuoys, spars, dinghy etc., were floating away down to leeward. But that mattered little. The main thing was to keep the boat afloat till we could get a bit closer to land. It was too far to swim from there.

"Go for it, lads, bail for your lives!" And we did, with pots and buckets and everything we could lay hands on. If we got another breaker now, we would never survive it; I groped in the water-filled lockers until I found our five gallon drum of whale oil. Then I attempted to pour it overboard on the waters to windward of us. But, of course, it was a hopeless task. The shrieking wind blew the oil back over my naked body and over the ship. What happened next would have been funny at any other moment but at the time the humour of it was not apparent. Crouching on deck – with the wind hurricane force it was impossible to stand up – I tried to get a grip on something to steady myself. But the ship was so slippery from being sprayed with the blighted whale oil that I could not get a hold on anything and the next thing I knew I was being blown – sliding on my seat – right down to the stern of the ship. There I luckily grabbed the horse, or I would have gone overboard.

With an axe I cut the boom, gaff, and sail from the mast and on a couple of warps I let the whole affair out over the bow to act as a sea anchor. But it made no difference. I let out more gear on ropes but she still would not ride head to wind. Our only hope was to run before it. I pulled in all the gear from the bow and let it out over the stern. It sounds a simple operation but it took a couple of hours to do. I could not afford to get any help from the other two, for they were bailing incessantly.

All our sails, spars, anchors, and oil drums were tied to ropes and let out over the stern until we had lines and ropes trailing behind. The move proved very effective and as long as we kept running dead before it the floating gear behind remained to windward of us.

It was now about 6 p.m. and getting dark. We carried on, I keeping the ship dead on in the ever-increasing seas, while Don and Eddie bailed for their lives. Down below it was utter chaos. Everything that would float was swirling about on top of the water. Lockers, drawers and cupboards were all being smashed and burst open by the force of water surging below as the ship rolled and pitched. The floating debris considerably hampered Don and Eddie in their bailing, and every now and then a bit of board or a locker door would come flying out of the hatch as it got in the way of their buckets. They stuck to it like heroes, carrying on hour after hour. It was a case of life and death and we all knew it.

The wind blew harder than ever. I had never known anything like it. I think it was also raining, although I could not distinguish rain from spray or anything else. It was pitch dark and there was no light of any sort on board. I steered by the wind on the back of my neck.

Endless hours went by and the water below was, if anything, gaining on us. We had shipped no seas, thanks to the gear streamed behind us, so we must have developed a bad leak somewhere. About midnight – we could only vaguely guess the time, our clocks and watches having become useless – I handed the tiller over to Don, while I crawled around the boat feeling if any of the ports had been smashed. But they were all sound. Then I remembered a little generating plant that I had recently fitted. Sure enough, the engine had come adrift and water was pouring in through the exhaust pipe. No wonder the bailers were making no headway! I plugged it up and resumed my steering.

Further endless hours dragged by. It was the longest night I had ever spent. So great was the force of wind that we were doing about five knots under bare poles and dragging all the gear behind. I could not look back, for the rain or spray, whichever it was – hurt too much, but I could take a quick peep now and then by covering my face with my hands and looking through the slits between my fingers. But all I could see was, naturally enough, fairly harmless.

At long last day dawned – a grey, cheerless dawn, but infinitely better than the horrors of darkness. We carried on all day, taking in turns to bail, bailing, bailing, always bailing.

About 3 p.m. the wind lightened as we got nearer the centre of the hurricane, but the seas seemed to get even higher and mounted and pitched upwards from all directions. But, with the wind losing strength, the seas lost some of their terrifying breaking crests which are so dangerous to small craft. During the comparatively calm spell the water was bailed out nearly down to the floor. We had a good pump on board, but with the mess that was now in the bilge, it continually got blocked and was useless. I took the opportunity of straightening out some of the rigging. A lot of the gear behind had broken away, but luckily the mainsail was still there. It was hauled in and fastened, with the boom and gaff, back in place on the mast. I climbed the gyrating mast and rove a couple of temporary halyards to haul the sail up if necessary, for we must be getting somewhere near the New Zealand coast and we might be wanting that sail soon.

It grew dark and soon after the wind started howling again, this time from the sou'west. But tonight it was not so bad. We had most of the water out and the ship was more buoyant. Again the night seemed endless. Towards morning I thought I heard the roar of distant breakers, but the night was pitch black and nothing could be seen. At the first sight of dawn I went on deck and looked around, and there, less than a mile away down to leeward, was the rocky New Zealand coastline, with merciless surf, clearly visible in the half-light, thundering in.

No time was to be lost if we were to avoid being wrecked. Luckily, the wind had now moderated and we could show a little sail. The staysail and double-reefed mainsail were hoisted; we had to try somehow to claw off that rocky shore against the high wind and mountainous sea. We plugged along, the ship being more underneath than above the water. The spray flew high over the masthead, but we were getting no farther from the rocks.

We shook out a reef in the mainsail and carried on under single reef. *Ngataki* knew what was wanted of her. She heeled right over and ploughed along. If anything carried away, we were done. But the gear stood up to it and I was grateful for the heavy mast and the stoutness of the shrouds and canvas. Our gallant little craft climbed up each wall of water, shattered the top of the sea and sank into the trough again. We were winning now – gradually drawing away from the hungry surf.

About 2 p.m., by the sun, Cape Maria Van Diemen was sighted through the haze. Once around there, we would be safe, but about five miles off the cape there is a shallow patch which breaks even in moderate weather. Now, as we drew closer, the seas became terribly confused and started to break in all directions. Suddenly a huge sea broke 50 yards away on our beam; then one broke on the other side of us. Our stern lifted high in the air and the bow went down so far I thought we were going to turn a complete somersault. With a roar we started to plane on the sea. The bow wave was colossal and there was a white streak of foaming water level with the deck from bow to stern as we rushed madly along at an unbelievable speed for nearly a minute. I threw every ounce of weight on the tiller to keep her dead before it. If we had swerved a fraction of a point we would have broached-to and all would have been lost. But we were lucky again and soon we were out of that ungodly sea. Darkness found us past the cape in the relatively calmer waters of the East Coast.

There followed three days of uneventful sailing down the coast. Conditions were fairly comfortable, as comfortable as wringing-wet clothes, wet bunks and water sloshing round the floor would allow, for the weather was by no means fine and we could do no drying.

At long last we reached port. Good old Auckland! There never was a crew more pleased to see it. Terra firma at last! There had been many times during the last few days when we thought we would never see land again.

Auckland had not suffered the full force of the storm, the centre of the cyclone passing about 300 miles away. Nevertheless the damage done around the waterfront was very extensive. When we saw the wrecked boats, the smashed retaining walls and other obvious signs of storm damage, we considered ourselves very lucky to have escaped with our lives.

Since that unhappy trip I have been very careful. Now I am a little afraid of the sea. Captain Slocum once said that a little fear at sea is a good thing for safety. I believe him. For just a little fear will keep you up to the mark. It will make you keep everything shipshape and it will make you prepared for anything ALL the time. In a wellfound boat, if you do this, no harm will befall you. But, if you do not treat Father Neptune with the respect he undoubtedly deserves, he will, sooner or later, creep up behind you with that lump of lead piping. And that will be that!

In 1977 Ngataki *was still going strong and sailing in the Hauraki Gulf. During World War II, Johnny Wray was in the Air Force, often overseas, and could not look after her too well. So she was sold. He checked her again when she was surveyed for a new owner after 45 years service and found her still sound, with no signs of rust from the fencing wire used for fastenings, no sign of leaks from the old pyjamas and shirts used for caulking. She was in excellent order.*

After the war Johnny Wray returned to the cottage he had built for himself at Waiheke. Here he built his second yacht Waihape, *a two-master 12.81 m long with a 4.03 m beam, both house and yacht being built of material found on local beaches. House, yacht and owner have remained in good order and the blue-painted* Waihape *is sometimes to be seen anchored off Auckland's St Heliers Bay as Johnny Wray revisits old haunts.*

First leg of a long journey

by ADRIAN HAYTER

From *Sheila in the Wind* (Hodder & Stoughton)

Adrian Hayter spent six years on his solo voyage home from England, interrupting the journey from time to time to earn enough money to continue. He endured many storms and tribulations, eventually arriving at Westport in May 1956, after a Tasman crossing which took 78 days.

This story describes the voyage from England to Gibraltar.

Hayter's yacht has belonged to a succession of owners since he brought her back to New Zealand. In 1977 she was a participant in the Devonport Yacht Club's two-person race around the North Island, sailed by a husband and wife team, Peter and Lyn Nelson.

ON Saturday morning, 12 August 1950, I slipped quietly away from the Berthon Boat Company, motored past the Royal Lymington Yacht Club unnoticed, much to my relief, turned off the engine and put on sail with two reefs down. The first thrill of this venture came as *Sheila* lifted to the swell and heeled to the first gust by Jack-in-the-Basket at the mouth of the river. The 1400 miles to Gibraltar seemed like a trip to the moon.

All that night I beat down Channel against a gusty sou'wester. It rained a lot, and I was twice nearly run down by steamers coming up from astern. It was so unusual sitting alone in the darkness of an exposed cockpit, huddled against the cold and wet and partly bemused by the one tiny compass light, that I felt I was a mere solitary atom in a great empty void and forgot about shipping. The noise of their engines made me turn around to see the red and green lights, with the mast-head lights in line.

I slept for an hour the next day but stayed at the helm all night; there was too much shipping about to sleep safely, apart from the fact that it takes time to get used to sleeping alone at sea, leaving the ship to look after herself. That night the mizzen crosstrees broke in a squall and next morning, being very tired, I decided to go into Teignmouth where there were friends.

On the 19th the Met. Office told me the weather was uncertain until the outcome was decided between a depression over Iceland and an anti-cyclone over Central Europe. The issue had still not been decided on the 20th or even the 21st, and so I sailed that morning. An extract from my diary written after sailing tells of that better than my memory now:

"It is a strange feeling starting off on a trip like this – God knows how or where it will end. I can still see the white houses and hotels along the front, the red cliffs, the steep forehead of the Ness, and behind are the green hills of Devon. It is a beautiful day, a light southerly breeze and a warm sun. As I was getting the dinghy on board before slipping the mooring a young chap rowed alongside and asked to come with me. A launch caught me up going down the Teign, a photographer on board, and two reporters (one a woman) sat below while the photographer did his stuff. Later they remarked on my books – Charles Morgan, Huxley, Plato, Shaw, Tagore, and so on. The man asked, 'Are you in search of a new philosophy?' and the woman, 'Is there a girl at the other end?' They were nice.

"Now the launches and speed boats have gone, I've had lunch, cleaned up, and am enjoying the sun, looking back over the England I've grown to love so much and wondering if I'll ever see it again."

During the first two days out of Teignmouth, the wind was erratic and I was continually changing jibs, reefing and unreefing, and snatching odd hours of sleep during daylight because of the fear of being run down at night. The glass dropped slowly and steadily, assuring me by the evening of the 23rd that I was shortly going to experience my first gale.

The gale developed next morning so I hove-to and for the first time changed to storm canvas. I had practised this in port, but it was a very different matter at sea. Before beginning I read it up again in the text book, and the only thing that this forgot to mention was the most difficult part of the whole procedure – how to stay on board while doing it. In such jobs, when both hands are used, you hang on with your legs, the crook of an arm, the point of your shoulder, and often use your teeth as an extra hand.

I had fervently hoped that I would not meet a gale until I had gained some experience of the sea, but running into one was the best thing that could have happened. I sat for hours in the open cockpit as *Sheila* lay hove-to under storm canvas, because being down below under closed hatches frightened me out of my wits. Whenever a breaker crashed on board it sounded as it the masts had gone, planking and timbers smashed to pieces and immediate sinking was inevitable. I'd rush to the hatch, tear it open expecting to see chaos, to view *Sheila* as if nothing had happened; and nor had it. Later, common sense told me that if a breaker did smash the decks I would know about it without the need to look above.

Also when below there was a feeling of neglecting the ship, of not being ready for emergency at the time it was most likely to happen. For the next 48 hours of that storm I hardly left the cockpit, and during that time I did nothing for the simple reason there was nothing to do. The sails were set hove-to, reduced to their smallest size, the helm was lashed, and I could do no more but leave it to the gods. I was wearing myself out quite unnecessarily and very stupidly.

"Our friends' kind thoughts seemed to be tinged with the colour of doom." Tom and Lydia Davis's *Miru* leaves Wellington on her storm-tossed voyage to Peru.
New Zealand Herald

"A pair of young greenhorn sailors sailed away in a home-built boat on a journey that took them round the world." Tony Armit *(right)* and "Tig" Loe — and *Marco Polo.* The photograph of the young New Zealanders relaxing on deck was taken in Florida. *John Mallitte*

This gale also gave me the essential confidence that *Sheila* could look after herself in big seas. Time and again a huge steep sea, a veritable wall of water, seemed to fill the sky above and I'd think, "She can't get over this one," but *Sheila* rose gracefully, somehow slipped around the jagged crest, and sank easily into the next trough.

I had no idea whether or not *Sheila* would sail in that weather under storm canvas, and there was only one way to find out; it was something I had to know for the safety of future navigation, when storms might catch me in congested waters or close in to a lee shore. That sail proved to be one of those thrilling, fantastic experiences you never forget – like your first solo loop in an aeroplane, your first fast run on skis, anything in which temerity and doubt are banished to leave a whole new field of adventure open to you. And adventure in this light is freedom.

I had splashed through rough seas in a motor launch around the coast of New Zealand, but here in the Channel there were noticeable periods as we climbed the hills. From the top was a view to all horizons, of the long lines of rolling white-topped seas and the deep watery valleys between them. Sometimes *Sheila* slid swiftly down the steep slope into these, at others her bow hovered before we fell headlong down a watery cliff to the valley floor below, only to land, it seemed, on rubber cushions. *Sheila* said, "You look after me, my boy, and I'll look after you." And that was fair enough; it was like being back with Gurkha troops.

Over the next two days I got very tired. I only slept by day in hour snatches and this robs sleep of much value, delaying fatigue enough to carry on for a few more hours but building up no reserve of energy. The long night hours in the exposed cockpit were bitterly cold; there was much spray, at times breakers smothered the ship, and heavy belts of rain added to the misery.

In these days too I overworked myself through sheer inexperience. I'd think the wind had eased, and change from storm canvas to the closely reefed mainsail only to overburden *Sheila* unmercifully, and have the weary process of changing back again. I had little knowledge of what stresses and strains *Sheila,* the rigging and the sails could take, which also led to much anxiety and needless worry.

(Prior to this voyage I had never been out of sight of land in a small boat. Since arriving in England a year before, I had sailed mainly around the Solent, putting the theory of the textbooks into practice; before that I had only once before stepped on board a yacht when a Christmas party had called at my home on d'Urville Island, New Zealand. We youngsters had gone on board to "see inside" – beyond this and brief outings in sailing dinghies my yachting experience was nil.)

I wrote, "I have to stay awake all night in case of shipping. It's bitterly cold and I'm not really enjoying this very much. There are several ports on both the French and English coasts within easy reach, but I know if I go into a port without beating this ruddy gale I'll never leave land again."

Then came the first Sunday, and a blessed day indeed, a beautiful sunny day with gentle wind, and the sea died to let *Sheila* sail herself happily towards Ushant. I brought out the soaking mass of clothing from below to dry on deck, and cooked myself a curry lunch. When stripped to change into dry clothes I was amazed to find that my body was black and blue from head to foot, and in the most unexpected places, from being knocked around during the rough weather.

That night I put lights in the rigging and slept dead to the world until 8 o'clock the next morning, and it was a beautiful morning. This was the first real sleep I'd had since leaving, and there was something wonderful and strangely exciting in waking to such a lovely day out of sight of land, of ships, of people. And that new world was me.

With dusk a strong westerly came in from the Atlantic, driving *Sheila* hard across the increasing seas to fly past the winking light of Ushant – spray flying, flashes of blue lightning and giant rolls of thunder, and sometimes the moon shone briefly between the towering white columns of the thunder-clouds to show the upward curve of the white sails, the wildness of the tossing seas and their racing black shadows. Ushant died astern and home waters were behind me.

The westerly continued all next day carrying huge seas before it, but lacking the viciousness of those in the Channel. I hove-to for a couple of hours sleep during the day, and sailed all through that night into the next dawn. I wanted to get out of the notorious bay as soon as I could, and there were another 300 miles to go. I slept for an hour after dawn but by noon was steering so badly, half-dazed with fatigue, that I feared that if anything went wrong I'd be in no fit state to put it right. And once my head nodded forward as a sharp sea lifted *Sheila's* quarter (the corner of the stern) catapulting me right out of the cockpit to land impaled on the lee stanchion. That was another lesson, and thereafter when tired in rough weather I always tied myself in with a lashing round the waist. I hove-to and slept again.

Two hours later I shot out of my bunk and through the hatch with the realisation that a loud hooting in my dreams was real. A big tanker (the *Shelldrake*) was rolling heavily beside me, the skipper peering over the end of the bridge right into my hatchway, and I heard his laugh as I appeared frowsy and alarmed. They must have had a discussion before leaving their course to investigate this lone yacht apparently unattended. I regretted the intrusion, but was grateful to a ship which troubled to ascertain that help was not needed.

The weather looked black to the south-west, and as the day grew old wind came. I tore the mainsail badly getting it up, so changed to storm canvas and let *Sheila* sail herself away from the shipping lane so I could get more sleep during the night. I was too tired to mend the sail then.

Next day was fine with a gentle breeze, so, I mended the tear and let *Sheila* sail herself to the south while I did all those things I ought to have done the day before. It is very damaging to morale to leave those things undone that you know ought to be done – "and there is no health in us". How exactly that describes the feeling, of apprehension, of "butterflies in the tummy". It is also (I have found) the basic cause of bad temper, even when alone. The solution is obvious.

I ran the engine to charge the batteries, filled respective containers with meths, kerosene and petrol from the bulk stocks, cleaned the navigation lights and trimmed the wicks, tightened the port shrouds, cut out some chafe in the starboard runner (an extra back-stay for the main-mast) and put in a long splice (copied from the book!). I gargled with antiseptic as I'd had a sore throat for a couple of days, washed up the dirty dishes and put them away, scrubbed out the galley, burnished the draining board and degreased the sink. Clothes and blankets were aired and re-stowed, spare sails neatly rolled and stowed, cabin tidied, ropes above deck coiled neatly, and the bilges pumped dry. In fact *Sheila* was as shipshape as the day she left, and after a shave I felt even better than I myself had on that momentous day.

Cape Finisterre was somewhere about 120 miles to the south, and as I'd now been four days out of sight of land I took a sun sight, the first ever. Before sailing from England I had started a correspondence course on celestial navigation, and gone to retired master mariners for instruction, but all these went far too much into detail for me. I can only understand theory when I put it into practice, and so having bought the unnecessary nautical tables and an almanac I threw the papers on board for further study when the time came. The risk of such a system I offset by planning to keep about 100 miles offshore after sighting Spain, to allow for errors while under instruction. It would be impossible to miss Gibraltar, wedged in between two great Continents.

The position line obtained from this sight ran near my DR position, and as clouds were coming up to obscure the sun I headed south-east to the shipping lane, which runs near enough in a straight line from Finisterre to Ushant. This line I crossed with the position line, and from the intersection laid a course for Finisterre. This showed up two days later.

The next four days and nights were spent mostly encased in a thick fog. There was a big lazy swell and little wind – conditions which give a sailor a glimpse of hell. If you leave the sail the rolling of the ship slams the sails and spars from side to side, jerking the blocks, wearing the sails, and chafing the gear; if you take sail down you understand the meaning of the term "rolling her guts out". The almost continual hooting of fog-horns on that busy shipping lane did not help to ease the strain. My fog-horn had made a raucous blare in harbour, but in that great white loneliness it sounded like a toy flute. Sometime ships passed so close, but invisible, that their breaking wash smothered the side-decks.

As each day and night passed with little change in conditions I reached a stage of frustration which nearly drove me mad, and the engine was not much help because I wanted to save at least ten gallons of fuel in case of need in the confines of Gibraltar Strait. The noise or movement made sleep uncertain, and any breath of wind I used to the full, at whatever hour of the day or night it came.

Then I began to feel really ill, and searched desperately for the cause. A few days previously the tea jar had been broken, and rather than throw the tea away I'd sifted the tiny splinters of glass from each lot before use; perhaps some had been missed. Or perhaps some tinned food had been faulty, or perhaps the remains of some dread tropical fever still lurked in my blood. It felt like all of these – a splitting headache, extreme lassitude and depression, and a wracked tummy which in five minutes miraculously converted all solids into liquid. So I took no food and increased my weakness further.

Yet the ship had to be worked and I must have made progress which my diary is too vague to show. My log tells me that I took sights two days later, putting me 40 miles off the Spanish coast, which was safe enough.

Before going below to make a cup of cocoa at dusk I took a routine glance around the horizon, and to my horror saw a mass looming out of the fading light broad on the starboard bow. Compass bearings and the pilot book told me that I was inside a crescent shaped chain of islands composed of Berlenga and the Farilhoes, about 40 miles north of Lisbon. There was no need to panic but that is exactly what I did.

I clawed down the sails and started the engine, turned north-west and tried to motor out against a steep sea and freshening wind. This was a useless waste of my limited energy and the engine's fuel, because *Sheila* can deal with conditions more efficiently under sail than power. So I stopped the engine, hauled up sail, put in two reefs, and went on to the port tack. Sometime during the blackness of that night we passed the outer-most rock, when and by how much I don't know. Short tacks would have eliminated all risk; I had effected only two and then left *Sheila* to sail herself, taking a chance on the wind not changing, and going below to the dimly-lit cabin too tired and ill to do more.

The next day brought the crisis. I was standing in the cockpit leaning against the coaming when my knees buckled. My mind was strangely clear and detached as it watched my body crumple and sink into a huddle on the cockpit floor.

I came to some time later, noted that there was wind and that for some reason the mainsail was down. I dragged myself forward to the halyards, not daring to stand upright for fear of falling overboard, but I had not the strength to pull the sail more than halfway up.

It is hard to describe that humiliation now and so I quote from my diary (written up later that evening): "How I wept today – I vaguely remember sliding on to the floor of the cockpit, my head falling on to my doubled-up knees and sobbing my heart out; I tried to stop and just couldn't. All my stupidities seemed too big and yet unended, just as people who knew more of the sea, more of the army, more of life, had predicted. My navigation is all to hell, I know nothing of handling a ship and have killed myself trying, my capital's gone – oh brother, are you a failure?"

I was laid completely bare and the whole world seemed to be in the watery sun looking down at me, so I went below as a wounded animal goes to hide in a cave, flinging myself on the berth as I thought to die. Then fatigue mercifully overcame the pain all through my body and I lost consciousness.

* * *

A round patch of light moved to and fro over the other berth as *Sheila* rolled quietly to the gentle swell. It was nearing noon, and my first realisation was that all pain had left me; I felt refreshed and at peace – and hungry. This told me that I'd been only a bit tired, nothing seriously wrong, and the black despair of failure and doubt had gone with the pain.

I fried up some bully beef and onions; it was good, but unfortunately fried bully tastes just like fried bully. At first I wolfed it down, but as soon as the first sharpness of hunger was gone, I started to put aside those horrid-looking bits of gristle and the flabby slivers of thick white skin, which make up heaven knows what part of an ox. This meal was a celebration, so ran to two courses, peaches and cream (condensed milk) with a cup of coffee after. Then I went back to bed.

I woke in the evening. After supper while the washing-up water heated I sat on the foredeck with a mug of coffee, watching the most beautiful sunset I'd ever seen. In its beauty lay forgiveness and the peace that came with it.

This experience of illness was invaluable merely from a sailor's point of view, and indeed was part of the very careful plan I had made before the trip began – to drive myself to the limit in order to find out just what I could stand under those conditions. It is essential to know this for safe navigation, in exactly the same way as if you have a car with a broken petrol gauge. Before you know how far you can go, what stretches of the journey can be completed without replenishing, where you must replenish and so on, you must drive that car from a full tank until it is quite empty. For the same reason I drove myself until I actually passed out from sheer exhaustion, although it was not recognised as such at the time.

After that I knew not only roughly how long I could expect to last under those conditions, but even better I now knew the warning signs of approaching exhaustion and its inevitable inefficiency, signs which came in time to anticipate and plan to avoid that final state of collapse, and to put my ship in a position of safety before that state did arrive. You can sleep as much as you like far out to sea, but near land or shipping it is stupidity.

There must have been fair winds during that week because I was then in the area of the Portugese Trades, which blow from the north-east. My DR put me 40 miles north of Cape St Vincent, the south-west corner of Spain and the last to round before the home run to Gibraltar. Land was beyond the horizon to the east, and at noon I took infinite trouble in ideal conditions with my first meridian altitude sight, which gives latitude. The line put me 40 miles south of my DR, exactly opposite the cape. I checked and re-checked the simple working, not daring to believe the gift of 40 miles, and turned east to pick up the coast to make sure. In the late afternoon the haze lifted to show the exact original of the sketch of the cape displayed in the pilot book. That night I passed south of the light, deliriously happy to be on the home stretch.

At 10 a.m. the haze lifted and gave me my first glimpse of the Rock, my goal for the past four weeks, which had been the hardest four weeks I have ever known. At first a wave of wild elation swept over me, then it changed to one of quiet content.

An hour before arrival I hove-to and prepared for entry into port.

After supper that evening I sat on deck as *Sheila* lay quietly to her anchor, watching the lights ashore, the car lights climbing the higher roads above the town, hearing the hoot of taxis, and music from a nearby ship – my radio had been out of action for the last three weeks and I had missed music greatly. I tried to believe that it was me who sat on the deck of his own ship at anchor, after a sea voyage of 1400 miles, and not the character of a book I had read. What is real? I thought a lot about going on alone.

There had been times during the voyage when I had said that I would end it in Gibraltar, selling *Sheila* for whatever I could get, and take a passage back to New Zealand. No, there could be no turning back, no giving up, and I thought deeply how best to express my reaction. Before sleeping I wrote in my diary: "I would not do that voyage again for five hundred pounds, but nor would I have missed it for a thousand."

To Peru through the Roaring Forties

by LYDIA and TOM DAVIS

From *Doctor to the Islands* (Michael Joseph)

Tom Davis left his home in Rarotonga at the age of 11 to be educated in New Zealand at boarding school and medical school, topped off by two years in Auckland as a house surgeon. He returned to Rarotonga 16 years later as a medical officer, taking his Dunedin-born wife, Lydia. In 1952 they departed from Wellington on a yacht voyage to the United States, where Dr Tom was to do post-graduate work in Boston.

With a small legacy from his grandfather, Tom Davis had bought a yacht he had watched being built in New Zealand 16 years earlier, the Soubrette, *which he renamed* Miru. *She was a 14 m ketch built for ocean cruising, of triple-skin kauri, sheathed in copper. To arrive in time for the start of the university year in September, they had to cross the Pacific in mid-winter, 6750 miles through the Roaring Forties, between latitudes 35 and 50. With them were their two sons, John (10) and Tim (five) and two crewmen.*

Just 12 months after their arrival in Boston Miru *dragged her moorings at Marblehead in another hurricane and was smashed to pieces.*

In 1978, Dr Davis became Premier of the Cook Islands.

OUR departure from Wellington Harbour was not the hilarious leave-taking that seemed to be the lot of other small craft off on a long cruise. Although our friends gathered at the wharf to wish us good luck, their kind thoughts seemed to be tinged with the colour of doom, and none of them could conceal that they thought we were all committing suicide.

Tom had now acquired two crewmen. There was no shortage of applicants – almost everyone we met longed for a sea voyage to America. Tom finally selected a young man named Neil Arrow, whom he had met at the sail-mender's. Neil had had a lot of experience and seemed a fine choice. The selection of the second crewman we left up to him, more familiar than we with New Zealand yachtsmen, and he soon settled upon Bill Donovan, a young man just 21.

We would sail at 1 p.m., and the land-lubbers milling all over the decks, slippery with the pouring rain, were not making things easier for the crew. Tom was worried over the weather forecast. Something was brewing outside the coastline, but, as our sailing date had already been delayed four weeks, we must go now or give up altogether. John could not have been less concerned at the commotion around him; he sat and read comics; Tim was curled up on my bunk, asleep. I accepted various small gifts from the endless stream of farewellers, and felt very brave and rather sorry for myself.

I retired to the main cabin and continued to knit Tom a storm hat. The emotions of Madam Defarge as she busily clicked her needles were as nothing compared to mine at that moment. If only I had the courage to grab the children, run ashore and say, "I'm not going, I'm scared." Pure cowardice in the face of the resulting scandal kept me at my knitting.

"If you want to take photographs, come up," shouted Tom from the deck. "We're casting off."

"Come on, John," I said, grabbing my camera and struggling into my mackintosh. "Don't you want to say goodbye to New Zealand?"

"Poof, I don't care about New Zealand," said John settling down to another comic. "When will we get to America?"

Only God could answer that one so I left John to the realms of Tarzan, and Terry and the Pirates, and prepared to take pictures. Bill had kissed his weeping mother for the last time, and was now aboard wielding the boat-hook to keep our bow from under the wharf. Neil was hoisting the staysail, and rather than ask Bill to assist him he was launching our vessel in blood; the staysail block had evidently connected with his nose, and he had smeared the resulting gore all over the rest of his face with a piece of cotton waste. Tom was performing a rather clever acrobatic; he stood at the tiller, shouting goodbye with one side of his mouth, yelled to Neil with the other, and gave orders to Bill through the middle, all while hanging over the side of the vessel to grab his cine camera which was being handed to him from the wharf.

We were away. Up on the masthead, a carved tiki that Ron Powell had given us for luck was screwed to face the bows, our home-made house flag also fluttered a tiki, St Christopher's medallion was screwed to the deckhouse bulkhead, and everyone's fingers were firmly crossed. As Wellington disappeared into the distance, I went below and made a nice cup of tea.

To me there is nothing lovelier on the sea's face than a harbour. The sight of rocks, buoys and other ships may worry the skipper, but for the cook how precious is the lack of motion in sheltered waters. My cooking facilities consisted of the barest necessities: two kerosene primuses swung on heavy gimbals, one pressure cooker, three saucepans, one frying pan, and a kettle. With such reliable tools I knew that nothing could go wrong. Let others have their alcohol stoves and their bottled gas, we would always have hot food. Making that first meal was easy, for even outside the harbour, despite the ominous skies and falling glass, the motion of *Miru* was comparatively gentle. But this respite was short-lived. Within a few hours both Timothy and I had succumbed to seasickness, Timothy enduring the sneers of the more hearty John, and I privately vowing that I would show no action in the culinary department until my interior had settled.

On deck, young Bill too was feeling the motion. Tom was undisturbed, as usual, but Neil, having read somewhere that a glass of salt water would settle the most delicate of stomachs, had made the mistake of swallowing a pint of sea. Whoever started that legend was only too clearly a liar. However, the boys had to keep working, taking watches, two hours on and four off, attending to the sail and attempting to clear up the gear still to be stowed. Rough weather was so speedy in coming that the men took the least line of resistance and jammed all the loose gear under the galley table. What their opinion of my defection as cook may have been I will never know, and at the time I felt too miserable to wonder.

After two days of complete neglect of my duties, during which the men cooked for themselves, I issued forth. Timothy was rid of his sea-sickness, and none the worse for the experience; John was getting in everyone's way on deck. Bill and Neil were still suffering from sea-sickness, but this had not impaired their appetites; for the last two days they had all been eating canned food, so I prepared to make up for my shortcomings. There was no stanchion beside the galley bench, and, as there was nowhere to wedge myself while cooking the meal, the best I could do was to pounce on my pots and pans each time the *Miru* rolled to starboard, the galley side. Despite this, that first day I produced an excellent chow mein and restored my status in the eyes of the menfolk.

We were carrying only 200 gall (900 litres) of fresh water; we did not want to ration this out to a set amount per day, preferring to refrain from washing and to drink as much as we wanted. The children, for whom there is no greater sport than sozzling with soap and water, were also put on their honour to leave the fresh water alone. The prospect of going without washing their faces delighted them and there was plenty of sea for sozzling purposes. I had planned on using no fresh water at all in the cooking, and washed our dishes in a saucepan of hot sea, liberally sprinkled with soap detergents. The dishes were reasonably clean, but as there was no place to set a dish down without its flying under the galley table, clean utensils were apt to contain a small lake of sea and soap upon their next presentation, for they could never be dried or rinsed.

Like most small boats, the *Miru* had no provision for a locker in which the men coming off watch could hang their oilskins or stow their seaboots. Consequently these large, cold and dripping wet pieces of equipment were draped all over the galley. The chart table, at which we ate our meals, was also in the deckhouse, so with navigation gear, oilskins, radio parts, and all other pieces of equipment that had to be left in readiness for any emergency, there was really little room in which to do my cooking.

I discovered very early that under the seat where Tom worked out his navigation I had stowed my most often used foodstuffs. If I said, "Excuse me, could I get the flour," I invariably chose just that moment to interrupt a delicate computation, which would have to be done all over again. If, to make room for a plate, I shifted something, it was apt to become irretrievably lost. Small cans of oil, or other liquids which must not be upset, found a resting-place on top of the gimbals; if I put them aside to cook a meal, they tipped over. It was all too clear that a small yacht out on the ocean is no place for a woman's business. How I longed for my sunny verandah in Rarotonga and the efficiency of Maria. A few days out from New Zealand, Bill left one of the hatch boards lying on top of the deckhouse and a sea swept it away. Now for the rest of the voyage I would have huge seas filtering on to my stoves and down the back of my neck, for the gimbals were set just below the main companionway.

One week out from New Zealand John suddenly became rather green and within a few hours he was covered with spots. He had picked up measles and at a most inopportune time, for the glass fell and we were in the midst of a hurricane. I shifted Tim over on to the bottom of the mate's bunk and installed John in my place, cramping myself up at the bottom, with my knees up to my chin and water pouring on to my head from that darn leaking skylight. I was too worried about John's discomfort and lack of the rest he needed to notice much about that storm. Tom saw more of it than I did.

The hurricane at least had one good result. I was so bruised from being thrown around the deckhouse when working at the galley that Tom had at last rigged me some support. This was a length of rope with a spring clip at each end attached to the porthole bolts above the bench, but it kept me in one place even if it did dig a ridge across my seat. Meals improved, and there was slightly less food on the galley floor. The storm had not been followed by a calm for the seas were still raging. Fortunately we all had our sea legs by this time, but the strain of always clawing one's way from place to place, coupled with the everlasting suspicion that the man on watch might have been washed overboard, was beginning to tell.

I had been obliged to shift both the children out of the forecastle which was soaking and still pouring in water with each wave coming over the bows. Tim was now permanently installed at the bottom of my bunk; when the skylight leaked he squeezed up beside me while, John, speedily convalescing from his spots, was occupying a makeshift bunk just aft of the forecastle. The arrangement worked reasonably well as the children could now play on John's bunk and keep out of the main cabin, allowing the men, exhausted from the strain of the storm, to get a little rest. The presence of Tim taking up a good half of my already limited sleeping quarters caused discomfort, but as there was no alternative for little Tim I kept quiet and wondered if the pains in my joints were really just cramps or whether I was succumbing to sailor's rheumatism.

The deckhouse and main cabin were now in a state of the most appalling untidiness. Even Bill, who had started out so neatly, had to remove everything from his locker to find what he was looking for. The cabin floor was three or four inches deep in water, and anything that slipped off a bunk or the table was immediately soaked. We wore sea boots all the time except in our bunks; Tom's textbooks, carefully brought along to be used at the all-too-distant School of Public Health, had fallen from the shelves and were ruined; everything breakable in the crockery locker had to be thrown overboard. From now on we would use the few plastic dishes. From the constant deluge of seas breaking over the decks, the two primuses in the galley poured soot all over the boat. Our new paintwork was black, and so was I. We were all suffering from "the itch" and in need of lots of soap and fresh water.

Bill and Neil always combed their hair before going on watch. They couldn't explain why; perhaps subconsciously they were hoping that we would pass a luxury liner, but luxury liners don't come down the Roaring Forties.

Timothy was the most fortunate. Being only five years old and consequently not far from the ground, he found it easy to clamber round no matter how marked the motion of the vessel. Both he and John were more than paying for their passage in fetching and carrying for us clumsier adults. Because of the continuous rolling of the vessel, there was no hope of John starting his correspondence lessons. He lived in constant fear that we might strike calm weather; he need not have worried, for three days after the first hurricane darned if we didn't strike another, this time much worse.

Tom ordered all sails down, lashed the tiller in an effort to head the boat up into the wind, and we settled into our bunks determined not to watch the glass but to pray silently that this storm would not last the four and a half days of its predecessor. Where earlier the winds and seas had caused us discomfort, this time I think that we four adults were actually afraid. The *Miru* was on her own. Could she possibly survive the pounding she was receiving? The wind, now raging at what must have been 90 miles an hour, screamed and whistled through the rigging, and breaking waves caught the *Miru* beam on. The effect on those below the windward bunks was like a punch in the chest. Expectantly, we sensed each wave a second before it broke. "Hang on!" someone would call, and Tom in the bottom bunk clawed at his bunkboard while I grasped the beams above me, tensing myself for the blow.

From John's bunk, in the comparative security of the leeward side, I heard, "I'll have Mr Snip the tailor's son, then I'll have Mrs Chop the butcher's wife." Busy playing a card game of Happy Families, the children were blissfully unaware that the rest of us were waiting each moment for our vessel to fall to pieces.

Hurricane or calm, we still had to eat; it wasn't so bad in the galley once I had climbed into the security of my precious rope. I managed to cook up some steak, peas and rice, and produce my usual brew of coffee. I admit to feeling rather noble concerning the preparation of this meal, for a hurricane is always considered the perfect excuse for the ship's cook to take a day off. After the meal I climbed back into my bunk and prepared to hang on for the rest of the afternoon. Tom teetered up into the engine-room to see how things were faring there.

No sooner had he left the main cabin than I found myself sitting on Bill's chest without the slightest recollection of how I got there. All my breath had been knocked out, my back hurt like the devil, and my shins were quite skinless. Dazedly looking round, I saw that the deckhouse table had been torn from its bolts and had crashed against Bill's bunk. I had been thrown bodily out of my top bunk, struck the table and torn it loose, and finished up with Bill.

The two crewmen, whom gravity had stuck fast to their leeward bunks, stared at me in bewilderment and a little fear. I was not seriously hurt, having added only a few bruises to my already alarming collection, but when I struggled to regain my own quarters, another buster caught us and over I went again, this time straight onto our kerosene heater, the only means we had of drying clothes.

John put his head round his corner. "Mummy, whatever are you doing? Why don't you go and lie down instead of falling all over the place?"

Not deigning to answer, I had made a third sortie and scrambled back to where I had started. During all the commotion, Tom had been having some private adventures up in the deckhouse. When the buster hit us he had been thrown across a can of oil, upsetting its contents all over the already swimming floor, then tossed on to the deckhouse pitched down between the unbalanced table and the side of the vessel, his head amongst the gear crammed on the leeward side, and his heels in the air. Stuck in this position he had not been able to come to my assistance, but when he had at last regained the upright and lurched down to the main cabin again, his reaction to my perambulations took me aback.

"For God's sake," bellowed Captain Bligh, "Who did that to the table, and look at my heater!"

Crouching in my top bunk and hanging on to the beams for dear life, I felt rather as if I had taken a little hatchet and systematically smashed things up. Reeling and crashing, Tom managed to dig up a piece of heavy rope and lash the wildly careering table to the side of Bill's bunk. Bilge had now collected to the point where with each roll of the vessel it slopped against the sides of our bunks. Tom returned to the engine-room and attempted to start the electric pump; when he came back he was speechless. Our pump had given up the struggle just when it was most needed. If this was the state of things below, what must it be like above decks? It was unsafe to go and look, but we prayed to God that the hurricane would blow itself out quickly.

After Tom and I had reinstalled ourselves, we took Neil's bunk board and wedged it on top of mine, which had proved so inadequate. Each breaking sea threw Tom on to the floor. It wasn't far to fall and he was not being hurt, but every descent threw him into ankle-deep bilge water.

He wiped himself off and climbed back philosophically. "Now we'll have to put into land, the nearest is Rapa Island, 1300 miles away. We'll have to dry out after this and get the pump fixed and that table bolted down again. God knows what the rigging will be like now, I doubt if we'll have much unspliced rope left. I never dreamed any yacht would stand up to this pounding."

Next morning the wind had fallen and the barometer was rising. The hull was quite undamaged but the decks had been swept clean. All gear stowed in the cockpit had gone. The pieces of sheepskin used for chafing-gear on the stays were snowy white. *Miru* had been under water right up to the masthead.

A Postscript From the Skipper

* * *

My tentative plan was to sail straight from Wellington to Peru in the Roaring Forties between latitudes 35 to 50, an uncomfortable part of the world for a 6750 miles crossing in midwinter. During our first three weeks in the Pacific, as Lydia has said, we struck two hurricanes. At the outset I followed the varied advice I had gleaned from reading the numerous "epic voyages", and in the process I lost all my spare lines and both my sea anchors as well as a couple of heavy sails improvised as make-do sea anchors. I also learned a lesson that none of the books had mentioned. I will not presume to lay down a law that this is the correct method of riding out a hurricane, but when the experience of others and my own invention had failed, then I discovered that *Miru,* left to herself under bare poles, settled into the safest position to face the winds and raging seas. She eased into just that angle where she would take the least movement in any part of her; my 24 oz (700 g) canvas, a weight fitted for the old giant barques, would not stand, my ropes shafted through. *Miru* made sure that I had expended every effort to help her, then turned round and showed me how it was done.

I do not say that during the hurricanes we were comfortable below; that is impossible on any vessel. Although in the rest of the voyage we ran into no more hurricanes, the regular 40 miles an hour wind that is part of the scenery in the winter Roaring Forties and the cyclones and high velocity gale we struck during the remainder of the journey, I handled with an eye to the lesson I had learned during the two hurricanes. Gale-force winds allowed the use of a riding mizzensail and no longer did we hang on to the sides of our bunks and worry as to how we might best help the ship; instead we read detective books and rested secure in the knowledge that the *Miru* knew her business and would bring us through safely.

Marco Polo puts to sea

by TONY ARMIT

As told to Loris Chilwell

On 18 July 1954 a pair of young greenhorn sailors sailed away in a home-built boat on a voyage that took them around the world. In Brisbane they were joined by Mick Earl (son of Jack Earl who had sailed around the world in Kathleen *at the end of World War II). He stayed with them as they sailed through the barrier reefs to Thursday Island, through Indonesia to Christmas Island and across the Indian Ocean to Durban, where he left them.*

Sometimes spending months working ashore, they continued to the West Indies via Cape Town; to Florida; through the Panama Canal to the Galapagos Islands, the Tuamotus, and home via the usual island beauty spots. The youngsters had become veterans and their adventure had lasted for three and a half years.

WHEN I was young the greatest achievement for most young New Zealanders was to sail the Tasman. I'd always wanted to do it and I worked and saved. I built my first boat when I was 13, bought and sold boats, worked all through school holidays. Once I had three jobs!

I was 18 when I started building *Marco Polo,* and it took me three years. The boat was designed by Bert Woollacot and it was designed for me because I knew what I wanted. I went to him and said: "I want a boat that's a bit bigger than *Nada,* a bit beamier than some other boats and a bit smaller than *Ladybird*", and I wanted various other things. The building went on in a backyard in Newmarket.

First I went and bought the trees, then had them milled. Now I had all the timber. It didn't cost much, just to buy the timber. I was doing accountancy when I started, earning next to nothing. I used to build the boat all night – I'd come home from the office and work on the boat until three or four in the morning.

Eventually, because I ran out of money, I lost interest in the accountancy thing and got labouring jobs.

My father was very good. He believed in the principle that if you wanted to do something, you should do it, get it out of your system, then come on and do something else. He said: "I don't mind lending you some money, but just go ahead and do it."

I got a lot of help from Bert Woollacot. I'd write out my questions at work and then go to him. I remember one day coming over in the ferry to Devonport. I asked Bert, "How on earth do I build the stern?" His daughter was there and looked at me as if I were completely and utterly thick and said "You just follow the lines." To make a long story short, he'd forgotten to give me drawings for the stern. By then we were at his house, so he rushed out to the kitchen, got some lunch paper and scribbled the lines on it and said "There you are, that'll do, you can do it from there." And so the stern got built.

I asked as many questions of as many people as I could until I became a nuisance. Eric and Susan Hiscock turned up, so I went down and gave them a hand – I scrubbed the boat – and then I said, "Would you come and have a look at the boat I'm building? See what you think of it."

So he came out and said, "I think you should put a knee somewhere there, by the mast – it might be a bit better." And he said, "Oh, that's a good sink – I wish we'd done that." This way you get a wealth of experience.

I think there was a lot more of helping one another then and you could get away with more. The pace wasn't as fast. I bought all the fastenings from a chap who was going to build a boat and never got round to it. He had boxes and boxes and boxes of screws and I bought the whole lot from him. You made all your own bolts from wire from the trolleys of the old trams. It was copper rod and when the trams came down there were great amounts of this rod to be had. I bought the copper rod, cut if off to size and threaded it all – and there were my bolts. I had friends who were boatbuilding apprentices and I'd borrow stuff from the Harbour Board – drills and big machinery – then take it back. In fact I had no valuable machinery at all. All I had was a bandsaw and hand tools.

When the boat was launched, it had no masts in it because I had to make them. In the meantime the boat was on a mooring at Devonport. A gale blew up before the masts were put in and the mooring broke. I got a phone call to tell me my three years dream was on the rocks.

It was blowing a stinking gale. *Marco Polo* had broken her moorings right off the Devonport Yacht Club, had floated in between all those outcrops of rock, had somehow managed to strand on a bit of beach and was then hard against the stone wall in the swell, thumping on the ground.

Some people I didn't even know smashed their way in because the boat was locked, grabbed the squabs and put them underneath the bilge and then got a wire right along the foreshore, back to the club winch. Another launch which turned up out of the night pulled the boat away a bit, got her out and around the rocks (it was the early hours of the morning by this time) and just towed her away, for which I am forever grateful.

The squabs all floated away and were all returned. I had my name on them. Some were picked up in the Rangitoto Channel. The side wasn't badly damaged. I just had to clean it off a bit and do a little repair at the bottom of the keel.

There were guys who came around because they wanted to come with me, but all those plans fell through until Brian Loe turned up. He was a rural field cadet doing farming and all he could offer was himself. He wanted to go sailing too. So he joined me. His name is Brian, but he is always known as Tig.

People were so very good. They gave us things. Our tanks were all galvanised iron, made by a friend (I think they were booked out to another job). The cockpit was lined by somebody else on some other job. I worked for the sail maker, Sandy Harold, who was to make the sails, so he said, "You may as well sit and work with me for two or three weeks." So I sat there and he showed me how to make sails. One night I met Tom Buchanan of *Wanderer* going up the street and he said, "You want a few things for the boat. Come down some day." He produced a compass plus a hand-bearing one and said, "I'll never use them. You have them." He introduced me to an auto electrician because we wanted a generator (which actually didn't go on the motor until we got to South Africa).

Things were so different. You made do with things – but they were solid and strong. We had no winches, just blocks. My father paid for the motor because he felt we needed one and I couldn't afford it. I bought an ordinary radio. We had no power, just one battery and we used it purely for the time signals on the radio.

We had no money and we worked at odd labouring jobs; we lived on honey, cheese, bread and milk, which didn't cost much. We were just 21, living on the boat on a Westhaven mooring, rowing in and out in the rain and going to our labouring jobs at 7 a.m.

Marco Polo was 28 ft (9.54 m) long, 8 ft 5 in (2.5 m) beam and drew just under 5 ft (1.5 m). She was ketch-rigged, with tan sails. To preserve sails you tanned them so that they would be easy on the eyes. This again was a Hiscock thing. I took the recipe from his book. You had to boil up a brew and paint it on. What a mess! It's all over everything! You have to turn it over and do the other side. Then the sails have to dry for two or three weeks. I took them all into the Victoria Cruising Club, with which I had no connection whatsoever, and hung them in the roof. The sails had no names or numbers and nobody knew whose they were.

These days everyone is so safety conscious. In those days one thought, "It's your life. If you want to go and drown yourself, good on you." Everyone said, "You go in winter. That's the time. Winter. It's always settled in winter." Yeah!

Then there were people who came down and scoffed, "Oh no, they'll never do it, they'll be back again." The worst offender was Mark Anthony, who had had a series of *Rangis* and wrecked the last one on a reef. He had just started a new boat and was going to England. I said "We might see you in England."

"Ha ha!" he said. "You won't get there, we'll see you back here."

It just takes something like this to make me determined.

We were very young and we'd had no sailing experience. In *Marco Polo* we'd done one thing – we'd been to the Barrier, that's all. On our first night we sailed up to Kawau. There was no light on Martello Rock then. We were ploughing through the evening. The whole boat was battened

She survived a complete capsize in a gale. Graham Eder's sturdy yacht *Pono.*
"Suddenly," wrote Eder later, "it was very quiet." *New Zealand Herald*

A New Zealand yacht in the Arctic. D'Arcy Whiting's *Tequila* dodging icebergs at Columbia Glacier in Alaska.

down. We had a wood stove and you can't start a wood stove when there's not enough oxygen. I think I was stark naked and the guy outside was clad in thousands of jumpers and oilskins. The stupid stove wouldn't light and I think we threw kerosene on it and the whole thing went woof and it lit and then all of a sudden one of us thought "I wonder if there's anything in the way up there". Then Tig said he heard waves and all of a sudden out of the darkness there's Martello Rock right in front of us. So we just gybed right around and the bottom of the rudder just clipped the rock. Passage Reef? Well we must have missed that!

When we left we had twenty pounds each. At that age you're basically pretty selfish and nothing really worries you because you can overcome anything. As long as you've got a place to sleep!

I think we were only out a day – it was a slog – and we were hove-to out by the Moko Hinaus. Of course boats don't heave-to between here and the Barrier now, they bash on. To heave-to is ridiculous. But there we were hove-to all night and half the next day and it blew!

We didn't hit anything, but we didn't really know where we were, for the navigation thing was a problem. Because we really never learned how to navigate! I'd sailed on *Ghost* way back and we were going to do the Tasman race, but it went wrong and we came back. We did the first White Island race, which went round White Island and back up the coast and finished at Whangaroa. But I had been 17 then.

Fred Norris was going to teach us navigation at the Devonport Yacht Club. We'd start off and every week somebody new would come, so we never got past lesson one. We had had over four weeks and we weren't getting any further, so I said to Fred, "Come out and teach us about this sextant thing."

So Fred came out in the boat. It was a winter's day and we sailed down toward Motuihe. He said, "Doesn't the boat sail itself?" I said "I haven't got the faintest idea."

"Oh, all these Woollacot boats sail themselves," said Fred. "You do this and do that and you pull this in and you do that and you tie this up here and you'll be right. Now have you got any rum?"

So we went to Motuihe drinking rum and it was raining. You can't read a sextant in the rain. He was half full, so we turned round and came back home. So we never found out which way the thing went. We did have all the notes, tons of notes and tons of books and we thought we'd read about it. But to go back to the story of our voyage.

The next thing I remember specifically is running in a big sea and wondering how on earth to get the sail down because at some stage soon we were going to have to. If we turn round and come into the wind? The seas are breaking! It's very dangerous! No doubt we'd probably run too long. We should have shortened down. Actually I think we clawed the sails down flat off the wind rather than wind back. In most cases we drove the boat far too hard.

So we plugged on, and Norfolk turned up more or less where we'd expected it. It took us days and days to get to Norfolk. And then we couldn't quite get there. The wind would head us, we'd go one side of the island, and we'd tack that way, and we'd tack the other way. We'd tack off each side and it took us two days to get in there.

We stayed a while and then sailed across to Lord Howe. It blew – just blew. We were hove-to one night and you could hear the waves coming and crashing and bashing and the next thing you'd hear would be a hissing roar and the whole boat filled up with water and – my goodness! By the time we got on deck everything had gone – the vents were gone and the dinghy was gone – and the sails.

We got to Lord Howe and there we picked up an artist, a chap a lot older than we were, but very interested in ocean sailing, so we took him to Sydney. He said he'd pay for the food. So he paid for all the food, but he couldn't eat any because he was sick as a dog and it blew all the way to Sydney. Eventually we got there.

There wasn't a skerrick of varnish or paint left on the boat! But the mast was still standing, and the structural breakages were actually very small. It was all caused by inexperience and continuous bad winter weather, and we were going more or less straight into the prevailing wind. If we'd headed north, as you would now, we'd have gone to somewhere like Brisbane. But we were heading south, into the winter.

The only things that broke were the goosenecks, and we lost the dinghy. We lost lots of dinghies though, because they were just little things. It used to take a day and a half to make one. So we never used to worry about them. Otherwise the boat all stood together well and we were really pleased.

The last leg

by JEAN COLE

From *Trimaran Against The Trades* (A. H. & A. W. Reed)

When they heard that their farm in Kenya was to be cut up for a government resettlement scheme, George and Jean Cole and their adult son, Charles, and daughter, Jane, decided to emigrate to New Zealand, where an uncle had preceded them, settling in Nelson. George, a merchant marine captain and hydrographic surveyor, had long had a dream of building a boat and taking it on an ocean cruise, so it was decided to make that dream come true. They chose a 12m Piver Victress trimaran design, built the hulls on the farm and finished it at Mombasa. They set forth from there on 8 January 1966, with Mr Cole's 92-year-old mother, Granny Emie, as passenger. They chose the shortest route, against the Trade Winds, from Mombasa to Australia, stopping at Mahe (Seychelles), Diego Garcia (Chagos Archipelago), Cocos (Keeling Islands) and Christmas Island en route.

In Trimaran Against the Trades *Jean Cole tells the story of the building of* Galinule *and the voyage to New Zealand. We find them at Brisbane, having navigated successfully down the coast from Darwin, between the islands of the Great Barrier Reef.*

THE Brisbane mooring was one of the most pleasant of the whole voyage. The banks of the Botanical Gardens slope down to a containing wall at the river's edge, with mooring posts about 60 ft (18 m) away. A row of tall shady trees stands along the top, with glimpses of blue jacaranda showing between. The cuckoo calls frequently, particularly at dusk, and it made George and me quite nostalgic for England. At night the gates of the gardens were closed and peace reigned; downstream the curve of the Story Bridge arches over the river, its lights at night like a string of beads, with the flashes of car headlights casting golden flickering reflections in the water.

Below the boundary of the gardens was the Edward Street ferry jetty. The bank was impossible at low tide because of the mud, so we used this jetty when going ashore. The ferry men were dears and took us under their wings. For the fortnight we were there, they became real friends. They were mines of information and looked after our dinghy, oars and outboard engine. Just by the entrance to the ferry were the Royal Australian Navy Headquarters offices, with the white ensign flying above.

There were many jobs to be done before we tackled the Tasman. The main one was filling the cockpit bilges with polystyrene foam. (We had thought of this before leaving Kenya, but had been unable to get the stuff.) Our bilge pump, wonderfully efficient machine though it was in operation, had sprung a defect, so we were even more anxious to avoid getting these spaces filled with water. We had to have three goes with the foam, as each time we thought we had enough (it was very expensive), there was always some space still left. George also checked on our plywood to be sure we had pieces big enough to nail over our windows, in case any of them should stove in, in the event of a tough Tasman crossing. Jane and I spent a long time going round the frames with a new kind of putty, in an attempt to prevent leaks.

The meteorological man confirmed 28 October as the best date for departure. We got our clearance amid many kind wishes for a good Tasman crossing; bonded stores were taken aboard on the 27th, a customs officer accompanying them and sealing up the cupboard. He was to meet us at the filling station down the river the next day to do a final check, presumably to see that we hadn't broken into the cupboard and auctioned the goods on the riverbank.

On sailing day we were up early getting shipshape for sea. A television crew had established itself on the next boat and a small bunch of people had collected on the bank. As we let go our mooring ropes and set off downstream, we saw people waving from the ferry and the hotel across the way. A yell from the sky called to our notice some figures perched on the very top arch of the Story Bridge, brandishing paint brushes; and the coxswain of one of the ferries lower down hopped out and waved the Australian flag. We dipped our ensign to the commander of the U.S. submarine *Tiru.* We had won through at last and were flying the blue instead of the red ensign, the warrant having been among our accumulated mail when we arrived.

New Farm Park had a row of huge jacarandas along the riverside standing in blue pools of fallen blossoms like reflections of themselves. We stopped at the filling station and had an orgy of fresh water while the petrol went in the tanks, washing down the decks and filling every available bucket, basin and saucepan.

There was quite a strong north-easter blowing outside. We spent a slightly rolly night off Moreton Island, our last in Australian waters, waking early to find it very calm. We had only one regret on leaving the Commonwealth; being so late on schedule, we'd been unable to get down to Sydney as originally intended, to see its wonders and to meet the numbers of kind people who had written hoping that we should go there.

The passage round the top of the island had been described to George, but as we began to round its corner it seemed unbelievable that the instructions could be right. The beach was very sandy and there was a strip of pale-coloured sea, usually a sign of shallowness, with a little further out an ominous line of breakers. The directions were to turn to starboard between the island and the broken water. Eventually, with George muttering "I don't like this one little bit", Jane put the wheel over. Soon we were cheered to see a number of fishing boats drawing much more than our few inches safely following the same passage, so we stood on feeling happier. There was no wind at all, so we continued under engine, delighted that the bilges were no longer gulping in water – it just flowed along the drain and out at the side. The coastline consisted of sand dunes interspersed with desolate clumps of moribund trees, with a pelican or two, and a solitary horse walking along the beach.

Just after we had passed Cape Moreton Lighthouse, a slight breeze got up from east-south-east, which was exactly our course. It was enough to allow us to set all plain sail, close-hauled. There was a gorgeous sunset and the full moon rose – a pleasant start to our return to night watches.

The next morning was lovely, though cool, the wind still easterly with *Galinule* sailing close-hauled. The breeze was light but strengthening and gradually it changed until Charles and George were able to set the genoa. By noon we'd accumulated a bonus of 14 miles of current, for which we were grateful. Meanwhile we had a train of shearwaters with some of our dainty petrel friends flitting among the waves, flashing white patches on their backs like little marine rabbits. It was beautifully sunny and calm, with a long swell. To our surprise we could still see the Australian coastline, our course having been at a tangent to the bulge of the continent.

At 9 p.m. I woke, thinking I was in a railway train, the noise of the water rushing under the hull gave me such an impression of speed. To add to the illusion, an empty plastic water can that was lashed to the handrail was bobbing up and down making a noise like the clackety-clack of a train. I got up and took over the wheel from Charles and drove the express through the moonlit night. She was doing six and a half knots all through my watch.

October 31 was dazzlingly sunny, the air cool and crisp with the distance still rushing by. As we went southwards it became light earlier and earlier in the mornings. The day's run was 141 miles, which beat our 134 of way back in the early days. We altered course a bit to be sure of avoiding the Elizabeth and Middleton Reefs, which have been the downfall of many ships – the Pilot warns about the exceedingly variable currents which swirl around them both. We were making full use of the big navy blue jerseys that Jane had knitted for us before we left, as well as our warm trousers.

The day after this we did 171 miles, passing Lord Howe Island just over the horizon and toying with the idea of dropping in, but we were doing so wonderfully well that we went on. On 2 November the wind was almost astern and *Galinule* was literally waltzing along under jib and mizzen and even more so on my morning watch, when the main went up. Things were flying about a bit in the cabin, but nothing messy. Charles saw our first albatross.

The third was grey, with sea and wind increasing in roughness. It was the sort of day which made tea-drinking hazardous; one either got nothing or the whole mug-full in one's face. The barometer was dropping considerably and oilskins were the order of the day at the wheel. We mustered three albatrosses with one petrel joining the giants, skipping along manfully against the gale, close above the white-topped seas. There was talk of heaving-to at one time and if we had been beating there would have been no question about it; but the weather moderated a little in the afternoon and, luckily, there was a gleam of sun just after noon, which gave George a sight!

The following day also started grey and rough, banging and beastly, and it began to pour and stream with rain just after I went on watch. I had dressed myself in full regalia, shirt and shorts, thick jersey and trousers, yellow suit and bobble cap. In addition to the rain, seas were breaking over and deluging the cabin-top and pouring into the cockpit. It is extraordinary how in the right rig one can sit in comparative comfort in so much wet. Jane and Charles had a job to get out of their cabin without being drenched themselves or letting too much water into their beds.

We were back in the conditions when to open a cupboard or the fridge was a hazardous action. I found myself pouring coffee into the mugs on the floor, with my behind pressed against a cupboard, legs spread wide apart, which suddenly reminded me of a giraffe splaying on his legs and putting down his head for a drink. Jane, ricocheting about in the galley, produced a masterly lunch.

There was no sign of the sun during the morning or at noon, so George said he would take a sight whenever there was a gleam. The log run was 136 miles, only 280 now to Cape Maria Van Diemen, one of the most northerly points of New Zealand. Of course George had just retired with a book to the House of Lords when there were yells of "Dad, the sun, the sun." "Action stations," he shouted from his hideyhole and shot out, collecting the sextant on the way.

He took three sights, with Charles taking times on the chronometer. The horizon was extremely difficult, but by this time he was an expert. A second series was possible when we had a 20-minute sun patch in the late afternoon, which gave quite a good fix, giving us 16 miles of favourable current and a position a bit north of the dead reckoning one.

In spite of Jane's and my efforts with the windows, they were still leaking and things were getting unpleasantly damp. The wind was increasing even more, the barometer still on the downward trend. After tea it became a bit too much and George ordered "Down jib" and we lay to, with the stalwart little mizzen only. We kept normal watches in case of ships on the Sydney-Auckland run.

George and Charles were able to set the jib and get under way again at the change of their watches at 4 a.m. They said it was almost broad daylight, even at that hour. I woke to bright sunshine and much less sea and wind, though the swell was still considerable. It was beautifully sparkling but chilly with the wind almost astern, still too cold for Granny Emie to be on deck, so she had to content herself with the cabin.

On the sixth, my mother's birthday, we altered the clocks another half hour, making us 11 and a half ahead of Greenwich.

This was an exciting day, as we sighted the Three Kings group of islands just after lunch, as expected, our first glimpse of New Zealand. The three albatrosses were still with us, one white and two brown. We saw a pintado for the first time, a smallish black and white speckled bird with round light patches on its wings, giving the impression of transparency as it flies above the waves. We saw some almost daily as we went down the coast. We also met a gannet new to us, the common one in New Zealand, with lovely glistening white plumage, a black bar along the after edge of its wings and an orangey-yellow top to its head. We were dashing along at a good seven and a half knots all the afternoon. Exhilarating to us, but this was the fourth day on which Granny Emie had been unable to sit on deck and she was getting a bit browned off in the cabin.

George sighted Reinga light at about 6.30 p.m. We had been straining our eyes to see the mainland since 4 p.m., but the general visibility was poor and a cloudbank obscured the land. I sighted North Cape at 11 that night and took bearings as instructed; Reinga was still clearly visible. *Galinule* was a brute to steer, she wanted to go to port all the time with the wind quite boisterous on the quarter or even astern of that. I called the skipper at a quarter to midnight according to his orders. He checked the bearings and ordered a southerly alteration of course, which brought the wind almost dead astern for Jane at midnight. George and I took down the main as it would have been crashing about and very awkward.

The morning was sunny and cold, with dim lumps of New Zealand visible to starboard. We altered course again to close the coast, and were able to pin down Cape Karikari from the chart. We were hoping to make the Bay of Islands by the evening.

The main was set although the sea was rough and the wind quite strong on the quarter and steering was difficult again as it had been in the night, *Galinule* surfing and yawing about from side to side. We eventually had to reduce sail during Charles's afternoon watch when she began to waltz rather more enthusiastically than usual and nearly broached to, taking a big splash over the side. This raised a sqawk from Jane, who had found a patch of sun sheltered from the wind and had stripped down to the basic bikini to get a few minutes warmth — she'd received a generous dollop of cold South Pacific.

We were able to sail right into our chosen spot in the lee of Moturua Island, dropping the anchor at 4.30, pretty good going with 158 miles done since noon the day before, 10,600 miles from Mombasa, and 1400 miles from Brisbane in nine days.

We could hardly believe that we had reached New Zealand. It had seemed such a remote idea for so long.

The voyage had taken 10 months.

The Cole family finally returned to Queensland and settled there. Sadly, Galinule *was driven up into the mangroves during a hurricane which hit Fiji in October 1972. She was badly holed and finally had to be written off. At that time the trimaran belonged to Mr Ross Wrightman, a former Mayor of Morrinsville, who had been using it for pleasure trips for visitors staying at his guest house at Nandi.*

Bebe

by ROSS NORGROVE

A peerless raconteur with a bottomless fund of stories, Ross Norgrove has spent a lifetime at sea, some of the early years in sailing scows. He has owned a variety of yachts, and has been seaman, mate and master on Auckland Harbour Board tugs. For three and a half years after World War II he was fishing in trawlers and obtained a trawler master's ticket. Putting his expertise as a yachtsman to good stead, he spent nine years as a charter yacht captain in the Caribbean on his 21 m schooner, White Squall II, *which he was bringing home to New Zealand when the events in this story took place. He now lives at Herald Island, Auckland, where he is writing two books.*

BEBE was a mere two days old when we first heard of her. She had just been christened, and was using an area of ocean 860 miles north of us in Fiji, as her playground.

She was small, relatively harmless – "winds up to 40 m.p.h. (64 km.p.h) can be expected within 20 miles of the centre," (so the forecast said) – and she was travelling south at a modest 5 m.p.h (8 km.p.h.). Also she was early, very early. Hurricanes are just not supposed to happen in the south-west Pacific in October, or so we had been told!

We pricked off her co-ordinates on the chart as they were given in the twice-a-day radio bulletins, and we watched her progress with a wary eye. She probably wouldn't amount to much, we decided. And we went on with preparations to leave for New Zealand within a week. Maybe she would fizzle out, or perhaps veer off towards the west, where the New Hebrides would cop it again. There was not much chance of her influencing our sailing date.

Aboard *White Squall II,* our 70 ft (21 m) schooner anchored in Suva Harbour, Minine and I, hindered a trifle by the attention that Clancy, our little black Skipperky dog was giving to the proceedings (he figures he's helping), went slowly about the familiar business of getting the vessel stocked up and ready for sea. For the first time since we left the Caribbean, nearly three years before, we were going to have to be careful of how we stocked the freezer. Any surplus meat, we had been told, would be destroyed by the agriculture inspectors on arrival in New Zealand.

Another first (for us), was the novelty of a crew. With the exception of one leg of our voyage from the West Indies we had sailed by ourselves. Now two old friends, Ron Chalmers and Peter Luxmoore from Tauranga, were flying in to sail south to Auckland with us. And they were to be joined by Alex Wotton, a friend of "Lux's", who was visiting Suva and planned a pier-head jump just before we sailed.

All were experienced ocean-going yachtsmen. We anticipated an easy trip with plenty of help. So why rush the provisioning, we told each other. Take it easy. With all that help coming, the whole thing would be a pushover.

In the space of another 24 hours, Bebe had matured into a full tropical storm. Adolescence was behind her. Now grown, she was a lady of awesome proportions. She gave a 100 m.p.h. (160 km.p.h.) scream that sent barometers plunging in every ship within a radius of 400 miles and, with a flick of her skirts, stepped out into the world to make her mark.

We were not the only boat preparing for the trip to New Zealand. Half the 20-odd yachts anchored with us, off the Royal Suva Yacht Club, had the same idea (others, anticipating the approaching New Zealand summer, had already gone), and among the dozen or so moored at the Tradewinds Hotel on the opposite side of the harbour, there was the same number getting ready for the long sail down south.

It was going to be hard to leave. We had spent a good year cruising in the Fiji Islands, and on our frequent visits back to Suva, had made many friends in this most hospitable of yacht clubs. There were farewell parties every night, and the fact that the only way to get a cab into town during the day was to use the phone in the club – and that's where the bar and the friends were – had to be considered as much of a hazard as a rock in a fairway or an uncharted shoal.

Our progress therefore, was slow but happy. There was nothing to worry about; nothing was going to happen. By the time Alex transferred his gear aboard and we moved the ship over to an oil company jetty to take on fuel and water, we felt we had a stranglehold on the whole situation.

Ron and Lux joined us just before we let go to steam back and anchor off the club. Minine, armed with passports, crew lists and ship's papers, headed in the general direction of the Custom House to obtain a clearance. We decided on one more fling ashore tonight, and that would be it – we would sail in the morning.

"... Funafuti flattened by hurricane Bebe, island completely devastated by winds estimated in excess of 120 m.p.h. (190 km.p.h.) ... coconut plantations and crops ruined ... full extent of damage or loss of life not as yet known ... latest reports are that Bebe, moving south-southwest at 10 m.p.h. (16 km.p.h.) is intensifying ... all inhabitants of Rotuma are urged to seek higher ground and prepare for hurricane ... island is in direct path ... "

"Just listen to that!" Lux turned from the radio, which at 0630 hours the next day, had electrified us with the news. "What's the deal, Rosco?"

"We stay where we are, sport. That's what the story is! Let's have a look at the chart." We congregated around the chart table, looking at that little dot less than 600 miles north of Suva that had suffered a direct hit from one of nature's most feared occurrences.

"Poor devils, it's an atoll too – seas must have washed right over it. Listen to this." Alex ran his finger down the page which described Funafuti in the Pacific Islands Yearbook, and continued. "It's small – says here that all the Ellice Islands are small – all atolls comprised of coral rock with only about 8 ft (2.4 m) of hard sand and a scanty supply of soil – only industry is copra – limited amount of well or rainwater and that's probably contaminated now."

He closed the book: "God they must've had a hell of a time, probably still are!"

I pricked off on the chart the distance from Funafuti to Rotuma: "Two hundred and seventy miles, and dead south-south-west. Twenty-four hours at ten knots – it'll be on them. We'll hang on where we are for the time being – Rotuma's about 360 miles north of here as the crow flies; our barometer's going down, but it's still too early to say what's going to happen. Let's clew up on deck."

We checked the ship's three spare anchors and cables, stowed awnings and jib below. We passed the mainsheet round and round the boom all 30 ft (9 m) along to the mast, lashing and frapping the sail as tightly as possible and using all the 300 ft (90 m) of 2 in (50 mm) circumference dacron on the job. The main and fore staysail got the same treatment.

We battened hatches and skylights with our new waterproof covers recently made in Miami – there seemed a good chance that they were to get an opportunity to prove themselves.

Then a thought occurred to me. I turned to the boys: "You jokers are all family men. It might be best if you sat out this blow ashore!"

They answered succintly, and they brooked no argument. So we brought the boarding ladder on deck and lashed it down, then the dinghy.

Now it was 1400 hours, Monday 23 October 1972. Our barograph, which had recorded a drop of 0.05 in the last 12 hours, and which seemed to have forgotten all about diurnal variation, now stood at 29.55 – a difference of 0.1 from the norm of a week before.

All around us, vessels were on the move – on their way to what they reckoned to be more secure shelter. A multitude of craft owned by the Fiji Government – lighthouse tenders, small cargo ships and barges – moved across to the western side of the Bay of Islands, about two miles distant. A number of yachts from around us went there too, or to the Tradewinds anchorage inside Admiralty and Snake Islands. Some of the shallower boats (5 ft 6 in – 1.6 m – or less draft), managed to get up the Kumbuna Creek, on the extreme western side of the Bay of Islands, and so availed themselves of the best shelter Suva provides in a hurricane.

We watched the mass exodus, but did not join it. There is no safety in togetherness – not in extreme conditions, that is, and the thought of being anchored on the other side of the bay when one or two of those big unnamed barges or lighters dragged anchor and came down on top of us in the middle of the night (it's always at night that these things happen), was enough to make a man count his beads twice over!

By 1700 hours the wind, which was steady in direction from the north-east – that is from the land immediately inshore to us, and which, according to the weather office, would remain in this quarter for the next 24 hours – had increased to Force 8 (34-40 knots), and our anemometer was recording gusts of up to 56 m.p.h. (90 km.p.h.).

We were lying in three and a half fathoms of water to our starboard anchor – a 150 lb (68 kg C.Q.R., with 45 fathoms of ⅞ in (15.9 mm) diameter chain out. Then just before night came, we dropped a 200 lb (90 kg) Danforth underfoot from the port hawse pipe, and left just enough tension on the windlass brake to hold the cable from running out. With the door off the chain locker below, and a piece of rope yarn tied to each cable, this gave us an anchor alarm. If we dragged or carried anything away, the Danforth would take the cable with no assistance from us, and the fact that the rope yarn had disappeared, or the noise of the chain going out, would alert us.

"We'll stand three-hour watches night and day until this blows over, with all hands ready to turn to at any time," I decided. "We'll run the main engine for half an hour at the change of every watch, to keep it warm and ready for full throttle if for any reason we need it. The guy on watch is to keep his eye on the rope yarn on the port anchor cable in the chain locker, and also the echo sounder – we'll leave it switched on."

The main saloon was snug and dry – the howling of the wind and driving rain was muffled by the ship's thick wooden hull – to a point where it could barely be heard – and then only when all conversation stopped. I remember that night well for the steaks from Savu Savu that Minine dished up, for the Tom Lehrer tape we had playing, and for the spectacular inroads we made into what was left of our West Indies rum. I also remember thinking before I turned in, that the weather conditions we had experienced so far, were possibly a preliminary before the main bout.

" . . . Hurricane Bebe over northern Yasawas . . . Rotuma lashed by 140 m.p.h. (225 km.p.h.) winds . . . flooding, much damage to plantations and crops . . . Director of Marine warns all vessels in Fiji Islands to seek shelter . . . hurricane still intensifying . . . hurricane force winds extending over an area 100-mile radius of center . . . center expected vicinity Viti Levu north coast tonight . . . "

This was the radio story early next morning and it was worse than we had expected – much worse. Fertile Rotuma Island, the most northerly of the Fiji group, had experienced Bebe's full fury. Now the beautiful Mamanuthas and Yasawas – stretching in a 70-mile arc from Viti Levu's north-west corner, were being lashed – and what was that the forecaster had said – intensifying, still?

"Where are you off to, Minine?" said Ron. "Going for a swim?"

The wind had increased considerably during the night and had pegged our anemometer, which records to 65 m.p.h. (105 km.p.h.); conditions on deck were miserable, yet after breakfast that morning as I came into the saloon from inspecting the chart, I was in time to hear my wife (surprisingly wearing a diver's face mask), reply as she headed up the companion way, "On deck, I'm going to give Clancy a walk."

Clancy is a Belgian barge dog, a breed far more at home afloat than ashore. He has thousands of cruising hours behind him and he can weather a gale in as seamanlike manner as any living creature, humans included. But one look at him that day, all 12 lb (5 kg) of him rigged out in his seagoing harness, was enough for anyone with half an eye to see that Clancy's heart just wasn't in the job at all. His instincts, which invariably lead him to the driest, most comfortable out-of-the-way corner aboard at the onset of bad weather (where he'll stay for days if necessary, defying in some mysterious way every call of nature), had given him the message long before the radio had given it to us: that deck was no place for a dog!

"Well be careful, or you'll both blow away! Why the face mask?" I said.

"I can look right into the wind and rain with this on – I tried it last night, I can see everything," Minine replied.

And that I thought, as she disappeared through the hatch with Clancy, is one for the textbooks. I can just see it in the pages of *Nicoll's Seamanship*, or in the preface to one of the *Pilots*: "The attention of mariners is drawn to the advisability of wearing diver's face-masks when endeavouring to establish their position in driving rain when in confined waters." Maybe it will catch on. Maybe in times to come it will be a common sight to see a whole lot of ships' officers, all wearing face masks, rushing backwards and forwards across the bridge of a vessel as soon as it starts to rain. The mind boggles – in really bad weather, they could use flippers and snorkels, too!

By noon our glass recorded 29.70 and was still falling. The wind strength was hard to determine, as our anemometer could not handle it, but I would estimate it as being all of 70 m.p.h. (113 km.p.h.). Constant rain whipped along the deck of the ship. At times it was hard to tell where the rain ended and the sea began.

We were in the lee of the land, however, and we were as steady as a rock as *White Squall II's* 60-ton bulk strained back on our faithful C.Q.R., which hadn't budged.

On our starboard side, about 200 yards distant, was the *Optiki,* a 36 ft (11 m) fibreglass *Cheoy Lee* ketch recently shipped from Hong Kong for her American owners Bob and Peggy – who, with their son and a crew member, planned to sail her to Boston. Bob, a professor at the Massachusetts Institute of Technology, was on a year's sabbatical leave and was delighted with his ship.

Ahead about 500 yards – was the 43 ft (13 m) schooner *Whistler,* from

Oxnard, California, with Pat and Polly aboard – the anchorage's most colourful couple. Polly, for 26 years a stunt woman in the movies, and who had figured in most of John Wayne's films, was equally at home standing on the back of a galloping horse, jumping from it onto a moving train, or taking a dive through a second-storey window. Pat, an ex-boxer, had 183 professional fights behind him. A hurricane was all in the day's work to those two!

Broad off to port was the *Natasha* – a small sturdy ketch. That made four of us anchored off the yacht club.

All afternoon we watched the barometer and listened to the weather bulletins. We got no consolation from either.

Bebe was attacking Lautoka, Nandi – and the north coast of Viti Levu, with torrential rain and winds estimated in excess of 180 m.p.h. (290 km.p.h.) . . . much property damage . . . rivers rising (the Rewa river eventually rose over 25 ft (7.5 m)) . . . villagers urged to move to higher ground . . . and just on dark, a yell from Alex, who was on watch, *"Optiki's* away! She's off – she's dragging!"

We rushed on deck, just in time to see *Optiki* disappearing at a great rate astern into the murk. Never have I felt so helpless.

With our big six-cylinder Gardner diesel, we are fully powered. But not in a hurricane – not with the windage of a 70 ft (21 m) mainmast, a 56 ft (17 m) foremast and a maze of rigging. To heave up and try to manoeuvre among the reefs of Suva Harbour at night in those blinding conditions was impossible – suicidal.

This was a job for a salvage tug, a good one, and as I knew it was no use listening for *Optiki's* call – she had no R/T – I tried to raise Suva Radio myself on 2182 kH. I had been calling for about ten minutes, and had received no reply from the station (which was little more than a mile away) when Pat's Irish-American voice came over the air.

"*Whistler* to the *Squall.* Hi-ya buddy!"

"Oh, hi Pat, I'm trying to get hold of Suva Radio. You're going to have to get off the air, mate. The *Optiki's* in trouble. She's dragging towards the reef."

"That's where we are buddy, hard and fast – just opened a beer and poured Polly a Scotch."

"What!! You're on the reef!"

"Yeah, can't go any further – blowing like hell out here. Got plenty of booze though."

What a curve – we hadn't even seen them go past!

"Pat – now listen, can you see anything?"

"Yeah, I see a light flash now and again."

"Then time the interval between the flashes and take a bearing on it."

Just then a Fijian voice came in. "Suva radio, ov-er."

Thank God for that!

"Suva, this is the schooner *White Squall II.* We are anchored off the Royal Suva Yacht Club – and report that two yachts have dragged anchor. One is already on the reef and the other must be close. The vessel aground has two people aboard, and the other has four. That makes six, and they're all in danger of losing their lives. We must have a tug immediately to rescue them. Did you get that? Over."

Unbelievingly, the voice came back. "Tug on its way, over."

We looked at each other in the ship's aft cabin.

"Impossible," said Lux. "They'd have to be clairvoyant. I don't believe it."

"Neither do I!" I picked up the microphone. "*Whistler, White Squall.*" Pat, have you identified that light yet, have you timed it?"

"Not yet buddy – can't see it now – can't see anything. Poured another coupla drinks though – come and join the party!"

"What kind of a bottom are you on – coral or sand?"

"Sand, pounding a bit, but the old girl's taking it!"

This sort of repartee went on for hours, Pat and Polly quite cheerful in the face of what seemed like his last fight and her last stunt, and with Suva Radio assuring us from time to time, "Tug is on his way."

It was just after midnight, with the barometer standing at 28.95 (an all-time low for us), and the wind screaming like a siren outside, when a new voice came on the air. "*Salmar* calling *White Squall II.* What's the story, Ross?"

Salmar! A powerful steel vessel, specializing in marine salvage. She was just the ship for the job. I described the plight of *Optiki* and *Whistler,* finishing with, "How long have you known of this, Ian?"

"About ten minutes," was his reply. "We'll get out there as soon as we can. It's pretty bad right now."

A masterly understatement, I thought, as Ron and I, equipped with face masks (by God, they *do* work), crawled along the deck once more to check the windlass. You just could not reconcile yourself to this wind, howling and shrieking around stanchions, masts, deck fittings, making a whistle out of everything. It tore the paint off the front of our main hatch scuttle – tore it off down to bare wood. And when Ron, who had been holding my legs down as I checked the tension on the port brake band, stood up for one uncautious moment, it picked up his large bulk and threw him end over end 30 ft (9 m) down the deck like a piece of paper.

For us, that was Bebe at her worst. By 03.00 hours, the wind had fallen away and was light south-west. We had hove our Danforth clear of the bottom, steamed up to windward and dropped it, and were waiting with both anchors out for the breeze, which the weather office told us (they had been extremely accurate to date), would not exceed 50 knots.

The hurricane, so the latest bulletin had said, was dissipating. But, just in case (for after the wind had swung, our position was far more vulnerable than before), we lay for the first time on two hooks.

Salmar came and hung off our stern on a bow line an hour or so before dawn. They had found the *Optiki* in the calm before the wind change, and had towed her into the Tradewinds anchorage. She had dragged into the main Levu Passage within minutes of disappearing from our sight, and just when total disaster, in the form of hurricane force winds and gigantic seas crashing onto Suva's barrier reef were less than 100 ft (30 m) away, their anchor had hooked into something on the bottom and held. Here they rode it out — like a little toboggan on a giant roller coaster.

And the *Whistler?* "Can't find them," said Ian (part owner and skipper of the *Salmar*), "but there's only one place she can be if she's on a sand bottom, and that's about a half a mile inside the entrance to the harbour — the safest place in the bay! We'll pull 'em off as soon as it gets light."

The luck of the Irish! A diver swam a line to them just after daybreak, and the *Salmar* towed them off with ease. Pat and Polly had had a whale of a hurricane party, even though all of their friends had been too busy to attend. *Whistler* had weathered the pounding she'd taken as well as her owners. Barring a few cuts and abrasions, she was in far better shape than many other vessels in the harbour after the blow.

It was later that day, after the anemometer had slowed to 55 m.p.h. (90 km.p.h.) . . . 45. . . . 40 . . . that the weather office bulletins pronounced that Bebe was over. But we knew long before that.

Our "all clear" sign had come when Clancy appeared from his favourite cubby hole at the foot of one of the aft cabin bunks.

He had smelled the warm, clear air, delicately tested the dry deck with one tiny paw. And then, bladder bursting, trotted forward to do what he had to do. He was safe. So were we.

The kind of scow described by Percy Eaddy in the story "Safety Over the Bar". This is the scow *Herald* under full sail, racing in the Auckland Anniversary Regatta in 1906.
Winkelman Collection, Auckland Institute and Museum

The three-quarter-tonner ***Welcome Home*** **in a spectacular broach at the start of a winter race on Auckland Harbour.** *Neil MacKinnon*

Suddenly it was very quiet

by GRAHAM EDER, as told to Loris Chilwell

PONO is a big, heavy boat, 35 ft (7.6 m) overall, 10 ft (3 m) beam, 5 ft 4 in (1.53 m) draft. She was designed by Jack Muir of Tasmania for Bass Strait conditions and built by Mick Orchard of three skins of kauri over heavy stringers and glassed right over. Her fine-grain hollow spika spruce mast was made light, but very strong, covered with five coats of dynel.

In 1973 I raced her to Suva and started on a short cruise with Tom and Margaret Brightwell and Michelle Renwick as crew.

We spent three or four days in Suva and then went to Kandavu, where we struck four or five days of fresh conditions, in company with a large number of other boats. From there we went to Matuku, to Torea and then to Ongea Levu. We anticipated calling there for a couple of days, but ended up staying about a week, it was such a fantastic place. We had a letter of introduction to the chief's son, had a great time and did a lot of diving.

We left Ongea Levu on 20 June, intending to go to Minerva on the way home. But the weather wasn't really suitable for Minerva. It was overcast and murky, so we gave that a miss and carried on. We had not had a weather forecast at all at the Laus because there were atrocious atmospherics at the time.

On about the 16th day it was flat calm and there was a really eerie sky. We motored all day and then a breeze gradually came in and we sailed through the night. Through the next day the breeze gradually freshened and freshened and freshened and we gradually reduced sail until we had the main reefed down to the spreaders and no headsail at all. There was quite a big building sea and we were pretty tired because as the girls hadn't been feeling particularly well Tom and I had been sailing the boat. We decided to heave-to and just lie a-hull. We lashed the boom down to the deck, took off the spray dodger, battened down and had a bit of a sleep.

There was a tremendous sea running and a screaming wind. You could hardly believe it when you looked out the window, for it was really comfortable down below, where we were all in our bunks. We'd be hit occasionally by a fairly big sea, but had no worries. At about 3 o'clock there was a tremendous crash, a lot of water pouring inside and we all ended up out of our lee cloths and on the cabin roof. I think now we had just had a bad knock-down – virtually went upside down and came back the same way – but at the time I thought we had been run down by a ship. All of a sudden there was a roar and a crash and then it got very quiet. The forward hatch had been washed off, the lee cloths had been torn, but we were ok. There was a lot of water down below.

I donned my wet weather gear and put my safety harness on, got out into the cockpit and got the boat running before the seas. Tom also came out and found that the forward hatch, though it had been washed off its hinges, was actually still tied by the lanyard to the rail, so we put it back on, got bits of wood and nailed it down. We then pumped the boat out. It took quite a while.

We had a couple of tyres and chain and all the things that Harry Pope had told us about, so Tom went below to rig all this up while I steered the boat. We were doing upwards of seven knots with no sail at all. We got our paraphernalia all sorted out in the cockpit, put a swivel on the outboard end and the two tyres shackled with chain to the swivel, and 120 ft (36 m) of terylene. I rigged up a bridle across the stern and got it all set up. We were still doing seven knots and we had to be careful when we dropped it over the side because it would race away. We got this out, but it didn't make a lot of difference. We were still doing about five knots. These were the steepest seas we had ever seen, with almost vertical fronts.

From the talk that Harry Pope gave, one then went down below and played cards and waited until the storm was over. However the bridle wasn't quite centralised and we weren't quite stern-on to the sea and on top of that we had a big sea build up behind and then a rogue sea came out of the side of it and it broke. It is hard to estimate the height of a sea, even though we have talked about it a lot afterward, but it was perhaps 10 ft (3 m), perhaps 12 ft (3.5 m) above the boat. It just broke right over the top. I held on to the rudder post in the cockpit and over we went.

We'd been doing a lot of diving in the Laus and we'd got to the point where we could dive for a considerable period, but I still tried to undo my safety harness because I didn't think the boat was going to come up. It got very dark as we went round and very quiet, because we had this screaming wind and then all of a sudden there was nothing. That's the thing that really hammers it home. I can remember the light gradually coming back.

Tom got washed out with the wave. When he surfaced he could see the keel of the boat sticking straight up above the water. Eventually she came up, after going right around and doing a 360°. Tom had his safety harness on and as the boat came back he just climbed over the side, because it happened so slowly.

The hatch of course was well shut. Our first thought was for the girls down below. We opened the hatch and apart from a few cuts and bruises they were ok. The boat was a real shambles. At this stage we had a lot of water in the cabin. It was up to the bunk tops. Everything had come out of everywhere; there was nothing in the chart table; the anchor chain, which had been stowed under the forepeak, was in the toilet compartment; there were no floorboards anywhere. There was nothing dry from one end of the boat to the other. Absolutely nothing dry!

So one of us continued to sail the boat downwind.

We eventually pumped the boat out and we rigged up another contraption. We had bought a little outboard motor for the dinghy in Suva. We put that over and another 120 ft (36 m) of terylene, dismantled all the self-steering gear and put that out on another line. We got all the chain out. We had 60 fathoms of $^5/_{16}$ in (7.9 mm) chain and we ran that in a big loop over the stern from the bitts up forward and we got things under control. We were down to about a knot or a knot and a half and you could still steer the boat.

About this time it got dark. We had no lights because all the batteries had been under water. Fortunately the stove still worked. We were able to get the girls wrapped up in woollen blankets, which were warm although they were wet. We put them in one bunk and tied them in and although they were wet they managed to keep warm. I made the mistake of putting on my wet suit. It was a very heavy one and after about half a day I started to get chafed under the arms and under the legs; but I was warm.

We continued to steer for 30 hours. A lot of the seas had three breaking crests down the face of them. We don't know how high they were – and talked about this too, and our estimate was 25 to 30 ft (7.5 to 9 m). As far as the boat was concerned, one battery had come out from under the floorboards and nearly gone through the cabin side. We managed to get things roughly sorted out down below.

On deck, both the aft lower stays had broken out through the thimbles and one had sprung over the top of the spreader. We had to throw a line through above the spreader and pull it back and make temporary repairs so that we could start sailing again. Amazingly, the mast was still up. We had a heck of a job to get that line. We didn't have anything very solid. All we found was a jandal.

The following day we put a light line on that and threw it up. It was like trying to thread a needle from 50 ft (15 m). It took us an hour and a half to get the line through there. It would wrap around the spreaders; it would do everything. We finally got it pulled back over and made temporary repairs – got lengths of chain and shackles and made the stays reasonably right. Through the night we both sat in the cockpit and alternately went down below and comforted the girls and made cups of tea or coffee or soup or something.

By the late afternoon of the next day we reckoned we couldn't stand another night of it. We were still getting swept from end to end about two or three times an hour. It was a risk opening the hatch. We'd sometimes wait for a quarter of an hour before we would dare open the hatch to go down below. We had no idea how hard the wind was blowing. We didn't have an anemometer and although we had a hand-held wind gauge and an underwater camera there was no way we even considered going below to get things like that.

So we decided to set some sail and we pulled up the main and we had to get all this gear in from over the stern. In the meantime it had all tied up in a knot. We could only get one turn around the winch and it took us a couple of hours to get it all in. It took us some days, later, to untangle all the rope. But soon we had it all in the cockpit. The carburettor had washed off the outboard motor (though with very little fuss, when we got home, we got it going again and we still use it. Good little outboard!).

Then we started to sail very slowly. We didn't know what had happened up at the top of the mast. We didn't have the strength to go up there anyway. Fortunately the two stays had been broken at the bottom. The wind had come in from the south or east-south-east and we were actually running parallel with the coast. We were in no danger of hammering into the coast, but after a while we would start to see Cape Brett everywhere we looked. There's no doubt about it, people give up before boats ever do.

Eventually the seas started to moderate and we took an R.D.F. bearing off Kaitaia and Whenuapai and got a rough fix about 65 miles off the coast, approximately due east off North Cape, and laid a course for Whangaroa. We still had the main reefed right down to the crosstrees and were sailing the smallest jib we had on board. It was lucky we did this, because we didn't find out till some time later that one of the joins in the mast had actually fractured. It wasn't until the boat was surveyed we realised this.

We made a landfall in Doubtless Bay late at night and it took us until about seven or eight next morning to get in to Whangaroa, by which time we were under full sail again in a very light breeze. We had to slog in a westerly through that little narrow entrance with the tide going out. We tied alongside a boat that, unbeknown to us, was on its way from Australia to Mururoa for the French Nuclear tests. All we wanted to do was sleep. Customs arrived from Whangarei in about an hour and we just booked into the hotel and had a good night's sleep.

Our last fix before we capsized had put us about 100 miles from the Moko Hinaus and 100 miles from Cape Brett, which gives you an idea of our position. According to local fishermen, there is a shoal there. Look at it on the chart. The water does shoal a lot and this would account for the size of the sea in relation to the wind.

The Brightwells had made friends with an American couple, Bruce and Sue Lamb, who had been visiting New Zealand for several months in their yacht *Iaorana,* a 30 ft (9 m) schooner. At exactly the same time as we were in trouble they were in the same area going in the opposite direction, to Fiji. And they had exactly the same thing happen to them. Their boat wasn't as strong as *Pono* and the roll-over opened up the cabin sides and carlines and they had a real job even staying afloat. They made it to Fiji, but their boat was almost a write-off. They spent a dickens of a time getting it right and then sailed back to Hawaii. As far as I know that's the last voyage they've made. Their story was almost exactly the same as ours. You strike a sea that's got no face in it — there's just a wall of water and it comes down on you.

I never lost faith in the boat, because it's so strong, but it took me a while to get my nerve back to go to sea again offshore. I had the opportunity of navigating *Kishmul* in the Sydney-Hobart race and I thought, "If I don't go now, I'll never go offshore again." So I did it, and I have been quite happy ever since. But it's shattered me a bit. Michelle would never go to sea again. For Tom and Margaret it was some time before they even went out in their boat after they got home. But they have a new boat and have completely overcome that now.

When Graham Eder sold Pono *he ordered a revolutionary new boat, a 12.8 m Bruce Farr design. He christened her* Gerontius, *and together they represented New Zealand in the Admiral's Cup series at Cowes in 1975.*

On 29 August 1977, while Pono *was cruising from Fiji to Vila in the New Hebrides, she hit an underwater object and sank in one minute. Her crew took to a liferaft and finally, after 15 days, drifted ashore at Pentecost Island. They were Paul Gedye (owner), his sister Jill Maddox, her husband Alan and Terry Byrne.*

With *Tequila* to Alaska

by D'ARCY WHITING

To be in the company of Auckland's D'Arcy and Mollie Whiting is to have fun. As yachtspeople, raconteurs, pranksters, amateur painters and warm friends they enhance proceedings wherever they go. This is what the "Baggywrinkles" column of the July 1975 issue of the Hawaii Yacht Club Bulletin, had to say as yachting friends made in Honolulu wished them a sad farewell en route to Alaska:

"A special trophy was presented to D'Arcy Whiting, wife Mollie, kids Tony and Debbie and crew Mary Hazard just before they left. I don't know when a group of cruising folk have become so dear to the hearts of so many members. As a group they added a great deal to our club — always willing to help out, always adding a note of joy to any event. If ever a family added much to a new place — the Whitings did. We love them and wish they could stay forever. Alaska may be a cold place but it will sure warm up when Tequila *arrives with her wonderful skipper and crew."*

TEQUILA was rolling gently in delightful Hanalei Bay on the island of Kauai, Hawaii. We were now well acquainted with roly-poly anchorages, for natural harbours are not plentiful in this part of the world, and the long Pacific rollers swing into most bays.

After three and a half months in the Hawaiian Islands, *Tequila* seemed to want to get going again. We had fallen in love with Hawaii and the Hawaiians. The Hawaii Yacht Club must surely be one of the great clubs of the world and we'd made so many grand friends that we could have finished the cruise there.

A meeting with John Guzzwell had changed all that. "Why don't you go to Kodiak, Alaska? Go, it's good — it's great." So we were on our way, once again in a different direction than planned.

"Try and arrive about the fourth of July," was John's advice. So at 1400 hours on 19 June we left Kauai under full main, No 1 genoa, wind north-east at 10-15 knots, just laying course 2400 miles away. The crew: Mollie, Tony and Debbie Whiting and Mary Hazard.

The breeze was slowly swinging aft and this was champagne sailing, with runs of 186 and 190 miles a day. By the 24th it was on the beam, so up went the kite. Fishing was great, with an abundance of tuna and mahimahi, Tony landing a 50 lb (22 kg) mahimahi and Mollie scooping up two huge glass balls.

With the wind now well aft of the beam, we were going (as John Lidgard would say) like a burnt boot, toasting the Great Sea God, when the smiles fell off our faces and we ran into a dense band of fog! And still kept the breeze! The temperature that had been 78 dropped to 66°F.

June 26: Lat. 39.23, long. 157.18 west, getting colder, entry in log says. Sailing through pea soup. Cold pea soup. Sea slight to moderate and no sun, just dense fog and wind and sea increasing. Went to poled-out genoa.

June 30: Lat. 50 north, long 154.10 west. Started cabin heater. Very cold: *Tequila's* watch system is: one on deck for two hours, then eight off. We'd gybed and were reaching under full main and No 1 genoa. Although I was asleep, I could hear Debbie winding in the headsail and bringing the main aboard and then I thought I could hear her crying. I shot up on deck and was met with an icy blast. With the wind well forward of the beam and straight off the ice, the cold was intense. Feeling a heel that I'd let a 15-year-old suffer this, I made up a hot water bottle and got Debbie in my bunk. Then I took over, and a few minutes later I wanted to cry myself.

Now hard on the wind and, hurrah, *Tequila* sailing herself. Blowing hard. Put two reefs in main and set spitfire jib. Had so many clothes on I could hardly struggle through the hatch. Although we could see no sun, we realised it hardly set. Night or darkness was only about an hour and a half duration. Still no sights. All dead reckoning.

I decided at 0300 on 4 July I'd better do something, so I had a rum and toasted the Great Sea God! At 0345 the sun rose in a clear sky, but from behind a great range of snow-covered mountains. Kodiak!

The day became sparkling clear. To the west stretched the Aleutian island chain. Ahead and to the east were towering ice mountains as far as the eye could see. Oh yes, we were excited!

At 1300 hours on 4 July, after 14 days and 23 hours, we motored into the harbour, jammed with huge fishing boats, and tied alongside *Compass Rose,* a sister ship of Eric and Susan Hiscock's *Wanderer IV.*

We'd only just got our lines ashore when a fishing boat came along and tossed a huge live king crab in the cockpit. It stretched the full width of the cockpit and we let it have the space on its own while we poked it with oars. King crab proved to be the most beautiful seafood we've ever tasted and we were given these each day with halibut, clams and salmon.

Kodiak had only seen the sun eight times since August last! And here we were in glorious sunshine. The country abounded in blueberries – and very big brown bears. Mollie set out to gather blueberries and, as Kodiak bears like blueberries, she took the coffee percolator half full of stones. When rattled, this was supposed to frighten a very big nasty bear. I wondered what would happen if she met a deaf bear!

So began two wonderful months cruising in the Gulf of Alaska. We anchored beneath huge glaciers in Whittier, cruised alongside huge icebergs and anchored near ice faces where great masses of ice plunged into the sea. The noise was continuous and startling. Rumblings, groanings and crackings and creaking, then the report like a cannon and a quarter-mile of ice would crash into the bay.

We saw a bear catch salmon and we saw the giant golden eagle swoop down and make off with a mighty fish. The days were sunny but the nights cold and the heater ran continuously. We'd anchor in bays of unbelievable beauty and we visited towns such as Cordova, where few, if any, yachts had ever visited. What wonderful folk are the Alaskans!

Float planes seemed more plentiful than cars and we were flown over glaciers 70 miles (113 km) wide! We saw herds of moose grazing.

I also noticed the birds heading south, and thought it was time to go. Ice was forming in some bays and we had to watch that wind changes did not close the leads or open-passage ways. Seals basked on ice floes, and Mary and Debbie took off in the dinghy to film them.

We had a short period of 40-knot winds as we crossed the Gulf of Alaska and then we were in that wonderful, interesting Intercostal Waterway. Oh, the delight of Stika, Glacier Bay, Gunea, Wrangell, Ketichan. But that's another story.

Safely over the bar

by P. A. EADDY

From *Neath Swaying Spars* (Whitcombe and Tombs)

Once an impressive sight in coastal waters, with their large spread of canvas, sailing scows are now only a memory. A few of the hulls remain on the water, converted to motor and used for various menial tasks around the harbours. Some present-day yachtsmen got their early training in sail on scows when they were just youths, and a good training it was in every facet of seamanship.

In 1904 Percy Eaddy shipped in the fore-and-aft scow Hawk. *At Tairua, on the east coast of Coromandel, they loaded all the machinery from a dismantled sawmill, even to the big steam boiler, the bricks which encased it and the dismantled mill buildings. They stowed the iron rails on deck first, then all the heavy material, finishing with the timber and corrugated iron of the mill itself.*

They left Tairua early one morning on their voyage to the Kaipara.

BY tea time the Barrier was well astern and the *Hawk* was tearing along under the three lower sails and three headsails, making splendid weather of it, but cutting up quite a dance in the big sea that we were in since leaving the Barrier astern. As usual old Dargo Bill took the wheel while all hands went below to tea.

Even seated at the cabin table we were put to no end of gymnastic performances in keeping our places and also rescuing runaway eating utensils, which kept up a continual scamper from one side of the table to the other. Suddenly a wild yell from the old cook at the wheel arrested the progress of our meal.

"The cargo on the lee deck amidships has shifted to blazes! boys, come up or we might lose half of it overside!" called Old Bill.

Barney, the skipper, was first up the companionway, we all quickly following.

"Strewth!" said Barney, taking in the situation at a glance, "get for'ard some of you, and stand by to tack ship."

Two or three of us scrambled for'ard over our awkward deck load, while the rest stayed aft to bouse in on the mizzen sheet as she came up into the wind.

"How are the centreboards, Frank?" roared the skipper as we were scrambling forward.

"Half-way down in the cases," answered Frank.

"Right oh, she's come round alright with them like that; sing out as soon as you are ready for'ard."

"All ready for'ard," roared Frank, as soon as we arrived at the lee jib sheets. "Lee oh!" was shouted from aft as the helm was put down and the big scow's head came sweeping up into the eye of the wind.

She was round on the other tack within a few minutes, carrying her way, in the sea that was running, equally as well as most round-bottomed vessels of her size.

Scows very seldom "miss stays", that is, if they are handled properly and their centreboards are lowered far enough. In our case we had commenced to surge forward again on the other tack, almost as soon as her sails filled. Once around, and the lee side that was became the weather side, we all congregated amidships to secure the part of our deck-load that had shifted.

It proved to be the huge mill boiler, which, rolling over its retaining chocks on the deck and parting the parbuckling chain which had been set up across it, had pitched up against the port main rigging. For the time being this held, until the ship had thrown it with a leeward roll back inboard once more.

By passing heavy wire lashings across it from side to side of the deck and chocking it off securely with some of the smaller pieces of machinery, we managed to make all safe again. The scow was once more put about on the other tack, heading her course to the north'ard.

The glass still continued to fall and the wind and the sea increased to a very considerable extent, so the skipper decided to run in and anchor at Whangarei Heads till the blow was over.

We lay three days at Whangarei Heads in the *Hawk,* and then one fine morning, with the wind round to the sou'west, we proceeded on our way towards Hokianga.

Fine weather took us up this picturesque harbour-studded coastline and then the North Cape was reached, our turning point, for now our course was about due west.

The wind freshened up into a good strong breeze from the sou'west as we slipped along in fairly calm water past North Cape, and our worthy skipper, who had been standing at the foot of his cabin assiduously studying the weather glass for the last ten minutes or so, called out to Frank, who was standing by the companionway, that he didn't think there would be much chance of beating down the west coast against it.

Coming on deck a little later he said:

"I think we'll stand-on on this tack well clear of Cape Maria van Diemen, and have a look at it. If it proves too strong out there we can easily run back into Tom Bowline Bay and anchor until such time as the wind shifts."

Standing out on the port tack, close hauled, with both centreboards down, we lay about as high as west-nor-west, but owing to the increasing sea, which caused the big scow to thump like a pile-driver and wallow unmercifully, we were doing no good at all, as far as proceeding on our way to Hokianga was concerned.

Towards evening we were well off-shore with the Three Kings group of islands under our lee. We tacked ship after tea, and seeing that it was hopeless, with the wind in the direction it was, to lay a course for our destination, with the wind a point or two free, we romped back towards Tom Bowline Bay.

For two days and nights we lay at anchor in Tom Bowline Bay and then early on the morning of the third day we were roused out by old Dargo Bill, who was busy with his morning task of getting the breakfast ready.

"Now then, my lads!" he bellowed down our companionway. "Rise and shine and get her out o' this, the wind's round to the north'ard an' we'll be on a lee shore if yer don't get a move on!"

Within half an hour we had the *Hawk* reaching out of Tom Bowline Bay with the wind freshening, about a point free on the starboard tack. Our steam donkey-winch had facilitated the getting under way operations, for with the fire under the boiler being kept banked, it was a simple matter to raise steam in a very short space of time. Then the setting of the three heavy fore-and-afters and the heaving in of the 45 fathoms of chain cable had been child's play.

We were just out of it in the nick of time, however, for the wind rising from this quarter made Tom Bowline Bay a most undesirable spot to lie at anchor in. Looking astern as we slipped away past Cape Reinga towards Cape Maria van Diemen, I could see the sea already pounding in on the sandy beaches.

"This'll fly round into the nor'-west and west'ard before long, so we'll have to drive her for all she's worth to get in over the bar at Hokianga before too much sea works up," said the skipper as he came aft, rubbing his hands and gazing anxiously to windward the while.

As we brought Cape Maria van Diemen abeam we gradually eased the sheets and hove the centreboard nearly right up. The big scow was now fairly flying along and when the cape came right abeam the patent log was set for the run down the coast in a south-easterly direction to Hokianga, about 70-odd miles distant.

With a fresh northerly breeze strong out on our port quarter, we coasted along the beach all that afternoon, and as night came down we passed close under Reef Point.

It was splendid sailing under these conditions; the *Hawk* surged along in great style, and with all the canvas on her that she could stagger under, she must have presented a fine picture from the shore.

Besides the three ordinary gaff topsails set above our three large fore-and-afters, we also carried two flying staysails, one between the fore and main topmasts and the other between the main and mizzen topmasts.

These two great sails ballooned out to leeward of the fore and main gaff topsails. They reached from the lower-masthead to the topmast head on their respective masts, and their sheets led aft to the deck outside of everything. They pulled like teams of wild horses in favourable winds.

I do not think that there are many fore-and-aft schooners in the world that carry more sail for their size than these sailing scows of the New Zealand coast.

Here was the *Hawk* with four headsails, three large fore-and-afters, three gaff topsails, and two flying staysails, 12 sails in all. And the vessel that was carrying this press of sail was a flat-bottomed scow that carried the whole of her cargo on deck, 300 tons deadweight, or 180,000 ft (54,000 m) of sawn timber.

The wind hauled a little more aft as the night drew on and the big scow made good time of it, as with the centreboards hove well up she floundered onward.

We slipped past the little port of Herekino, known as False Hokianga from its remarkable likeness to that place when observed from seaward. In fact, this likeness was so pronounced that on more than one occasion vessels from overseas, bound to Hokianga to load, have run for this entrance and have been in imminent danger of stranding.

At midnight the skipper came up for a look around. After studying the drift of the clouds across the sky for quite a good while, he went below and we could see him striking matches and gazing long and intently at his weather glass at the foot of the cabin stairs.

Coming on deck again, he gave orders for the three gaff topsails to be taken in and furled (the flying staysails had been doused at sunset).

After taking in the gaff topsails, we also hauled down and stowed the jib topsail and outer jib.

"We'll dodge along slowly until daylight; by the looks of things astern I think we are in for a hard blow from the nor'-west, the wind is hauling more aft all the time," said the skipper.

And he was right too, for before daylight the three booms swung over to the port side with a tremendous bang that shook the scow from stem to stern.

"Give her half the centreboards and flatten in on all the sheets, we'll hang to windward of the bar now till an hour or so before high water," called out the skipper to those of us who were for'ard hauling the head sheets over.

It was only when we brought the big scow up into the wind close-hauled that we felt the weight of the wind and the sweep of the rising sea. She shouldered her way to seawards manfully, however, slinging great showers of flying spray all over herself. As dawn broke we were forced to put a single reef into the three fore-and-afters. This eased her considerably.

It was high water at 10 a.m., but by the aid of the glasses we could already see the signal "Put to sea" (two balls horizontal on a yard on either side of the mast) hoisted on the signal station on the South Head.

"Put to sea my foot!" muttered old Barney as he gazed at the signal. "Not with this unhandy conglomeration of a cargo, anyhow," he added.

In any case the chances of our putting to sea were completely squashed just then by a yell from Frank, the leading hand, who was making his way aft over the deck-load.

"Let fly the main-sheet, the weather main chain-plates have carried away!" he sang out.

"That settles it," said Barney. "Stand by to wear ship."

"It's take the bar now, or die in the attempt! A couple of hands aft here to tend the mizzen sheet, lively now, men!" he called, as he swung the great wheel over.

Off went the scow's head, with her bluff bows snoring away down into the hollows of the big sea that was running. Then with a wild giddy rush, up she came into the wind on the other tack, with her long bowsprit stabbing madly at the low flying clouds, and her booms swinging tumultuously over to leeward.

With big Dargo Bill, the cook, and Walter the Dane at the wheel, we charged in towards the bar, which could be seen breaking heavily down to leeward. The skipper had taken up his position on the top of the after deck-house and from this point of vantage he waved directions to his two hefty helmsmen, who strove mightily to keep the scow's head down on for the entrance. The rest of stood by on deck for'ard, ready to jump for the fore-rigging as we neared the bar.

As we bore down towards the line of white foam that marked the bar, we drew closer to a stranger, which we soon recognised as the scow *Bravo*.

"Are you going in?" he signalled.

Barney jumped below for the signal book, and on reading the message, came up with the affirmative pennant under his arm.

"Run this up, young fellow!" he called to me.

On hoisting this reply, down came the *Bravo's* hoist, and as we drew within speaking distance, her skipper, a Portugese, called out through a megaphone:

"I don't alik' a dar look, what'a for you go in, Barney?"

"Starboard main rigging gone!" yelled Barney in reply, at which the Portugese skipper threw up both his hands in a gesture of despair.

"He won't come in after us," said Barney to me, as I put the signal book and flag away.

"Anyway she's a hold-scow and can weather it out with the best of them, old Joe won't risk too much."

Shortly afterwards we saw the *Bravo* come slatting by up into the wind, and stand out to sea again on the starboard tack. She passed to windward of us, and the antics she was cutting up almost made one seasick to look at her as she battled her way out against the high flung "white horses" of the west coast.

As we swept onwards towards the South Head, close to the deepest channel, the great ocean combers towered menacingly astern of us. We had shaken the reefs out of the fore-and main-sails to hurry her in ahead of these big seas, but even then she did not move fast enough for our skipper's liking.

"Up aloft there! A couple of you loose the fore and main gaff-topsails, get them out on to her as quickly as possible, men, and then give her the outer jib and jib topsail," he called out as the scow's stern rose sluggishly – only just in time to miss a huge breaking sea.

From aloft the whole scene was laid out in glorious sea panorama. The high bluff of the South Head capped with its white building and flagstaff of the signal station seemed remarkably close, the white seething line of foam marking the bar stretching away to northward on our port hand, the big, confused sea rolling in astern of us, and ahead and inside of us the peace and calm of Martin's Bay, just inside the entrance.

With the extra sail on her we simply flew before the might of those high curling breakers, but just before we reached the bar itself an enormous comber picked us up and on its crest we flew along at the rate of an express train. It won, however, eventually, passing underneath us and tearing along to break in a smother of foam a half a mile ahead.

Our stern settled into the trough and before she could lift, the big sea's successor had towered astern and, curling over with a curious sibilant sound which seemed to speak of disaster, crashed all over our devoted craft, flooding her fore and aft.

I looked from my perch in the fore-rigging for the helmsmen and for the skipper, but luckily all were safe.

The skipper had seen the oncoming sea and had jumped for the weather mizzen rigging, while both Big Bill and Walter had previously secured themselves with lashings to the after railing.

Bill's cursing could be heard above the crashing of the breaking seas, but both he and Walter handled the helm of the big scow on that mad wild rush in over the Hokianga Bar like the veterans of the sea and sailing ships that they were.

As we shot into calm water inside and looked astern at that seething maelstrom through which we had just passed, we realised how close disaster and total loss are to vessels negotiating these dangerous bar entrances.

We hauled the *Hawk* in and beached her at high-water, so that an early start could be made discharging our cargo next morning.

A slight ground swell coming in over the bar caused the scow to grind and creak for awhile before she finally settled down, hard and fast ashore for the night.

Ocean racing yacht clubs in New Zealand

by LORIS CHILWELL

WHEREVER there are yachts there are yacht clubs, but some are of more than local interest, mainly because they sponsor glamour events which transcend class racing.

The royal yacht clubs are not so named by accident, but because they have a royal charter; their members are permitted to fly the blue ensign, provided they fulfil certain other conditions and obtain a warrant to do so through their club. First they must have their boat measured and obtain registration as a British (or New Zealand) ship with the Marine Department. The ensign must be correct according to the description in the club's charter and it may be worn only when the warrant holder is aboard and so long as he or she remains a financial member of the sponsoring club.

There are three royal yacht clubs in New Zealand – the Royal New Zealand Yacht Squadron, the Royal Akarana Yacht Club (both of Auckland) and the Royal Port Nicholson Yacht Club, of Wellington.

Senior club in Auckland is the Royal New Zealand Yacht Squadron, founded in 1871 as the Auckland Yacht Club. In 1901 it became the New Zealand Yacht Squadron and in 1902 was granted a royal charter on the occasion of the coronation of King Edward VII with permission to fly the blue ensign undefaced. In 1971, its centennial year, "to mark the squadron's 100th anniversary, Her Majesty the Queen graciously authorised the squadron's flag officers to wear on board their vessels the white ensign of our New Zealand fleet".

In 100 years many traditions have become established, and the squadron's racing programme adheres to these traditions. Summer sees a points programme of Saturday harbour races interspersed with passage-races to a destination in the Hauraki Gulf and a few "family cruising" races to gulf destinations. On Boxing Day a race goes off to the Bay of Islands and in February the club meets for several days' racing at Kawau Island, a great spectacle and social occasion long known as "Squadron Weekend". Recent additions to the programme are the substitution of Olympic courses for some harbour races, and a ladies race on the Waitemata harbour.

Squadron racing members are devoted to their points programme, and large fields of seven divisions turn up on every occasion. The first Olympic points race in 1972 drew 200 entries. Saturday races leave Sunday free. Sunday "cake days", when the ladies join the yachts for a day cruise, usually to Motuihe Island, are another popular squadron tradition.

The squadron does not undertake a stringent offshore programme. But it sponsors one such race annually, the Poor Knights – Cuvier coastal race. An innovation was the first race to Rarotonga in 1974, planned to take place every fourth year.

A proud part of the recent history of the R.N.Z.Y.S. is its sponsorship of successive international challenges and defences of the One Ton Cup (which Chris Bouzaid won for the club and for New Zealand in *Rainbow II* in 1969 and in *Wai-aniwa* in 1972) and the hosting and organising of this international contest in 1971 and 1977.

In 1977 the squadron accepted a request to be host for eight weeks to the Whitbread Round the World Yacht Race contestants, who arrived in November and December on the second leg of their gruelling contest. The squadron was ideally located to play host from its clubrooms at Westhaven Boat Harbour, to where it moved at the end of 1976 after 100 years in city headquarters.

Situated at Okahu Bay Boat Harbour, handy to the starting tower at Orakei Wharf, the Royal Akarana Yacht Club is innovative where the R.N.Z.Y.S. is traditional.

Founded at Devonport with 25 racing members in 1894 as the North Shore Sailing Club, it later became known as the North Shore Yacht Club. The club changed its name to Akarana in 1922 when it moved across the harbour to Mechanics Bay, and obtained its royal charter in 1937. (Akarana is the Maori word for Auckland.) The blue ensign of the Royal Akarana Yacht Club is defaced by the club's crest, a native sailing canoe surmounted by a naval crown.

Whereas the R.N.Z.Y.S. was purely a men's club until 1975, when it started admitting a few full lady members, the Royal Akarana has been a family club with voting lady members for many years. Over the years this club has put greater and greater stress on its offshore racing programme and on racing to the International Offshore Rule (I.O.R.). The summer programme consists of offshore races and cruising races on alternate weekends, with six weekday races for lady crews. The rules for ladies' races read: "Only one man is allowed on each vessel and he may give ADVICE, if requested. He is NOT allowed to give physical assistance on sailing the yacht except in case of emergency and if for any reason such assistance is given, the yacht concerned MUST retire immediately."

R.A.Y.C. pioneered winter racing in Auckland and holds a series of eight Sunday divisional races with up to 200 yachts entered on alternate weekends, with races for lady crews interspersed.

Since 1974, R.A.Y.C. has held in October its very popular Feltex Regatta over two weekends, including Labour weekend. This event is for

Two veterans, *Ariki* (A3) and *Ranger* (A22) duelling on the Waitemata Harbour off Rangitoto for the Royal New Zealand Yacht Squadron's A-division points prize in 1967. They have been rivals since 1937, when *Ranger* joined the fleet. *Ariki* had been the champion since her launching in 1905. Still with gaff rig and powered by block and tackle, *Ariki* was still competing in 1976 against *Ranger*, whose owner-builder-skipper Lou Tercel has now passed 80 years of age. *J. E. Farrelly*

Younger duellists. *Northerner* (Boyd Hargrave, foreground) and *Kahurangi* (Lawrence Nathan) competing for the R.N.Z.Y.S. A-division points prize off Rangitoto in 1967. *J. E. Farrelly*

They say that "Flap" Martinengo knows every tidal quirk, current and rock around Auckland. This is his champion 6.7m (22 ft) mullet boat *Tamariki*, **which he campaigned so successfully in 1950, seen here racing on the harbour in the 1930s.** *Auckland Institute and Museum*

A photograph taken several years after the events described by Peter Mander in "The Debut of *Intrigue*". **Here** *Intrigue* **races on Auckland Harbour in 1954 to win the world 18-footer title for the second time.** *Ian Mason*

A sight to sadden any yachtsman. *Northerner* **raised from her resting place off Tiritiri Matangi Island after her sinking in 1964.**
New Zealand Herald

one-design and level-rating classes only, and also draws about 200 contestants from Admirals Cuppers to trailer sailers.

Unlike the squadron, which limits race entrants to member yachts, except for its recently started Wednesday evening races, Akarana accepts entrants from other clubs (at double entry fees), even in its classic races such as the Balokovic Cup and the White Island race.

A pioneer in regular ocean races to overseas destinations, the R.A.Y.C. held its first race to Suva in 1956. This race became so popular that, in conjunction with the Royal Suva Yacht Club, it was decided to hold the race every two years from 1977 onwards. So many entries were received in midwinter of 1976 for the 1977 race that a second destination was planned at Lautoka to take the overflow.

Another overseas race sponsored by the R.A.Y.C. is the Hobart-Auckland race, which takes place every second year after the completion of the Sydney-Hobart race, the final event in the Southern Cross Cup series held in Sydney.

Akarana, as it is commonly known, usually has overseas trophies on its display table. In 1976 it held the World Quarter-Ton Cup, the Coupe de France, the Southern Cross Cup, several other trophies from the Southern Cross series and trophies from the recent Vila race.

One of the club's most rewarding non-sailing achievements has been the publication of the *Coastal Cruising Handbook*, a description of passages and anchorages from East Cape to North Cape, well into its enlarged second edition.

Founded in 1883, the Royal Port Nicholson Yacht Club did much to foster yacht racing in Wellington in the early days, and continues to do so. The royal title was obtained in 1921 and permission was granted to wear the blue ensign undefaced.

Planning yacht races on Wellington Harbour is made difficult by the geography of the area, fierce squalls from the surrounding hills making some areas unsuitably hazardous for small craft. Sometimes huge seas build up on leeward shores and sudden cold comes down in southerly wind changes. Wellington yachts and yachtsmen have to be tough to sail in the conditions so often prevailing in the harbour. If they go cruising, they have to brave Cook Strait, notorious for its gales.

Nevertheless the Royal Port Nicholson Yacht Club sponsors a very full programme of harbour and offshore races. Wednesday evenings in the summer and alternate Sundays in the winter see the keeler fleet out racing on the harbour. Summer offshore races go across Cook Strait through the Tory Channel to Te Awaite; to Nelson (on anniversary weekend); to the Wairau River and The Brothers Islands (three miles east from Cape Koamaru) and back; to Port Underwood 16 miles south of Tory Channel heads; around Kapiti and Chetwode Islands; to Picton via Kapiti; to Ship Cove.

On alternate Christmas-New Year holidays the club races to and from Gisborne and to Akaroa, starting from the clubhouse on Boxing Day. The Gisborne race starts concurrently with one from Auckland to Gisborne and the race home starts on New Year's Day.

For many years the headquarters of the club has been at the Clyde Quay boat harbour, moving from a building at the eastern end of the quay in 1955 to its present site. Races are started from the starting box at the clubhouse.

There are some full lady members; but most are listed as associates, being wives or under-18 daughters of senior members, who do not have voting rights. They race annually for the Kirkcaldie Cup and the rules state: "The lady sailing any yacht must not be the regular helmsman of any racing yacht during the season."

A newcomer compared with other ocean racing clubs, the Banks Peninsula Cruising Club was formed in 1932 and the next season held its first race to Akaroa. This was to become an annual event. The club's summer programme consists of harbour races and short coastal races outside the harbour, and weekend races to Port Levy and Pigeon Bay. As a prelude to the Commonwealth Games in 1974, the club organised its first race from Auckland to Lyttelton, started in conjunction with Royal Akarana in January 1974; at that time it was the longest race ever held in New Zealand waters – a distance of 675 miles.

In 1951 the Banks Peninsula Cruising Club organised the Canterbury Centennial Race from Wellington to Lyttelton to coincide with the Lyttelton Regatta and local celebrations. An unseasonal five-day southerly gale of great intensity turned the event into the greatest tragedy in New Zealand yachting history. Two yachts, *Husky,* from Lyttelton, and *Argo,* from Wellington, disappeared and no trace of their crews of four and six was ever found.

Once outside Lyttelton Harbour, the yachts are racing in the open ocean and the club yearbook reminds its members that: "Those who earlier learned to handle a vessel in extremely heavy winds in sheltered waters must realise that in the open sea, where there is a long reach to build up waves, or superimpose waves to confuse an old wave pattern, or where deep water waves are accentuated by shallower soundings, damage to spars and gear is to be expected and solid masses of water can do immense damage very unexpectedly."

The club's general committee, if it thinks fit, may request the owner of any yacht proposing to proceed outside extended harbour limits, to cancel his or her proposed trip if, in its opinion, the yacht in question is "unsuitable or incapable of making the trip or that the crew lacks sufficient ability".

Headquarters of the Banks Peninsula Cruising Club is a delightful building extending over the water in the small craft mooring area of

Lyttelton Harbour. The club has a full social programme and an active band of associate lady members.

Other clubs whose programmes include ocean races of general interest include:

The Onerahi Yacht Club of Whangarei, whose race to Noumea is equal to Akarana's Suva race in popularity. This club's 100 mile race around the islands adjacent to Whangarei Heads also draws many contestants from other clubs.

The Devonport Yacht Club, near the Naval Base opposite Auckland City, which sponsored New Zealand's latest ocean classic, the two-person round North Island race. The inaugural event, timed to start on the morning the Queen and Prince Philip arrived on the Silver Jubilee visit in 1977, was started by Prince Philip amid a lively scene and a harbour crowded with spectator craft.

The Tauranga Yacht and Power Boat Club, which held it's first race to Vila, in the New Hebrides, in 1976.

The Gisborne Yacht Club, sponsor of the bi-annual Boxing Day twin races from Auckland and Wellington to their home base.

The New Plymouth Yacht Club, with its four-yearly singlehanded race to Mooloolaba, Queensland, first held in 1970.

The Evans Bay Yacht and Motor Boat Club of Wellington, inaugurated in 1919, which started racing across Cook Strait to Port Underwood in 1920. This club sponsors the annual race to Nelson in conjunction with the Royal Port Nicholson Yacht Club and the Nelson Sailing Club, and an annual race to The Brothers Islands.

Before leaving the subject of yacht clubs and yacht races, it may be as well to give a short explanation of the International Offshore Rule, known as I.O.R. This rule was formulated to enable yachts of different design and size to be given a constant handicap to enable each one to compete against any other one so rated.

To obtain an I.O.R. rating, each yacht must submit to an "I.O.R. measurement", each measurement taken according to stringent specifications by trained measurers, including measurements of spars and sails. The number of sails carried is restricted and certain furniture and equipment is mandatory. The resulting figures are put through a computer and reduced to a constant, which is the rating. From then on the yacht races with this rating and its handicap remains the same until the yacht is sold or anything is changed. At this point another measurement or inspection of gear must be made and the results revised. This method of handicapping is used in most international contests.

A yacht may race in any type of race (offshore, cruising, harbour) under either or both its I.O.R. rating or a club handicap. If racing under its I.O.R. rating it can compete only against other boats also racing under their I.O.R. ratings. If racing under a club handicap it is racing only against non-rated boats or other rated boats which are not using their I.O.R. ratings. Therefore it is possible (and frequently done) for a boat racing in one race to be competing against two different sets of competitors, provided the owner has paid his two entry fees. The club sponsoring the race will decide and publish in its racing instructions whether one or both of these methods of handicapping will be used.

Yachts which race beyond harbour limits are also obliged to have a safety inspection of hull and gear and to conform to current safety regulations.

Banks Peninsula cruising guide

by IAN TRELEAVEN

From Banks Peninsula Cruising Club History (Pegasus Press)

BANKS PENINSULA, rich in legend and rugged scenery, reaches well into the windswept South Pacific. It comprises more than 330,000 acres (133,000 ha) with a shore line that abounds with inlets, small and large bays and places of wonderful interest. Since 1932 these have been the home waters of the Banks Peninsula Cruising Club. Most cruising men like to make the passage from port to Akaroa at least once a year, while the bays this side of Long Lookout are their weekend haunts.

Outside Lyttelton is "blue water", with a coast line that can be difficult if one doesn't know the sheltered anchorages. Anything from flat calms to full gales and winds from every quarter can be experienced on the passage to Akaroa that nearly boxes the compass. Five miles from Lyttelton, your ship reaches the Heads. The Whistling Buoy (Thorpe's Cow, after an early harbour master), moans to the easterly roll and, if the roll does things to your breakfast, there is a nearby haven – Port Levy one mile wide and 4 miles to the shelter of Horomonga Island. In the days long past, the Ngai-tahu tribe lived there and often fought bloody battles with the Ngati-mamoe. Later it was a haven for whale ships.

From Port Levy, Blind Bay and Double Bay give way to Little Pigeon Bay, a fine haven in a southerly buster, with a stony beach which the coaster *Storm* was lucky to hit when she mistook her bays. Just around the corner, 4 miles from Lyttelton Heads, is Pigeon Bay, the third largest inlet on the Peninsula and so named by early whalers for its flocks of native birds. At the head of this inlet is Holmes Bay, a place of great peace, which is broken only when the cruising fleet arrives. Pigeon Bay was one of the places first settled in Canterbury, originally by the Hays and Sinclairs.

Outside again are Menzies and Decanter Bays, unhealthy places for small craft, so you free sheets and run into Little Akaloa, a tiny but delightful place for swimming, and if you are lucky you may catch a crayfish. Beware of northerly winds in this bay. Close by is Long Lookout, a narrow peninsula capped by a long line of pine trees – a familiar landmark to all skippers and the playground for schools of porpoise who frolic in the strong tidal streams. Then sail on past Raupo and Stony Bays, not to be deceived by the realistic Sail Rocks off the entrance to Okains Bay. This bay looks inviting, but has poor holding ground and is never quiet. The next landmark is Pa Point, then

Lavericks Bay, then round into Le Bons Bay, which is about halfway to Akaroa and good shelter in south and north-west winds, but a poor proposition in north and east winds, although possible if one can stand the motion. Le Bons can be dangerous in south-east gales.

From here on the swell takes on a longer deep-sea look and its colour changes to a deep indigo. Now you are off Steep Head, the eastern extremity of the peninsula and a sheer 600 ft (180 m) rock face topped by East Head light, your departure point if bound south. There is no more shelter until you reach Akaroa, so if the wind is north-east, up with the spinnaker and leave astern Hickory Bay with its 500-year-old nikau palms, rock bound Goughs and Fisherman's Bays and Paua Bay where the ancient Ngati-mamoe Pa was established around 1700. Pompey's Pillar, a needle-like outcrop, points the way to Long Bay, Sleepy Cove, Stony Bay, then the frowning 500 ft (150 m) cliffs fall away to Flea Bay, which despite its name is quite a beautiful spot. The cliffs rear up again and reveal the amphitheatre, where one can almost see the rows of ancient Maoris, with their thumbs up or down, depending on how you are feeling.

Suddenly the Akaroa Lighthouse appears on its low short promontory and across the entrance the oppressive Iron Head. If you are thinking of cutting the corner, beware of Longboat Rock below the lighthouse. In north-west weather expect violent squalls out of the harbour. In southerly winds, or following them, a very confused sea can be experienced, so keep a good offing before altering course for harbour. Another 5 miles up the harbour is Akaroa township and the wharf, with picturesque streets and houses topped by high green hills and many areas of native bush. The origin of the town is steeped in French history. Many of the quaint old homes have a distinctly French character. Even the streets have French names, such as Rue Jolie and Rue Lavaud.

There is good holding ground here and good shelter except in heavy southerlies, but it is possible to ride these out, especially by moving under Greens Point, near the Glen. Akaroa Harbour is extensive and has many spots of beauty as well as of historic interest. On Onawe Peninsula at the head of the harbour can still be seen the remains of the fortification dug by the Ngai-tahu when they were beseiged by the North Island chief Te Rauparaha and vanquished in a bloody battle. Up the harbour on the starboard hand is Takamatua Bay, with deep water in a channel near the cottages and good shelter in all winds.

On the other side of the harbour, opposite Akaroa, is Wainui, with no shelter but a good beach and then further up is Te Kao and Broughs Bay with good shelter and then beautiful French Farm, where one must keep in the channel for deep water and good anchorage. Above this bay the harbour is only navigable for keelers at high water, but some delightful sailing can be experienced with views of picturesque hills and bush-filled valleys. Moki and butterfish can still be caught with set nets nearer the heads and setting pots for crayfish is well worthwhile. At times there are flatfish in the upper harbour, but apart from the occasional red cod or tarakihi line fishing is poor.

There is much interesting cruising along the south side of the peninsula past Iron Head and in north-east weather this little-known coast is well worth a visit. Fascinating names such as Snuffle Nose Point, Tumbledown Bay and Murray's Mistake remind you of the early whalers. In fact, on St Patrick's Day 1835 the first shore whaling station in the South Island was established in Peraki and whaling ships used to hang out in southerlies in this bay. Rusting ring bolts in the rocks bear testimony to this and whale bones can still be found on the beach, reminding one of the hard life led by Captain Hempleman and his crews.

Just a little guile goes a long way

by O. P. MARTINENGO, as told to Loris Chilwell

"Flap" Martinengo is one of the best-known yachtsmen in Auckland, both for his racing prowess and for his many years as custodian of the Westhaven Boat Harbour, bossman on the tractor for hauling out and launching, and arbiter of fate for supplicants needing a marina berth in time of stress. On his retirement in March 1977, an era was ended on the waterfront.

Fortunately he did not also retire from sailing. Known by many epithets starting with "cunning" and "wily", he is said to know every tidal quirk, current and rock in the waters around Auckland. In his Jim Young designed NZ37 Namu *he is a constant prize winner with R.N.Z.Y.S., Akarana, Richmond and the Kawau Island yacht clubs. He is also an expressive conversationalist with many a tale to tell.*

Over the years he has owned a variety of boats, among them the large mullet boat Starlock *and the H28* Patricia. *His* Tamariki *needs no introduction to most yacht-loving Aucklanders. She has been a winner under a succession of owners, several times of the coveted Lipton Cup, and is still racing on the Waitemata.*

I'D like to tell you the story of the mullet boat race to Leigh in 1950. That time we had the 22 ft (6.7 m) *Tamariki.* She was a good boat and we had been racing her around the buoys with success.

This race to Leigh at Easter time was the third Leigh race. Prior to this the mullet boats used to race at Easter to Coromandel; but for some reason or other they changed the venue to Leigh.

On the day in question we had a perfect trip up and arrived there first.

The prize for finishing first consisted of a dozen bottles of champagne, all packed in a wooden crate, each one wrapped in straw. We duly took delivery of the vintage brew and, being teetotallers at that time to a man, we unpacked it and stowed it below the bunks, not knowing that the right thing to do was to shout all the other competitors. This no doubt raised a few eyebrows and caused us to be cast in an unfavourable light.

We went to the prize-giving at the hotel the next day and we were presented with the cash prize, which we proceeded to put in our pockets and not spread it around the bar. This further increased our unpopularity, but of this we were blissfully ignorant.

On the Sunday the club was to stage a sweepstake race back to Lidgards bay at Kawau, to start with a gun outside the hotel. There was to be another prize of two crates of beer for the first boat out of the harbour. The idea was that we all had to tear down the road, hop in our dinghies, row madly out to the boat and start sailing out into the bay.

The previous night I thought to myself, "Well, we're anchored well in the harbour, there are boats anchored much nearer the heads than we are, so we had better rectify this disadvantage." We joined all our spare rope, of which we had great quantities aboard, and at dead of night we tied it to the bollard. Then we quietly rowed out and anchored the end of it near the entrance. We left our main pick down as before, on a short warp.

Being honest and believing in doing everything according to the rules, we all left the ship the next morning and went up to the hotel for the start of the race. There were others not so honest who left a man or two aboard.

The gun went and we all ran off. Some took short cuts and ended up in the blackberries. The boats with men left aboard had their sails up very quickly – some even before the dinghies got back to the boats.

We only had a small dinghy, so we had to make two trips. Nevertheless our sails were up before the second load arrived back. Quickly we pulled up our main anchor and started to pull on the long warp and were off straight up the bay at about three knots. The others were taking much more time, having to tack with a little puff here and a little puff there.

We beat the rest of the fleet to the outside of the heads by about five minutes and were off across Omaha Bay to finish first outside Roy Lidgard's house at Smelting House Bay.

The Lidgards were great and invited us all ashore to their house for the evening and turned on supper. By this time I was clued up on the mistakes I had made before, and when I was presented with the two crates of beer that were the prize, I said, "Come on boys, open them up and be in." So then I managed to retrieve quite a bit of the popularity I had lost earlier.

There were some 26 ft (7.9 m) mullet boats in that race, and we beat them all too, so we felt we had had a most successful Easter.

The debut of *Intrigue*

by PETER MANDER and BRIAN O'NEILL

From *Give a Man a Boat* (A. H. & A. W. Reed)

A champion yachtsman and designer in centreboard classes, Peter Mander represented New Zealand in three Olympic contests and won an Olympic Gold Medal in 1956. He also skippered the winning eighteen footer (5.48 m) world champion Intrigue *in 1952 and 1954.*

IT looked as if we were running out of classes to race in for national trophies.

The eighteen-footers (5.48 m) had what they called a "world" championship. Although that was drawing the bow a bit, at least they carried with their biennial contest the cachet of international competition. They also provided an opportunity for us to see whether our knowledge, experience and ability were adequate when they were pitted against Aucklanders and Australians who had developed and raced these thoroughbreds over a period of many years.

There was a tiny eighteen-footer society on the Waimakariri River, but we had little to do with it until 1951, when my brother Graham designed a boat for one of its members. I decided I, too, would design an eighteen-footer, build and sail it, not on the Waimak but in the heart of eighteen-footer country: Waitemata Harbour.

The eighteen-footer world sailing championship began in 1938 when four New Zealand boats went from Auckland to compete against Australian boats at a carnival regatta to mark Sydney's 150th anniversary. Two America's Cup contestants – Britain's Sopwith and America's Vanderbilt – showed an interest in the contest and at one time there was a possibility of an entry from Hong Kong. The founder of the New South Wales Eighteen-Footer Sailing League, James J. Giltinan, gave a magnificent trophy for an event which was, with typically Australian entrepreneurship, cited a "world" championship.

As it happened, only Australia and New Zealand were able to compete in the first contest, which was won by Australia's *Taree.* The Aussies crossed the Tasman the following year and had the trophy lifted off them by the Auckland boat *Manu.* War interrupted the series, which was resumed in 1948, when Australia returned to Auckland and took the trophy home with a boat called *Crow's Nest;* and in 1949 at Sydney, an Australian boat, *Top Weight,* was winner.

In 1950, when the contest was won by the Aucklander, Jack Logan, sailing *Komutu,* Fiji competed for the first time, its representative being

O-Vuka, a new boat designed and built by one of the fathers of the Royal Suva Yacht Club, Alex Bentley. The 1951 winner, and the holder of the Giltinan Trophy, which we hoped to have a crack at, was *Myra Too,* from New South Wales.

The eighteen-footers were something to stir our blood, excite our interest and provoke our participation. A purblind landlubber could thrill at the sight of a mountain of graceful white sail billowing atop the low, open hulls as they leaped over the water; a yachtsman, particularly a designer-builder, could find the freedom of scope for his lines and ideas in both hull and sail plan, an outlet for his talent.

Competitors and observers had learned much from watching developments in the class and the result had been steadily-improving boats and the appearance of a number of interesting designs. We had heard, too, that the eighteen-footer contests were free – unusually free – of the snarling, the dissension, the inconsistent rulings and soul-destroying acrimony that all too often accompanied the measuring of boats before national class contests in New Zealand.

In the eighteen footers, bright schemes were what was wanted, and when you went to a contest you went to sail hard, not to argue. As each contest had gone by, more and more youthful yachtsmen had learned the thrill of matching speed, resourcefulness and experience against those of fellow-sailors of some of the fastest craft for their size in the world.

We had some thoughts about making them even faster: to construct a first-class hull whose properties would be assisted by as many gadgets as we could devise and for years had been itching to try, but had been prevented from doing so in established New Zealand classes. We believed we could whip up a disciplined crew. It would have to be – six men in combination, having understanding and lightning response to the requirement of the moment.

The scientific application of body weight is the main factor affecting the maintenance of speed in a centreboard yacht and it was a factor that I personally considered had not been studied or applied sufficiently. After all, the crew weighed something approaching half a ton all-up, and their continual action made them a shifting, fluid cargo which had to be taken into account. The more that hull could be kept on an even keel, notwithstanding the vagaries of the wind and the movement of the crew, the better the yacht would keep under way. A boat that yaws and plunges, heels over hard and swings in the wind, is alternately stopping and starting, losing vital seconds each time it decelerates; the seconds, cumulatively, build to minutes . . . Good crew response would overcome this.

It was teamwork from the word go. As an eighteen-footer required a lot of thought and effort to construct, we decided to form a partnership, complete with formal memorandum of agreement. The main members were Bill Nicholson, a shipwright, who was responsible for the hull construction; Brian Wall, an electrician by trade but a veritable Mr Fixit, who was responsible for fittings and metalwork; and myself, engineroom, for that is what a sail department is.

As it turned out, the boat we ended up with was – as planned – extremely steady, but in retrospect I feel Brian's lines would have made an even faster hull. However, that was only one of many lessons learned from that period.

It was built at Dad's place. We all weighed in with much of the work involved in the three departments, but each chap was boss of his own section. If he decided a fitting should be constructed in a certain way, a piece of wood used in a special place, a particular stitch or cut required in a sail, his say-so went. At the weekends we worked on the hull; at nights we spent our time on sails and fittings.

We would think of something, talk about it, argue, debate, draw, and finally make it – only to discard it. It was experiment, experiment, experiment, but in the end it reached the water and as there wasn't, in our own area, any competition to try it out against, and as we felt we had to find out how we were ticking, we hooked it on to Ian Smith's 1934 Vauxhall 14-6 and he towed it through the North Island for our debut at the Auckland anniversary regatta. For an unknown quantity, what better name could we have chosen than *Intrigue,* with a distinctive marking – a gigantic question-mark – on the mainsail and spinnaker?

In addition to Bill Nicholson, Brian Wall, Ian Smith and myself, there were my brother Graham and Marsh Neilson to make up the crew. Graham had just ridden up to Auckland on his motor-bike from the Idle Along contest at Petone. At Paraparaumu, at about eleven o'clock at night, he ran out of gas and was picked up by a Good Samaritan who took him home to his place and fixed everything up. In conversation, Graham mentioned he came from Christchurch and had been yachting. The helper asked Graham if he might possibly have heard of his cousin, John Pickering.

"Yes," replied Graham, "he has been one of my crew all the week."

When we lifted *Intrigue* off its 8 ft (2.4 m)-wide trailer, we sailed to Westhaven to compete in a race a couple of days before the regatta. It was a hard, damp westerly, with an astonishing number of leads. Jack Logan and his crew in his skimmer *Tarua* sat on their gunwale like sparrows on a rail, smoking pipes with bowls down and hardly seeming to work. When we came to slog into the wind, on one of the few short beats, we had to work like the devil. The only comfort was that we made better time than a Tornado, a new boat hot off the press, trying to sail in the same direction. You might describe the Tornado as a prototype Flying Dutchman. One of the few Uffa Fox designs that went wrong, it was being promoted as a two-man international class, but never caught on.

Downhill we seemed to be going ok, but upwind was another tale and a sad one at that. Our full sails, inherited from Idle Along and fourteen-footer (4.27 m) practice, lack of trapezes, the complete absence of self-baling venturis, all meant the boat shipped water. The sail area was only 250 sq ft (23 sq m), but with its narrow, high-cut headsail and over-full main, it was more than we could handle. We weren't helped by our large-section mast, which, while it was very light, contributed unnecessarily to windage (and that would be the understatement of the day). The Auckland boats had begun using trapezes, an innovation we could see we would have to make as well.

Because there were no venturis, or other self-baling devices, we had to pump out all the water we were shipping aboard. Most boats had pumps which ranged from the purloined milkshake container on the end of a stick, to hefty, man-sized wooden-box pieces made at home, but among the gadgets aboard *Intrigue,* useful and otherwise, was the most marvellous double-acting diaphragm pump of immense capacity. It would pump more water for less effort than any other pump I have yet seen in a boat. This was, of course, in theory.

Alas! The outlet was at the bottom of the chamber instead of at the correct place, the top. The result was an airlock which made the handle feel like a piece of india-rubber and just about as effective. The pump was like everything else in the boat: thought about, pushed in and not tried because there wasn't time to test it before leaving home. The long and short of it was that after the pump did not come up to expectations and I tried to improve its operation by vigorous pumping, the handle came away in my hand and we had no pump.

At this point we became indebted to Des Skelton, who helped us more than anyone when we were in eighteen-footers. Skelton was a controversial Aucklander who owned a boat called *Norseman,* a 30 square-metre, an unusual type of craft for the Waitemata, where unusual craft abound. He had done a lot of organising for the Eighteen-Footer Flying Squadron and, as is often the case, had become unpopular in certain quarters. He finally gave up this part of sailing administration. Skelton knew a lot about eighteen-footers compared with our crew of new chums and, in his typically generous and open-handed manner, lent us a vortex rotary pump which we screwed to the top of our centrecase.

Regatta day was a battle through steep seas. We shipped water by the hundredweight and Graham was constantly winding the handle of the vortex. Its rated capacity was a ton in seven and a half minutes – just a toy when it came to removing the water in the amounts we were taking. It was a calamity-day all right. The screws came out, the pump jumped off the case, and Graham continued his work flopping about the bilges, standing and sitting on brass screws, some of which went up the spout, gallantly working the machine under one arm. The pump would jam and the water would rise in the hull to a good foot of slop.

At the end of the first windward beat we were, to put a chartitable phrase to it, somewhat behind the rest of the fleet, which, I may say, had thinned out considerably, rough seas and fresh wind having taken their toll. We came around the mark and I ordered a small kite, a 200-footer (18.5 sq m), to be hauled up. As the spinnaker broke out it lifted the boat with a jerk and Graham went sliding along the bottom of the boat, his back in the bilge, until his feet braced against the centrecase, where he just managed to hold the spinnaker sheet. I'm not easily shocked but – perhaps it might be better to pass over his actual words in the face of our hilarity.

We did, however, gain ground as we ran down before the wind and came up with Howard Pascoe's boat *Result,* first of the small-stern eighteens. Suddenly, while on the wind, his centreplate broke off flush with the hull – whether from stress of the weather or from the boat's proximity to Bean Rock, I don't know to this day – and *Result* limped off in the direction of Kohimarama.

As we came past Orakei Wharf on the final beat, we had had it; all of us were completely, absolutely, utterly – as Peter Jones might say – tired out.

The boat was banging and shaking everything loose as it jumped from wave to wave. The bilges were flexing inwards in a most disconcerting fashion. A good nine inches of water in the bottom was surging and splashing from side to side around our legs. As the mast vibrated in its step, the alloy crosstrees were coming to pieces. The tiller was waving me about like a rag doll. It was five o'clock in the afternoon and *Intrigue* had to be aboard the inter-island steamer express at Wellington, at the other end of the island, 22 hours hence. We had found what we needed to know – that we and the boat were no damn good. We looked at the Orakei Wharf where we had launched and we couldn't get there fast enough.

Everything seemed misery. Everything had gone wrong. The pump. We couldn't hold the boat. We couldn't get the water out. We couldn't sail to weather as we should have. If it hadn't been for the damage to the rest of the fleet, we wouldn't have been anywhere. I was most unhappy about the sails, which were largely responsible for our performance. A world-beater we'd been aiming for, and what a thrashing we'd taken.

We had a semi-formal meeting over tea on the top floor of the Farmers' building, looking disconsolately out over the city and the beautiful harbour. Where did we go from here? Was it worth while carrying on after such a shambles? Or should we just go home and forget about the whole thing and take up Idle Alongs or golf or something? The world championships were five months away, at Suva. None of us had been on a South Seas holiday; so we decided to go for one. And take the boat with us.

In fact the crew returned home, revamped their boat from the lessons learned and went on to win the series in Suva.

Raced to the bottom

by MAX CARTER, as told to Loris Chilwell

A bluff, chunky man, with an Irish heritage and mountains of drive, Max Carter has had a varied career in the boating world. A successful boatbuilder, he gave up his yard, where he employed 54 people, in 1968 and went to Fiji to take over management of a shipyard there. Here he did ship repairs and also hauled out about 100 yachts a year. At one time the famous American racer, Ondine, *was on the slipway, where her bow was cut off and altered to improve her rating for the Sydney-Hobart race.*

On his return to Auckland, he took over management of Yachtspar, and in five years the staff had increased from eight to 28. He goes away twice a year to Taiwan, Hong Kong, Japan and other points east to collect export orders. The famous shipbuilding firm of Cheoy Lee is among his clients, and nowadays it is commonplace for Cheoy Lee boats to have New Zealand-made spars.

"I was talked into going to Fiji, and stayed there three years," he said. "I only left because we had to send our children home to school and it was breaking my wife's heart. I loved it in Fiji, but it is better to break up a business than a marriage."

This is the story of Max Carter and Northerner.

NORTHERNER was one of the fastest boats in Auckland at the time I sank her. She was a real glamour boat and the only boat in years that could beat *Ranger.* We used to take it in turns to win, week after week, and Lou Tercel used to come over every week to talk it over. I put her in the water for Boyd Hargrave on 5 November 1963, and I lost her on 8 February 1964.

This time we were starting in the Balokovic Cup. Boyd Hargrave had to go to a wedding at Dargaville, but his son Don and his brother Win were in the boat. The others in the crew were Peter Hay, Michael Williams, Neill Mills, John Roxborough, Ron Feisst and Philip Hawkins.

The race started on a day with about 10 or 12 knots of wind and soon after the start we had taken the lead and slowly opened a gap. We were first around the Cow and Calf. The boat was one of the first in New Zealand to have a Brookes and Gatehouse speedo, but it would only read up to 10 knots.

It was a slog in a light north-easterly out to the Cow and Calf and then it was a reach up to Canoe Rock and on the way there we had the speedo off the clock and we had to guess how fast the boat was going. We were disappointed on reaching Canoe Rock to find that we had only been going a little over 10 knots on average, about 10 and a quarter, I suppose. To the Cow and Calf we had also found the speed was less than we had anticipated.

When we took a compass course to come back to Auckland, the wind had increased and a bit of an easterly swell had come up. We put a spinnaker on the boat and started to surf continuously on the waves. We estimated she was doing about 11 knots.

We couldn't see Tiri Light, so we decided we would run for one hour like this and then, if we still couldn't see Tiri Light, we'd take off the spinnaker and head for Tiri Passage. It was very dark, the moon hadn't come out and it was raining a light drizzle. Fifty-eight minutes after leaving Canoe Rock, it was at 8.28 p.m., and we were about to take the spinnaker off, there was a great boomph and we hit Bollons Rock. It turned out the boat had actually been averaging about 13 knots!

Northerner was shooting a wave and heeling over at about 16° when we hit. It was very hard to see ahead because of the terrific amount of spray. I think the wave carried us up over the rock and then dropped us down on top of it with that tremendous crash.

The bow went down and the stern up and I flipped over the wheel. The crew, who were all in the cockpit, were hurled off their feet and against the bulkhead. I'd ordered them all down there earlier because if we'd lost a man overboard in the dark there'd be no chance of finding him. *Northerner* stopped dead. Luckily no-one went in the water. I managed to gybe her free, from starboard to port, and she slipped off the rock. With a heavy starboard list, we started to sail for Tiri at a speed of about half a knot.

Water began flowing in. We bailed with buckets, biscuit tins and anything we could get our hands on. We went below to try to find the hole in the hope we could jam some life jackets into it. We couldn't find any hole, so I presumed the crash had forced the rudder up and water was coming in there. We did two tacks of about a quarter of an hour each and kept bailing all the time. We tried to keep sailing, but we had no rudder and no motor working. The decks were awash and after about a half an hour she went down with all her sails up. She stood 72 ft (22 m) high from the bottom of the keel to the top of the mast, but the mast disappeared beneath the water.

We had tried hard to stem the damage, but it turned out it was under the water tanks. Anyway we went in to get bearings on land so we could know where we were. But the rudder had been damaged and it was hard to make headway. It was still pretty dark.

In those days life rafts were not compulsory bits of equipment. There were nine of us on board and we only had a little fibreglass dinghy. We got six of the fellows in that. We also had a 20 ft (6 m) spinnaker pole. It was hollow and supported the rest of the crew.

Before we took the dinghy and the pole, we sent up a couple of flares, but there was no answer, so we held on to the rest of the flares. About 20

Two years later ***Northerner*** **is racing in the 1966 Auckland Anniversary Regatta with other A-class keelers.** *From left: Ranger, Hinemoa, Jupiter, Northerner, Arohia, Ta'Aroa, Ariki, Moana.*
J. E. Farrelly

Revisiting Captain Cook's anchorages. Philip Houghton's *Murihiku* **in the entrances to Acheron Passage in Dusky Sound.** *New Zealand Herald*

minutes later one of the Union Company freighters, the *Kawerau,* who was coming in from north, altered course. They had seen our flares and the S.O.S. sent out by Don Hargrave with a torch. I have to praise that skipper, Captain Stevens, for the way he manouevred to pick us up.

We were pretty close to Tiri, but there was still a bit of wind and sea. We couldn't row the dinghy, or it would have sunk, we just had to keep her so she would bob up and down in the waves. Altogether we were in the water about 40 minutes.

When we got to Auckland, we couldn't get off the ship until morning because we were on a foreign-going ship and Customs wouldn't let us get off until all the papers were straightened out. We finally got off in the morning, which was Sunday.

That day we went out in the tug *Sierra.* There were Boyd Hargrave, Bob Stewart, who designed her, and various others. We dragged with a grapnel on a long line for two and a quarter hours and found her. She was standing dead upright, mast and all. The divers did an inspection and left marker buoys. There was a hole in the port bilge and the keel was damaged. We took the sails and main boom to relieve the pressure from the tides.

On Monday we went out again. We removed the mast and all the rigging intact and it was towed back to Auckland.

The next two days it was blowing hard and they were very bad days, so we couldn't go back to salvage *Northerner.*

We went out on Thursday very early in the morning with one of Harry Julian's tugs, *Sea Toiler,* towing the Harbour Board crane, and one of Subritzsky's little boats, *Greyhound,* with Warwick Dunsford the insurance surveyor, Rex McCoomb, Harry Pope and Les Subritzsky. We went straight to the markers, and there she was sunk in 120 ft (35 m), or something of that order.

We managed to get a strap under the boat. We virtually had to burrow under the boat – she had wriggled herself down into the mud among the scallops. We had scallops and eggs for breakfast. The eggs had survived the pressure of all that water, although the water tanks had collapsed.

The crane winched her up. Harry Pope, who was a boatbuilder with Baileys then, nailed wooden plates backed with felt over the holes. Harry, Rex McCoomb and Les Subritzsky were all under the boat with scuba gear. We got petrol pumps and pumped the water out of her. Then we brought the boat back and hauled her out at Percy Vos's yard. We put a sail on to come back up the harbour, just for the hell of it. Later we trailed her out to my yard at Penrose.

She wasn't as badly damaged as the newspapers made out. They said she had twelve holes, the biggest 5 ft (1.5 m) long by 6 in (150 mm) wide. Actually most of the damage was water damage. The physical structural damage was not very great. The major damage was to the wiring. The engine was full of water and all the electrics had corroded badly in just that length of time.

We were back in the water again a few weeks after we sank her in early March. The starboard bilge had been replanked, the hull refibreglassed, the interior stripped right down and a new auxiliary motor fitted, the whole boat repainted. We got a second that day in a race to Kawau from Auckland.

They tell me Boyd Hargrave came back from the wedding and went up to the racing tower to see how *Northerner* was placed. "Oh she sank," said the race official casually without turning around and went back to the time sheet. Boyd Hargrave is a wonderful fellow. I couldn't have got a better guy to sink a boat for.

Northerner *remains one of the leading yachts in the first division of the Royal New Zealand Yacht Squadron. A 14.9 m sloop, she continues to race on the Waitemata. In 1977 she carried the white ensign of her new owner, the commodore, Hugh Littler.*

Cook's anchorages revisited

by PHILIP HOUGHTON

From *Land from the Masthead* (Hodder and Stoughton)

In 1966 the author and his mate, Mike, circumnavigated New Zealand in Murihiku, *visiting anchorages used by Captain Cook. A doctor of medicine, Philip Houghton is at present engaged in research in the anatomy department of Otago University.*

WE entered Preservation Inlet, passing several fishing boats coming out for the day. Some came alongside to see if we were happy. We were. In the anchorage we ate a breakfast of crayfish and blue-cod fillets someone had tossed aboard. Then slept.

I woke with a vague awareness of being somewhere unexpected and delightful, but in the first sluggish stirrings of consciousness could not orientate myself. Rectangles of sunlight lay across the cabin and swung from floor to lockers as *Murihiku* rolled slightly. A mess of clothing lay scattered around the floor and on the ends of the bunks. Mike, his head shoved in the shadow of a corner, snored gently. It was mid-day. Rather blearily I went up on deck, and Fiordland was there.

Not a cloud crossed the sky, and the sea breeze came in quite strongly to the anchorage. The broad expanse of the sound ran back between hills of the richest green, rising steeply from the water for two to three thousand feet before flattening and turning brown with tussock. The sun was warm, and I hadn't felt real sun for weeks.

I lit the primus and poached some crayfish, then woke Mike. We sat in the sun on the hot deck and ate the white flesh. Afterwards, with difficulty, for our sense of lethargy was great, we weighed anchor and ran into the sound with the sea breeze. Like the others northward – a dozen of them – it runs well inland, more than 20 miles. After two hours fair sailing between islands and close under bush slopes we came to a deep bay where a long beach of white sand fronted a flat-floored valley that promised an evening stalk. As happens commonly in the fiords, the soundings came up rapidly, from fifteen fathoms to nothing in a matter of yards, and after nearly putting *Murihiku* on the bank we pulled her back to fifteen fathoms where she lay out of the wind and with the chain vertical. Bush, hills and the calm of the late afternoon were liberal reward for any number of endured westerlies.

Driftwood littered the beach. In the evening we lit a great fire and baked bread, and Mike floundered back into the bush, through masses of waist-high fern, and shot a couple of deer. This solved the meat problem for a while, but there were lots of others, for our abrupt departure from the island had left us short of provisions. There was wholemeal enough to bake a vast number of loaves and a mere half-kilogram of butter to coat them all. We had no vegetables beyond a cabbage that was starting to look like a mouldy football. But as long as we possessed a fish-hook there was no chance of starvation, for all the tall stories about fishing in the fiords turned out to be short of the truth. It simply came down to the fact that if a hook lowered over the side didn't have a fish on it in 10 seconds the bait had come off. In point of fact the time interval is nearer five seconds, but one mustn't stretch people's credulity.

In the morning we went back down the sound on the same sort of day, cloudless and hot, with a light sea breeze. I wanted to get a photo of *Murihiku* under full sail, not an easy thing with two aboard, and the only time I had seen her thus, from the sinking dinghy in Paterson Inlet, photography had been far from my mind. But she had looked magnificent leaning to the westerly under that spread, lee rail under the white tops, with the sandcoloured decks, the blue trimmings to the coachroof, the red throats of the ventilators and beyond, the darkness of the cloud and the Ruggedies.

I rowed off in the dinghy and Mike made a few turns back and forth across the mouth of the sound. He was away across the other side when one of the fishing boats came into view across the mouth of the sound, just drifting, the crew on deck repairing craypots.

"That's not you, Tim?" I said.

"Indeed it is," he said. "And what in the world brings you down here?"

"The old insanity," I said, and heaved myself over the rail.

I hadn't seen him in a long time, the square face, the archetypal seaman's face.

"How are you off for supplies?" he said.

"We left the island in a hurry. We've no butter," I said. He gave us a lot of supplies, and during the weeks in the sound every other boat seemed to do the same. Some chased after us when we were doing five knots up the coast, just to throw crayfish aboard. "If we kept painting the boat a different colour," said Mike "we could live for ever around here for nothing."

The weather office maintained faith in their imminent nor'wester. We, at the fringe of the western ocean, couldn't see it, but wanting to enter Dusky Sound on a clear day, made out of Preservation, across the mouth of Chalky Inlet and inside the rough tops of Balleny Reef. Captain John Balleny of the *Eliza Scott,* a sealing vessel in the 1830s, named it, but Cook himself saw the danger much earlier. In the *Resolution* on his second voyage he made his landfall a little far south, intending to fetch Dusky but finding Chalky. It was misty: "Fearing to run, in thick weather, into a place to which we were all strangers, and seeing some breakers and broken ground ahead, I tacked in 25 fathoms of water and stood out to sea, with the wind at N.W. This bay lies on the S.E. side of Cape West, and may be known by a white cliff on one of the isles which lies in the entrance of the bay."

The breakers and broken ground would have been the Balleny Reef, and Cook added, with customary frankness: "This part of the coast I did not see but at a great distance, in my former voyage; and we now saw it under so many disadvantageous circumstances, that the less I say about it the fewer mistakes I shall make."

We lost the wind and motored in an uncomfortable fashion across all manner of confused waves and currents at the entrance to Chalky. Beyond the white-cliffed islands which identify it we found a light southerly and made northward up the Fiordland coast. It is not really characteristic here, in the 20 miles between Chalky and Dusky, running in nearly a straight line without any worthwhile indentation and coming in low cliffs to the water. Even beyond the coast the land rises only slowly, and without the usual chasms and summits. Only about halfway to Dusky does any sort of headland protrude, and this is Cape West; again, no very significant thing, but it did mean that *Murihiku* had rounded the four extremities of the land. It is a curious thing that the two capes of the south, which by and large has a more formidable coast, should be less remarkable than the two of the north.

A couple of hours beyond the cape we lay opposite Dusky and if, in retrospect, we had to say that any one moment of the cruise stood out above all others – in truth, that would be a hard question – it was this moment. Dusky lay before us. It is immense. We were lost in the width of the vast entrance and the sound seemed as wide as deep; but not of course in fact, for the sea cuts deeply beyond the concealing islands. Within the farspaced entrance points we saw a calm expanse of water strewn with dozens of islands, large and small. Behind rose the sharp peaks of Resolution Island and the mainland. The nearer greens of the land changed to brown and purple with distance and at this season only a few scraps of snow lingered around the highest summits. Not a habitation, not a boat, and the white standard of the light on the southern entrance point must have been the only addition, the only thing changed in the scene since the *Resolution* entered nearly two centuries before. The *Resolution* and not the *Endeavour,* for Dusky was only viewed and named on the first voyage.

Night came as the *Endeavour* approached the land, and she had been blown northward by morning. But from its position, in the track of the westerlies, Cook perceived its potential as a harbour for sailing vessels; "It is about three or four miles broad at the Entrance, and seems to be as full as deep. In it are several islands, behind which there must be shelter from all winds, provided there is a sufficient depth of water." And of course this last is no problem. Rather, there is too much water; a hundred fathoms will not find bottom in places within the sound, and it is necessary to moor close in, with a warp ashore. Making the bay from southward on the second voyage the *Resolution* found water enough, 40 fathoms at the entrance and then no bottom at 60.

Inside the entrance point we lost all wind and started an untraditional engine. *Murihiku* came abreast of the entrance to Pickersgill Harbour. It is an indentation of the shore partly shielded from the main reach of the sound by a small, high island, Crayfish Island; only partly and not adequately, as we were to learn. We looked at the narrow entrance to the west of the island. From the journals it seems clear the *Resolution* was sailed in, and not towed by the ship's boats. For us there was not a breath of wind so, shamefaced, we chugged through.

Within, we drifted to a halt on the calm water, wanting to moor precisely where the *Resolution* had, but not sure where to go. None of the journals was specific on this point, simply talking of "a cove" or "facing Astronomer Point", which is ambiguous. A number of minor promontories with intervening creeks faced us. The nautical chart showed Astronomer Point clearly enough, but not the anchorage, and in any case seemed not very accurate. In the end we turned to the facsimile of a chart drawn by Henry Roberts, a 15-year-old draughtsman on the ship, and only here did we find firm evidence of the place, in the cove south of Astronomer Point. We dropped the bower anchor in eight fathoms and then, using the dinghy, warped *Murihiku* in by the stern until she lay a few yards off the rocky bank, in four fathoms, much as the *Resolution* must have done. Thus secured, we sat on deck in the sun and looked around at the historic place. After the immediate entry to the sound it was, I think, the supreme moment of the cruise.

But we were to learn that the popular conception of the fiords as vast havens for vessels, full of splendid anchorages, was fallacy. To some extent this may be true for ships, of something more than, say, a hundred tons. But for boats, for small fishing vessels or something like *Murihiku,* this is just not so. In all of Dusky there is only one anchorage beyond criticism, and that is Luncheon Cove, and similarly most of the other fiords seem to have only one acceptable anchorage.

Cook, while surveying the south-east side of Anchor Island, where a confusion of rocks and small island lie, wrote: "I found here a very snug cove sheltered from all winds, which we call Luncheon Cove, because here we dined on crayfish, on the side of a pleasant brook shaded by the trees from both wind and sun."

Without any canvas up we motored through the narrow entrance of Pickersgill Harbour, and straight away things went wrong. Tide and wind against her, *Murihiku* was not happy, and out there it was blowing far harder than I had realised. She kept on course for a moment and then slewed to port. With the wind abeam and the tide pressing on her long keel she defied correction and just ploughed on for the cliff face. There was nothing to be done, there was no room to wear ship, and I simply pushed the engine revs up to the limit and leaned on the helm. The rock came up and I remember thinking, rather sadly, that it was at least a noble place to finish. Then, just a few yards short, *Murihiku* felt the rebounding wind off the wall, and this sufficed. She answered, the whole hull churned round, and we ran into the wind alongside the steep-to limits of the entrance, so close we could just put our hands out and touch the rock.

Billy flung us a line. With our 30 horses and his 60 champing we plugged across the sound. I can't imagine what it was like at sea. Here, in the sheltered waters of the sound, the air was white with spray willy-waws swept over us, and three or four times *Murihiku* was close to lying on her beam ends. Then we came between the small islands and into Luncheon Cove, and a few minutes later *Murihiku* sat comfortably alongside Cardie's large and luxurious *Minerva.*

Here we dined in the evening while the wind howled beyond us, occasionally dropping into the cove to toss up a bit of spray. It had not been a proud day, towed across Dusky after near-disaster. What would Cook have thought?

Aboard a 727 in 72 knots

by JIM BOLLAND

From *Sailmaker*

Of all the many nasty days that made up the 1975-76 yachting season in Wellington one in particular will be a lasting memory for Jim Bolland, who sailed on Dennis Dodson's Farr 727 quarter-tonner Blue Streaker. *The events described in this story took place on a typical Saturday in December.*

AFTER two and a half months of 20-knot plus racing, this particular December Saturday was not outstanding because it was already blowing 25 knots at 10 a.m., but more because of the state of health of *Blue Streaker's* crew.

For the first time that season, Friday evening social life had reduced all four of our crew to shadows of our usual healthy, enthusiastic selves. Procrastination set in (also for the first and happily that season the last time) with regard to firstly, should we go and after deciding that with the championship points at stake we had to *!?**!! well go, the second problem was with what rig?

Because of procrastination we were late implementing the belated decision to reef the No. 2 genoa and put one slab in the main. Procrastination then took its usual course and turned into panic and in the ensuing melee some "body" removed a reef lacing eyelet and large portion of 120 g Hood cloth from the mainsail. So it was deep reef, like it or not.

By this stage, of course, we were late for the start.

Shortly after crossing the start line we got a taste of things to come and changed down to No. 3 genoa. There was some real weight in those squalls from the north-west, but we had our ears pinned back now and were starting to gather the opposition in. Fresh air and cold water was working wonders on our Corubarized constitutions.

We rounded the weather mark at Ngauranga in a squall harder than any so far and as we bore away for the run to Hope Shoal Light (in the Wellington Harbour entrance) we noticed the leaders in real trouble trying to carry spinnakers in the strengthening wind which was now swinging further to the north and blowing steadily at 40 m.p.h.

We changed back to the No. 2 genoa and poled it out for the run – and what a run. The seas got bigger and the wind continued to increase. The 727 was in its element and we all but ran Russell Cooney's Harmonic 24 to the ground by the time we reached the leeward mark.

Now it was blowing! We reefed No. 3 and deep reefed the main, and we just staggered in the hard bits. The Harmonic was in trouble, her keel would come out of the water and she would slide slideways. Although staggering, good old 727 was still sailing and sailing away from the opposition.

Our next mark was the buoy at Korokoro (near Petone) and it looked a long way to weather through the white haze of spray now covering Wellington Harbour. As we cleared Somes Island we were hit by the full force of the gale now blowing and we wondered just how much more we could take and keep racing.

It was a long beat to Korokoro. By now we knew our boat would keep sailing as long as everything held together. Discussing the race afterwards we discovered that everyone on board was talking to the rig and praying that it would all hold together.

It took over an hour to reach that weather mark and it was with no small amount of elation that we eased sheets for the run to Evans Bay. Changed again to No. 2 genoa (thank you gemini foil) and off we went.

And then it happened. The wind which had been blowing constantly at 50 m.p.h. and above decided to get serious.

By the time we reached the entrance of Evans Bay the seas were big and nasty and the wind was something else! We could not see the western shore of Evans Bay because of a 30 ft (9 m) wall of spray lifted by, as we discovered later, 70 to 80 m.p.h. squalls.

The skipper decided that the No. 2 genoa had to come off so we hoisted the No. 3 to leeward (thank you again gemini foil) and then I went forward to remove the No. 2. We flew over the top of a steep one and dived into the sea ahead, and that was the first of many broaches.

The next 15 minutes was the most exhausting harbour racing I ever want to know about. We were knocked *flat in the water* by the worst squalls, our windex was snapped by the force of the top of the mast hitting the water and our little portion of exposed mainsail had two seams torn apart.

As we broached our way to that leeward mark the crew actually hung on to the stanchions to stay on board and on one occasion we sailed a circle and a half, gybed back and carried on.

Our mooring was but two minutes from that leeward mark, the finish line a beat away at the top of Evans Bay.

Oh! if we had been third or fourth we would have gone home but no – we had not quite forgotten about those championship points so on the wind again!

That weather continued. A week after the events described in this story, Blue Streaker *broke away from her mooring in Evans Bay and was extensively damaged. She returned to racing in time to hold her points lead in the Wellington Harbour third division championship and went on to win by a handsome margin.*

The owner's brother, Harry Dodson, was so impressed with Blue Streaker *that he ordered one for himself. He named it* Plonk *and raced it to high placings in Auckland waters.*

Endless summer

by PENNY WHITING, as told to Loris Chilwell

"O.K. girls on the main, take out the battens. You let the outhaul go, Margaret."

A calm, unhurried voice, a little husky, with an encouraging upward inflexion. Into view around the stern of her Westhaven marina neighbour glides Avian, *a 14.3 m Spencer-designed sloop painted pale blue. At the helm is the owner, Penny Whiting, returning to the marina after the morning session of the Lady Penelope Sailing School. It is 12. 15 p.m.*

No time is wasted.

"You girls hop off with the headsails and fold them neatly; take the pin out of the lock, Mary. You take the halyard off the cleat, Helen. Roll the main neatly girls, in nice big flakes — that's a lovely job."

In seconds all sails are neatly folded and placed on deck and the crew has departed. Avian *is spotless, shipshape, uncluttered.*

At this stage Penny has taught about 4000 people to sail and crew on keelers at the rate of about 150 per week, three lessons a day from each October to April. She started in the family yachts, first Coruba, *then* Tequila. *A week before her family departed for overseas in* Tequila, *she bought* Avian.

Avian *has a large, roomy cockpit. "It has to be big," says Penny. "It has to have room for 16 people."*

Sometimes Penny and Avian *are out on the harbour until 11.30 at night, in all kinds of weather. Today it has been too calm. "See you on Wednesday. Then we will learn tacking," Penny has promised her pupils as they depart.*

In her mid-twenties, blonde, tanned and attractive, Penny has grown up in an uninhibited family where all the offspring have been encouraged to try their wings. Like brother Paul, she has been outstandingly successful in the yachting world. A first-class crewperson, she has crewed in top racing and cruising yachts at home and abroad.

Here Penny recalls some of the experiences which highlight her memory.

WHEN I was fortunate enough to be chosen to crew with Jim Davern to represent New Zealand in the Congressional Cup in California, we flew up there and were given a Cal 40, as were the other 15 competitors from other countries. We were all given identical boats with identical sails, jib sheets, water, food, fuel — all was identical on board. The officials would come down each day and measure the waterline between the bow and the stern just to make sure we were all identical.

With a course of about 12 races — match races — we were only racing against one other boat. The idea is that you've got to start before he does;

so the tactician on the boat is even more important than the helmsman. He calls all the shots and you juggle for line positions even about 10 minutes before the start.

We did manage to win our first race and then we didn't win any others. The competition was just so hot – but we were never more than about 10 or 15 seconds behind, that's how close it was.

As I was the first woman to ever sail in a Congressional Cup race there was quite a lot of publicity and interest, especially as I was working the foredeck. Most women on boats seem to work in the cockpit, but I like foredeck best and I was always up there doing whatever was necessary. After the contest I was asked to go up and say a few words at the prizegiving on behalf of the competitors and it was all televised. I got lots of offers after that to go and race boats or skipper boats in various parts of America. Some came from Miami, from San Diego, California, a couple from up in the north of California and one from Vancouver.

As I like Vancouver terribly much, I decided to go up there. I became the sailing master (or mistress) on the former *Dame Pattie,* which is now called *The Endless Summer.* I had 22 male crew on board, plus another helmsman, but I was just the sailing master.

The owner wanted us to win the Swiftsure race, which is a North American classic. He'd been trying to win it for about 15 years, but he had never had a boat that could win the race. This year we had the boat and we had the crew and he even allowed me or agreed with me that we should fly crew in from Australia, California and all over the place. So I rang various friends and got them up there to race this boat.

We actually did win the Swiftsure race and broke the record by an incredible number of hours. I just read this year, 1976, that *Kialoa* didn't get anywhere near our record and that was made in 1972. That was a super race.

We sailed *The Endless Summer* around the gulf islands off Vancouver and around Juan de Fuca Strait for quite a while and then I decided I wanted to get cracking and get on a boat for the Bermuda race; so I accepted an offer I'd previously had to deliver a boat from Miami to New York and then up to Newport to get ready for the race.

It was a C and C 42, and we cruised it up the coast to New York, half in the intra-coastal waterway and half outside, and then up to Newport where we did the Off-Soundings race. *Buccaneer* was there with a lot of New Zealand crew.

Two days before the Bermuda race was to start, while we were also racing, a nicro block exploded on my ankle and cracked my Achilles tendon. So I was unfortunately unable to take part in the race. However the owner was good enough to fly me to Bermuda, so I could still be part of it.

From Bermuda I decided I would accept an offer to sail in the World Half-Ton Cup for Canada, so flew over to Sweden for that. Afterward we cruised on down to Bayona, Spain, on the Atlantic coast near the border with Portugal, where the boys that left from Bermuda were doing the Trans-Atlantic race. There I got on the crew of *Windward Passage* and we cruised from Spain and Portugal down to the Mediterranean. *Windward Passage* is an American boat, from Lahaina, Maui, in the Hawaiian Islands. She's supposedly still the world's fastest boat.

She's 73 ft (22.2 m) long and 22 ft (6.7 m) wide – an incredible boat.

Well, that was in those days.

This year I left New Zealand and went up to meet my parents in Miami because we planned to cruise the whole of the intra-coastal water-way between there and Nova Scotia. There were my parents and my sister Debbie on board and we set off with all of *Tequila's* 7 ft 6 in (2.3 m) draft in that 8 ft (2.4 m) deep waterway.

We had a blackboard in the cockpit, striking off every time we hit the mud – about six times a day – and sometimes we'd have to stay there all day. The tidal difference is only 6-12 in (150-300 mm), never any more.

However we cruised from Miami to Fort Lauderdale on the outside and then we went inside. It is actually impossible to use sail in the intra-coastal. It's all motor. We realised that to do any sort of tracking to get to Newport to meet my sister, who was doing the Tall Ships race from Bermuda, we'd have to motor 12 hours a day in the intra-coastal. We ran watches just as if we were at sea. It was all done in the most terrific heat.

The waterway goes through unbelievable country with beautiful trees, rising 20 ft (6 m) on either side, towering way above the mast. It goes through the loveliest little towns and villages, through mangroves and then back through the bush. These man-made canals are about five miles inside the coast all the way from Corpus Christi, Texas, right round the Gulf of Mexico up to Miami and then to Nova Scotia.

After about five days we were all getting pretty sick of motoring, so we decided we'd go out to sea for a few days. We sailed out from Norfolk, Virginia, up the Chesapeake Bay to Annapolis, Maryland, where we had a lot of friends. We then decided to go inside again to Delaware Bay. Delaware and Chesapeake Bays are dotted with American history. It's beautiful and we had a lovely time there.

There is a canal connecting the two bays. There are the most glorious swinging bridges, pivoting bridges, hoisting bridges. Hoot your siren three times and they open up and then you go in a big lock and you drop 12 ft (3.6 m) and then you come out. And to think we hadn't even known it was there. We even caught fish there!

We came out of the intra-coastal system by New York, approaching the city in dense fog, no wind, incredible conditions – trying to work out a harbour we had never seen. All we could see were many flashing lights of the sky-scrapers above the fogline. The first landmark we saw was the Statue of Liberty.

We went right up New York Harbour, up the East River, under 16 of the hugest bridges you've ever seen, all in the matter of about three miles, with a 12-knot tide underneath us. It took Father and me each one side of the wheel to hold us in the whirlpools. We went up to the Larchmont Yacht Club and stayed quite a long time, sailing in Long Island Sound. Beautiful cruising!

Then we went up to Newport to see the finish of the Tall Ships race. Debbie was on a boat representing Holland. The tall ships all arrived and we were anchored out in the middle of Newport Harbour with the tall ships all around us. And then the Trans-Atlantic single-handers started arriving about two days after the tall ships.

After the festivities there, we decided we had better join the Fourth of July parade in New York Harbour, so we whipped back down there and paraded around with all the royalness of that celebration.

Then it was time to start back down to Miami and then to Corpus Christi where we were going to meet Paul for the World Quarter-Ton Cup. We set off on the outside and then Hurricane Belle came through, which meant that we didn't want to be out there. Hurricanes in that area are very well forecast. We decided we had better dive into the intra-coastal waterway and do a few more thousand miles in there.

We went in at Prince Rupert, just north of Cape Canaveral, having to sail through a channel that the chart said was only 8 ft (2.4 m) deep – with about a 5 ft (1.5 m) swell running. We either had to weather the hurricane or go in this channel. Father decided that we were going in, so Mother and Debbie both went below. Father watched the depth sounder, I took the helm and we went roaring through these great waves and only hit the bottom once. But once we got in we were stuck off Cape Canaveral for about 22 hours.

Once we were in we were right, away from the hurricane, which was further out to sea.

As soon as we eventually got off the mud (we had about three speed-boats zipping around us, one boat towing our mast over, a big power boat pulling us and Father rowing the anchor) we did another 500 miles along the intra-coastal, up some beautiful bays.

Back in Miami we met all our friends and I did some sailing lessons – both times. I had done some on the way up and by the time I got back they forced me to do a whole bunch more. Once again I was sailing in 8-9 ft (2.4-2.7 m) of water – in a boat like *Tequila* that's very difficult. The whole of Miami harbour, which would cover a great area – like the whole of our Auckland harbour plus the gulf – is only this deep. So I had to have Father along in case I hit, to help me get off.

Then we decided to whip across the Gulf of Mexico to Corpus Christi non-stop. We just got round the Florida Keys when another hurricane sprang up. We didn't get the centre of it, but we did get about 60 knots for a long time and that belted us across.

We got halfway across the Gulf of Mexico and sailed among the oil rigs there. We saw about 500 rigs, but there would have been about 5000 we didn't see that were on our course. At night the ocean is just a mass of the lights of these rigs. If we ran out of coffee we'd go up to an oil rig and ask for some.

We arrived in Corpus Christi harbour about a week before *Magic Bus* arrived and before the boys arrived. We stayed there, acted as mother ship, fixed all their gear and did jobs for them. Then I flew back home, to start my lessons once again.

The success of Penny's brother Paul in Magic Bus *in the World Quarter-Ton Championship at Corpus Christi is related elsewhere in this book.*

The price of safety

by LORIS CHILWELL

YOU have received a notice of a race to a destination in the South Seas and you have stars in your eyes. You visualise the start in goodly company and you can smell enticing tropical perfumes and feel soft, warm, tropical moonlight, see it shining over a palm-fringed lagoon. Stop dreaming, yacht-owner, and calculate the cost, before you commit yourself to a venture you can't afford.

Ocean racing does not come cheaply in the 1970s. Quite apart from the fact that racing puts a far greater strain on expensive boats and gear than the cruising you have been enjoying, ocean travelling itself is likewise harder on boat, gear and crew than coastal cruising. Once it was possible to take off in a home-made job with minimal safety aids – but not any more. Over the years more and more stringent regulations have been written and more sophisticated gear has become mandatory before the Marine Department is willing to give the ok to Customs officials to issue an exit permit.

To begin with, in 1975 international laws were introduced to require that no yacht would be admitted to a foreign port without being registered in its country of origin. To obtain registration as a New Zealand ship, a yacht must submit to a Marine Department survey and have its registration number carved into the bulkhead. This is only the first expense. The yacht receives its registration number, but it is not necessarily eligible for clearance to go overseas.

Since 1956 Royal Akarana and Onerahi yachts racing outside harbour limits have been required to comply with safety requirements laid down by the Offshore Rating Council of the New Zealand Yachting Federation. In 1972 the N.Z.Y.F. adopted these rules for all member yacht clubs. Category one carries the most stringent requirements and it costs about $2400 to outfit a yacht with equipment for this category, which includes ocean travel.

It is doubtful if any of the yachts that set sail in the Royal Akarana Yacht Club's first Suva race in 1956 would be allowed to leave today, equipped as they were then. Most did not even have a self-draining cockpit! When the 1977 race went off with the largest number of yachts ever to sail from New Zealand for overseas, they had to comply with new O.R.C. safety regulations adopted by the New Zealand Yachting Federation in September 1976.

Inspectors based at the Royal Akarana have been entrusted by the

N.Z.Y.F. (for racing yachts) and by the Marine Department (for other yachts leaving for overseas) to carry out these safety inspections for the Auckland province. Affiliated Onerahi and Royal Port Nicholson Yacht Club inspectors cover their areas. Under the chairman, Robin Coleman, a dedicated band of yachtsmen qualified in various boatbuilding skills spend a great deal of what would otherwise be their leisure time carrying out these inspections at very small charge. They are kept particularly busy before major ocean races. Quite apart from the competitors, many yacht-owners plan to start their island cruises to coincide with the races, so as to benefit from the safety aids provided by the race mother ships with their radio communications.

In spite of the stringent regulations and meticulous checks, wild weather takes its toll. Every ocean race has its mishaps – its broken masts, torn sails, damaged rudders and minor gear failure. Newspapers are livened up with daily accounts of the progress of contestants limping back to the nearest port for repairs or retirement from the race.

From major expenses such as radio-telephone and life raft to the lowliest flare or flashlight, every item on the safety list is important. The regulations cover the type and location of seacocks, the method of installation of gas stoves and bottles, the number of water tanks and the amount carried, the contents of medical kits, prescriptions for storm sails and many other items besides an exhaustive description of the type and quantity of gear required and mandatory structural features.

The regulations clearly define the owner's responsibility:

"The safety of a yacht and her crew is the sole and inescapable responsibility of the owner, who must do his best to ensure that the yacht is fully found, thoroughly seaworthy and manned by an experienced crew who are physically fit to face bad weather.

"He must be satisfied as to the soundness of the hull, spars, rigging, sails and all gear.

"He must ensure that all safety equipment is properly maintained and stowed and that the crew know where it is kept and how it is to be used."

It was a wet beginning. Johnny Wray's *Ngataki (left)* **and George Dibbern's** *Te Rapunga* **on Auckland Harbour at the start of their race from Auckland to Melbourne in 1934.** *Auckland Star*

The start line of the first race from Auckland to Suva in 1956. *Edelweiss* (C.10) and *Matuku* (skippered by the young John Lidgard) cross the line together. Alone at the line is *Wanderer*, skippered by Tom Buchanan, who bashed the yacht through strong gales to take line honours unexpectedly.

A hit-or-miss affair

From the *New Zealand Herald*

Although trans-Tasman races are today regular and highly organised events in the world yachting calendar, the first race – in 1931 – was a pretty informal, hit-or-miss affair.

IT all began when an Australian auxiliary ketch named *Oimara,* flying the burgee of the Royal St Kilda Yacht Club (Melbourne), entered Auckland Harbour. Her owner-skipper, Mr F. J. Bennell, challenged all comers to race to Sydney.

The challenge was immediately accepted by a visiting Norwegian yachtsman, Mr Erling Tambs, who was in Auckland during a round-the-world voyage in his sailing craft *Teddy,* a converted pilot cutter.

Auckland yachtsmen were slower to pick up the gauntlet. At the last minute the owner of the yacht *Rangi,* Mr W. A. Leonard, hastily recalled his craft from a cruise in the Hauraki Gulf and rushed her on to the slipway for a 24-hour clean-up and refit. The *Rangi,* a 37-year-old converted fishing vessel, had been bought by her owner for £300 in 1928.

By working day and night, the crew of the *Rangi* and volunteer yachtie helpers managed to complete the refit job and get the boat off the slipway only half an hour before the starting gun was fired at 2 p.m. on 14 March 1931. The *Rangi* was crewed for the race by four seasoned Auckland yachtsmen, Lieut-Commander W. C. Juler, formerly of the Royal Australian Navy; E. Spraggon, D. Kirkcaldie and A. Clarke.

The Royal New Zealand Yacht Squadron would not agree to *Rangi's* racing as its official representative. The squadron officers decided that the vessel's speed and displacement "did not represent the best that Auckland could offer if larger boats were available." Despite this, the *Rangi* flew the Akarana Yacht Club burgee from her truck and was generally regarded as the New Zealand entry in a three-nation race.

Rangi was beset with bad luck throughout the trip, alternately becalmed in windless areas and battered by raging Tasman storms. If this were not enough, it was discovered that her navigational equipment – hastily fitted at the start of the race – was defective.

The Australian boat, *Oimara,* also had a rough crossing, but she got the finishing gun in Sydney at 10.40 a.m. on 26 March – after a passage of 11 days and 20 hours.

The sturdy little *Teddy* crossed the finish-line two days later.

Not until 5.30 a.m. on 3 April did the *Rangi* sail into Sydney Harbour.

Based on handicap times, the *Teddy* was declared the winner, with *Oimara* second and *Rangi* third.

After spending almost a month in Australia, *Rangi* set sail on her return trip on 2 May. Again the New Zealand boat was unlucky. First her radio fused, cutting off all contact with other vessels and shore stations. Then she ran into fickle winds and calm which restricted her to logging only 20 miles on her first day out. For several more days she contended with winds veering and backing from north-east to south-east.

Finally, *Rangi* weathered the North Cape of New Zealand and a day later anchored in Russell, Bay of Islands. On the return voyage she had taken 19 days and logged 1620 miles.

Describing the *Rangi's* performance in his book *Little Ships,* Ronald Carter says:

"There is no doubt that *Rangi* was dogged by ill-luck in both the trans-Tasman race and her passage home. Poor navigating instruments, defective wireless equipment, and long calms interspersed with gales and persistent head winds were deciding factors against her putting up a good performance at any stage of the voyage . . .

"Fortunately the *Rangi* was manned by an expert and stout-hearted company who acquitted themselves in the best traditions of the sea . . .

"The yacht proved conclusively that she was well able to withstand the harsh treatment received while crossing the stormy Tasman Sea.

" . . . This little 38 ft (11.5 m) cutter, through the efforts of her crew, has written a splendid page in New Zealand yachting, which will surely be remembered for all time.

"In pioneering the trans-Tasman yacht race, *Rangi's* name automatically heads the list of those yachts which will undoubtedly follow in her wake through the coming years."

A wet beginning

by GEORGE DIBBERN

From *Quest* (The Bodley Head)

George Dibbern spent several years cruising from Germany to New Zealand in the early 1930s in his yacht Te Rapunga. *In* Quest, *published in the 1930s, he tells the story of this cruise and subsequent events.*

In December 1934 Dibbern's Te Rapunga *and Johnny Wray's* Ngataki *raced across the Tasman to take part in Melbourne's centenary celebrations. Here they accepted another challenge, to race from Melbourne to Hobart, described in this story.*

The crew of Te Rapunga *in the race to Melbourne were the skipper's nephew Gunter (the mate) and three New Zealanders – Fred Norris, Austin Vail and Noel Tatterfield. Fred then had to return to New Zealand. The "visiting cards" mentioned in the story are two bottles of beer in a brown paper bag.*

AS crew member in Fred's place, I decide to take Betty Rohr, a friend's wife. I still believe that the right kind of woman on board is an asset, because the whole tone of the ship is raised; and if we want a free world, first we will have to have free women, not merely females, but big, broad-minded comrades. Betty has never done anything like this before, and I think that the trip of about five days will be a fine experience for her, something that will keep on living in her memory. At the beginning the crew, of course, is against the idea, but finally they agree.

And so dawns 22 January. As there are only two boats, almost equal in size, and about a 500-mile race, a second on the start is neither here nor there, so they decide to do away with the bother of starting-boat and gun shooting, and hatch out the bright idea of starting the race from the club bar of the Royal St Kilda at 6.30 p.m.

When I leave the boat early in the morning to buy provisions, get my clearance papers, and do the many things a skipper has to do before he leaves port, I beg my crew to make everything ready for a nice sportsmanlike start.

Truly the Good Book says: "The spirit is willing, but the flesh is weak," for when I come back at 5.30 the boat is in an indescribable condition. All the friends of the *Te Rapunga* have come with their well-known visiting cards to say farewell to the crew, and the friends of the *Ngataki* also have come to us – can it be to help my competitor? The result is that on board the *Ngataki* everything is clear from stem to stern, but my bonny boys simply have had to celebrate departure. I thank God that they are at least still alive, and apparently still able to tackle the hurricanes and whirlpools of the Royal St Kilda.

Here it is that *Ngataki* has a great advantage; Johnny is the strongest on board and so everybody obeys him, and they all drink slowly. One may say that they sail in well-measured tacks towards the start. I, on the other hand, am the weakest on board, which means that my boat will not obey the rudder; it takes over great waves of liquid and does not seem able to stand this kind of weather much longer. All I can do is to plead with my crew to hang on.

There are farewell speeches which I try to answer, and all at once it is 6.30 p.m. "Clang!" goes the bell, followed by a cry of "They're off!" And that is the start of the race from Melbourne to Hobart.

Johnny immediately gets hold of his boys by the scruff of the neck, prods them down the staircase, and soon they can be seen tearing along the pier, which is black with people. Not so my little lambs. They are leaning out of the window to watch, and almost kill themselves laughing. Expectantly the people on the pier await our quick appearance. Vainly do I beg and scorn and try to persuade. We are surrounded with friends, who refill our glasses, shouting, though some call it singing, 'Why are they born so beautiful, why are they born at all?"

And we have to drink, drink, drink; and there is no "No" as an answer. We see the *Ngataki* set sails, shoot away like mad, and suddenly stand. Has a miracle happened? What is it? The boat is pulled back again, and amid gales of laughter from the spectators up comes the stern anchor, which has been forgotten, or which some kind person has secretly dropped overboard. Then they are off and away.

Finally, finally, when the *Ngataki* has almost disappeared, and people start to leave the pier, I have Austin and Tat so far that they promise me on their honour to go back on board, where the lonely Betty is patiently waiting and wondering why the *Te Rapunga* doesn't sail. The appearance of Tat and Austin immediately recollects the crowd. Now I implore the mate, who suddenly becomes serious and says, "All right, I am coming. There is only one little thing I have to do yet – well, something you couldn't refuse even a criminal. Then I'll come!" And I, fool, believe him.

On board is a terrible muddle. Not a single halyard is clear. It is unbelievable how much can be messed up in such a little space of time and like children, Austin and Tat are giggling and waving to the shore, and pulling here and there and tangling things up still more. In vain do we wait for the mate. I am about boiling.

"I'll run back and get him," volunteers Austin, but seeing the gleam in his eye, I have more sense than to let him go.

"You stay right here. Otherwise we won't sail at all. Savvy?"

Slowly I begin to get order into the tangle of ropes. Time passes, and the *Ngataki* is far off on the horizon. "When are you leaving?" shouts someone from the shore.

Suddenly a great cheer goes through the crowd. Away down the pier is the mate, loaded with a heavy deck cargo – a heavy sack – and with a still heavier list, tacking from one side of the pier to the other. That he reaches the boat at all is a miracle, a marvel of navigation. Now he is alongside. I try to help him – nothing doing – we can't separate him from his cargo of beer bottles. So we have to heave the combined dead weight on board. First he carefully stows his beloved bottles, and then, following my urgent pleas and orders, he joins the other two in setting sails.

"Hoist away mainsail!" I let the mainsheet go, and the mate, who is pulling on the boom lift instead of the halyard, disappears over the side. A loud cheer greets this spectacle. He begins to pull himself up by way of the anchor chain, which is up and down, full of black mud; and in his once white clothes looks a glorious sight. We heave him on board again – the sails are up – without orders someone lets the mooring lines go. The mainsail is not clear – the anchor drags through the water – to clear all this I have to sail round and round, doing my best not to bump against any of the many boats that are near. Still the anchor drags through the water. And all the time I have to keep my eyes on my little angels to see that they don't drop over the side.

"Haul in that anchor!" I shout, desperate.

"Aye, aye, sir," the mate responds and, all eager obedience, sways forward. Just as we pass the end of the pier, and the first swell meets us, he bends down and heaves. The bow makes a sudden dip, and he is gone. Fortunately the end of the anchor chain is belayed to the bitts, and so eventually we get him and the anchor back on board again. A fresh thundering cheer rewards this manoeuvre. The mate, like an actor taking a bow, is frantically waving, all smiles and friendliness; the next minute he has disappeared and gone to bunk, where – thank God – he is out of all harm's way.

And now the flag on the masthead is tangled up, just as I want to dip it, and as I can send nobody else aloft, I have to go up myself. So with this last exhibition of acrobatics, amid final cheers we close the performance, and bid farewell to this town of terrible dangers. I feel like Ulysses did when at last he had succeeded in escaping all snares and had his crew safely together again on board once more.

A little later darkness envelops us, and, continually tacking, we believe we have passed the *Ngataki* by midnight, and manage, the following forenoon, to reach the entrance just after the turn of the tide. Before going out, just as we pass a Hamburg-American freighter, and the tide is already coming in, and the sea steep, we must break our forestay. But thanks to our parallel stays, in no time we have reclipped the forestaysail, and the damage is soon mended.

We romp along as hard as we can, are soon clear of the coast, and set course. Betty, not being seasick, and having taken over the provisioning, prepares a marvellous meal.

"If you want to win a man's heart," so runs the good old saving, "feed the brute," and she sure wins all of us. The crew brightens visibly, and it is not only the meal that does it, but Betty's smile and cheerfulness. We are in high spirits.

We fly past the Strait Islands during the day and the night, and the following day we sweep through the Banks Strait. During the next 24 hours it blows harder and harder, and so we keep close to shore till it becomes too rough, and we prefer to go inside of Schouten Island into quieter water. And all the fourth day we tack south.

On the morning of the fifth we reach Cape Tasman, but no sooner have we poked our nose into Storm Bay than we begin to toss to and fro. Wind against us, a wild unruly sea, and later on, noon calm, prevent us from making progress, and only in the evening, in the shelter of Bruni Island, does the old girl get into her stride again. The water is almost smooth, the wind strong offshore. This pleases the old girl and she snorts along. Under a specially clear, beautiful lunar rainbow she bolts towards Hobart, the water on her stern churning almost as if she were a motorboat. Motorcar lights on shore morse us to come in.

At 1.30 a.m. we cross the finishing line, and soon are safely moored at the pier – once more the first boat in.

Now they come on board to welcome us in a Tasmanian way. The heads of the club and Austin's brother, Hilton, bring on board Tasmanian food, already cooked, young potatoes and mint, green peas, fresh meat and Cascade beer; it is dawn before we finally enjoy a well-earned rest. Next day the boat is full of people coming and going. Everyone wants to welcome us, and a great deal of honour falls upon the woman member of our crew, who has been a first-class cook, provision master, and comrade. All agree, in spite of previous misgivings, that with her happiness and humour she has never been anything but a blessing on the trip; and we are sorry that she will have to hurry back again by plane to Melbourne. If duties did not call her home we would like to take her on to New Zealand with us.

The *Ngataki,* with a 12-hour handicap, does not come in the next day, nor the day after. Finally, on the fifth day after our arrival, she is reported, and we sail out to meet her, escort her in and hear her tale.

We find that she left Port Phillips some hours later than we, as she missed the tide; she made good time to Cape Pillar, where she met such a buster that she was driven 60 miles out to sea. Next day one great wave put her almost on her beam-ends; it smashed her dinghy, ripped away her sails, and half filled her with water, while down below Johnny was thrown clear across the cabin and almost broke his back. Since then they have had a very rough time, tacking back against mountainous seas.

To both boats an official welcome is given, so warm and so whole-hearted that it takes first place of all official welcomes that have been granted to us.

The first Suva race

From JOHN LIDGARD'S logbook

The first yacht race from Auckland to Suva, run by the Royal Akarana Yacht Club, started on 12 May 1956 with 13 competitors. Eleven and a half days later, on Thursday 24 May, the first boat finished.

Increasing in popularity with each event, subsequent Suva races took place in 1966, 1969 and 1973. Then Royal Suva and Royal Akarana decided to make it a two-yearly event starting in 1977. So great was the response that a second venue near Lautoka was organised to take the overflow from the limit placed on contestants by the accommodation available at Suva.

Lessons learned from the first race and in succeeding years have made the organisation much more complicated and the entry requirements much more stringent. When over 100 yachts crossed the starting line off Orakei Wharf on 30 April 1977 they were accompanied by two radio relay ships with the most up-to-date radio equipment and were expected to answer regular radio schedules.

There were few radio telephones among the competitors in the first race back in 1956. Gear that became commonplace later was not in evidence. The mother ship, Ngaroma, *was actually never in contact with the contestants.*

Among the competitors was a blue-grey sloop, Matuku, *owned, built and skippered by young John Lidgard, then of Kawau Island. His crew consisted of Alan Draffin (mate), Basil Pollock and Jim Dawson (co-navigators) and Bill Harford (cook and bottle washer). Their log tells the day-to-day story of the race.*

MAY 12. Race started 1.30 p.m., breeze light southerly. Seas calm. Sundown one mile north Shearer Rock, course 350°. *Edelweiss* lies two miles north-north-east, making east of Little Barrier. *Reliance* lies one and a half miles east-north-east slightly ahead, making east of Little Barrier. *Wanderer* and *Taurangi* on starboard quarter one and a half miles. *Glennis* to port passed inside Little Barrier and Tiri. *Daydream* one mile astern. *Ranganui* appears to be creeping up the shore after *Glennis* and carrying every sail ever invented and some that just happened. Several nav. lights after dark, two ahead, one abeam, two astern.

May 13. Passed Moko Hinaus at 4.45 a.m. Wind flukey, seas calm. Sunrise three boats to leeward and astern. Course north-east, average speed today five knots. Noon, 120 miles out. *Wanderer* came from leeward and is about a mile straight astern. Holding us. Basil and Tim took first sights although land is still in sight. Wind north-west light, seas disturbed, barometer steady. 2.30 p.m., wind is slowly freshening. Holding on to full mainsail and genoa as long as we feel able. 5.15 p.m., things are starting to clatter and bash, so one reef in mainsail. Very fast reefing by crew, wind was never out of sail. Timed them two minutes, 30 seconds. However *Wanderer* came from astern and drew level. Slightly ahead at 6.15 p.m. (about two boat lengths). Next man on watch bore away from foul wind and drew level under *Wanderer's* lee. At dark still neck and neck. Tom is going exceptionally well as we have won all our races in this sort of stuff. Hope we are not overloaded. Seasickness taking its toll, four down, one to go.

May 14. 5 a.m., genoa doused, small jib on, three reefs in main. Wind freshening rapidly, seas breaking aboard more frequently. Nearly lost Allan over the pulpit during sail change. However he held to pulpit and skipper held to Al, he amused, I a bit shaky. Main taken off. Fresh winds north-west, sailing all day under storm jib. Seas appear to be getting bigger. The watch is a misery, two long, shivering hours. And even below this business of going to windward in a gale is tiring; pounding, bashing and getting knocked flat by the odd crest (well, pretty flat). Bare-poled from 6 p.m., towed warp, but still kept pointing in the right direction. 10 p.m., Jim woke me and suggested setting staysail again. He earned his place in that minute. We carried it alright and soon got all excited and set trysail. Midnight, passed yacht hove-to stern on. As we got closer there was an excited muttering aboard *Matuku:* "It's *Glennis*". She was showing foredeck lights under crosstrees, also cabin lights. Bas and Jim thought she was a ship at first and so flashed torches and blew hooters, much to our chagrin, as it woke the opposition and got them moving.

May 15. Much better day although a big sea still running. Wind dropped by 12 noon, put on main and genoa. North-west to north seas moderate. Midnight, breeze seems to be easing.

May 16. Wind dropped away 6.30 a.m. Doused all sail to avoid chafe. Big confused jumble of sea. Must be between two depressions. 7.30 a.m., light south-east gradually increasing but still light at 10.15 a.m. Full sail and genoa but wind backed to east-north-east – just too tight for spinnaker. Burning question: where are the other boats? And where are we? Sighted third albatross of trip. No sight of sun again today. Light rain, grey skies. Sighted whale about one and a half miles astern. Several beautiful blue dolphins. Basil tried the spinner but no luck. The boys are feeding the albatross. They are very partial to cake. Coming close enough for Basil to feed one from his fingertips. Good photo. Not my line – they may feed on one's fingertips. I cooked what Bill described as a nice greasy meal. No one else is quite up to it. Bacon, eggs and fried bread. Tim is trying to fix the radio which packed up on the 13th (second day out). Wish the wind would get up; the rolling is annoying and some of the more seedy members are stumbling about all over the place. Heavy rain. 3.25 p.m., at long last easterly wind. Off with a hiss and a roar. Course 340°. Rain very heavy, making good progress toward Suva under main and genoa. Bill feels it is probably the trades. We would like to believe him. But Allan sows a seed of doubt. 5.45, wind dropped. No trades these. Running under boomed genoa. Lowered mainsail to ease chafe. Made 11½ miles while the wind lasted. Heavy rain. Must get under way as soon as possible. Even our seven albatrosses have left us. Barometer steady.

May 17. Bill says the trades at last! Spinnaker, genoa and mainsail. Right direction. Plenty of albatrosses around us. No sun yet. Wind back to north-west. Where have the trades gone? Rain squalls coming across quite regularly. Coming up starry. Wind switched to south-west. Doused genoa and carried on under main. Average estimated speed 6 knots. Wind increased and bent trysail; later reefed same. Going like a train.

May 19. Beautiful day, still fresh, full trysail, spinnaker soon. It's up now and is most exhilarating, but perhaps a little hard on the gear. Running 2/6 sweepstake for the first person to sight land. Rolling was rather bad, but the kite has steadied that! Barometer rising. Estimated speed touching 8 knots. Spinnaker blows off after two hours. Clips were seized with heavy marlin and newly done but it has parted twice now so we will have to leave it off for a while. 4.30 p.m., wind is still the same but we can't stand it any more without the kite. It has been down about six hours. Up again, down again, seizings again! Have stripped other gear of small stainless shackles and shackled them on, up again. Biggest albatross of voyage. The kite is doing a wonderful job. I was too timid before and this could cost us the race. *Kismet* and *Edelweiss* will be making the most of this. Now the wind is easing.

May 20. Wind fluffed. No good for the race, but at least we are getting clothes, etc. dried out. Everyone has shaved and cleaned up. Very sweet with baby powder floating around. Should sight Kandavu Tuesday night or at dawn. Barometer rising. Got "accurate" sights today. 144 miles noon to noon.

May 21. Wind direction still easterly. Seas smooth, still a swell. A flying fish on deck during early morning watch. Several more during day. Weather definitely warmer. I feel these probably are the long awaited south-east trades. E.T.A.: sight Kandavu midday Wednesday the 23rd. Speed seven knots.

May 22. Light wind variable east to south-east. Dropped main to repair seizings on track slides. Noticed beam of light astern 6.45 p.m. Could be a frigate or possibly a yacht with spotlights. Trying to get the radio going again. No luck.

May 23. Day of days. 12 noon, Allan sighted a coconut. 12.30p.m., Allan sighted a Sunderland flying towards us. Circled, took photos and then disappeared into east. 1 p.m., Allan picked out a blob of land which has turned out to be Kandavu (we all spliced the mainbrace twice). Weather very warm and hot down below. Sailing with main and spinnaker set. Genoa up too and seems to be doing some good. Passing Lolo light 10 p.m. Suva is not far now. Flat run for the passage, picking up the lights midnight.

May 24. Lined up leading lights and laying straight in. Well, we didn't win the 1956 Suva race. *Wanderer* arrived two and a half hours ago. We are second to get here. Pleased and yet not so pleased. *Wanderer's* crew came aboard at 4.30 a.m., which called for drinks all round. Photographer came and snapped us. *Nina* finished 12 hours after us with *Mink* eight minutes behind him. Unless *Kehua* finishes tonight, the first three will remain the same (i.e. *Wanderer, Nina, Matuku, Edelweiss,* in that order) on corrected time.

May 30. Prize-giving today. Tom Buchanan spoke well. Peter Fletcher *(Dayream)* received a turtle-back for the last boat to finish. Made a comical speech. Barry Trigg got set of pots and pans for last cook home. We received Royal Suva Yacht Club pennant and £710 for second to finish. No sleep tonight.

While the crews in Suva were getting read for the prize-giving, Adrian Hayter arrived at Westport in Sheila II, *home in New Zealand from his six-year solo voyage from England. At this time two yachts not heard from when the other contestants had finished at Suva,* Aoma *and* Kehua, *had limped back to New Zealand, damaged by heavy seas and gale-force winds.*

Back in Suva, the boats started to disperse after the prize-giving, most to take island cruises before returning home. Matuku *took a 25-day cruise around the eastern and central Fijis. This time the crew included Heather Lidgard. On the day they left Suva the log recorded "Heather took her first watch". This was to be the forerunner of many others.*

Matuku *left Suva again for Auckland on 2 July, arriving on 19 July. The trip had started John Lidgard's inventive mind working on improving gear and layout for ocean sailing, ideas he was to incorporate in future yacht designs.*

Leading lady

Milestones in the career of HEATHER LIDGARD

When John and Heather Lidgard returned home from Suva after the 1956 inaugural race they were both sold on ocean cruising. But they had a young family to bring up, and it was not until the first race from Whangarei to Noumea in 1964 that they sallied forth again, John to race in his own designed 9.9 m Takiri, *and Heather to join him in Noumea for a short cruise before sailing home via Norfolk Island. This trip convinced Heather that she would participate in the next race. She learned navigation and became Auckland's first regular lady racing navigator.*

Heather was navigator in the next Suva race in 1966 in Taonui *and on the cruise around Fiji, New Caledonia, New Hebrides, Brisbane and Sydney which followed. In a succession of Lidgard boats —* Renegade, Runaway, Demijohn *(owned by Jack Allen),* Imp *and* Result *she has navigated in almost every major ocean race since then, has guided* XYZ *to an owner in Honolulu, completed nine Tasman crossings to attend Sydney-Hobart races, Southern Cross series, or on yacht deliveries, has taken part in the first two-person race around the North Island.*

In home waters Heather takes full part in all local races and pulls her weight in the actual building and maintaining of each current family yacht. She has also taught navigation classes. In all traditional women's roles she also gets full marks.

In the following story, Heather tells of her ocean-going experiences from the time she returned home after the first Noumea race.

A RUSH followed to build a new, faster, bigger yacht for the next Suva race in 1966. The 40 ft (12.2 m) sloop *Taonui* was the result, and in this race we set off prepared for an extended cruise with the family — Kevin, then 11 years, and Duthie, nine years, joined the yacht at Suva. We were well organised this time. I was now taking an active part in the race, having taught myself navigation.

Taonui performed well in spite of calm conditions during the race and finished 12th overall and first in the A-division.

We spent the next eight months cruising at our leisure around Fiji, New Caledonia, New Hebrides, Brisbane and Sydney, and we had by this time decided to try our luck in the 1966 Sydney-Hobart race. We were quite pleased with our first attempt in this race, being fifth yacht to reach Hobart, which was not too bad for a yacht described in a pre-race review by a Sydney yachting reporter as a family cruiser.

However we made up our minds during the Hobart-Auckland race which followed to build more of an out-and-out racing yacht, designed to the I.O.R. rule and to have another try from Sydney to Hobart.

Before we sold *Taonui,* we took part in the second Whangarei-Noumea race, in 1967, and gained ninth place overall. *Taonui* was sold towards the end of that year. John had built a Ron Swanson-designed yacht for Lyn Carmichael, *Castanet,* and was crewing in that. *Castanet* was chosen with *Rainbow II* and *Satanita* to represent New Zealand in the first Southern Cross series in Australia.

In spite of *Rainbow II* winning the Sydney-Hobart race, the New Zealanders did not bring home the cup. But *Castanet* won the Hobart-Auckland race which followed.

Two years later we represented New Zealand ourselves in our new One Ton Cup yacht, *Renegade,* in the second Southern Cross Cup series, with team-mates *Rebel* and *Outrage.* The year previously we had done a Sydney-Hobart race in *Renegade* and had won the Royal Akarana Yacht Club's top award, the Rothmans Gold Cup.

It was not until we represented New Zealand in the third Southern Cross Cup series in *Runaway,* our next one-tonner, that we finally scooped the pool, with *Pathfinder* first, *Runaway* second and *Wai-aniwa* third in the 1971 Sydney-Hobart race.

It was certainly my best achievement in navigation.

We always took part in the Hobart-Auckland races, which were more of a relaxation after the series in Australia, except when we raced in *Renegade* in January 1969 in the Hobart-Wellington race to celebrate the Evans Bay Yacht Club's 50th anniversary. We won this race despite considerable gear damage and decided to stick with the Hobart-Auckland races in the future.

We sold *Runaway* in 1973 but sailed in her in the Sydney-Hobart that year with the new owner, Ian Gibbs. We had moderate success with a third in the one-ton division. John had now notched up six Sydney-Hobarts. I had done five.

For the 1973 Suva race we were without a yacht, but John had just built a new half-tonner, *Demijohn,* for Jack Allen, so we both crewed on this for the race. *Demijohn* performed well, winning C-division.

At the end of that year we had a change of scenery. Instead of entering the Southern Cross series, we were delivering a yacht built at the yard to a Honolulu owner. The following year this yacht, the *XYZ,* won the 800 mile Honolulu classic, the "Round the State" race.

We now owned a cruiser-racer, the 33 ft (10 m) *Imp,* which was built as a fill-in type of yacht while we made our minds up about a new one-tonner. The local races were our main attraction at this stage, but we could not resist the 1975 Noumea race, with another short cruise around New Caledonia and the New Hebrides. We did not get the weather we were hoping for – fresh, fair winds – and finished 12th overall. *Imp* was a particularly easy yacht to handle and steer, and John and I decided to sail home from Vila on our own. We found this moderately easy and managed to get *Imp* to sail herself a lot of the time.

After our return to New Zealand, we flew off to Honolulu, where John participated in the "Round the State" race in *XYZ,* finishing second this time. We also managed a short trip to Japan on the way home to study the production boats being built to our design, and we had some sailing around Japanese waters.

We entered *Imp* in the second Auckland-Lyttelton race in December 1975 and had a win in rough conditions, with only three yachts out of seven finishing. The cruise around the Marlborough Sounds and later up the west coast of the North Island made the trip worthwhile and a pleasant change.

Imp was sold later to a Christchurch owner and so we were without a yacht once again. While planning a new one-tonner, we were fortunate enough to crew on *Demijohn* again for the first Tauranga-Vila race. This turned out most successfully, for *Demijohn* won the race overall.

Looking back, I see we have done most of the major ocean races around New Zealand over the past few years, missing only one Suva race, one Noumea race and the first Auckland-Rarotonga race. We had made nine Tasman crossings, with trips to and from Sydney for Hobart races and yacht deliveries, and are now planning a new one-tonner with the two-handed Round the North Island Race in 1977 as the first challenge.

During the 1976-77 Christmas cruise period, John and Heather Lidgard stayed home to finish their new one-tonner, Result, *so as to be ready for the start of the two-handed race in February. They worked hard. When their tanned friends arrived home from their cruises, they found John and Heather looking thin and uncharacteristically pale.*

Result *was third boat to finish in this race, beaten to the line by* Gerontius *and* Warchild.

It's all done for fun

by MIKE SPANHAKE

From *Sailmaker*

The author is one of Auckland's most sought-after crewmen. This story is his account of the Devonport Yacht Club's Two-Person Round the North Island Race, which left Auckland on 22 February 1977. He sailed in the Cavalier 36 Warchild *with the owner, Peter Smith, the voyage taking nine days, five hours and 22 minutes.*

ON Friday 18 February three months of insomnia suffering was brought to a head with the official and very formal briefing conducted by the race committee at the Devonport Yacht Club. A roll call was taken to ensure all competitors were present and the various articles and aspects of the race were discussed. Captain John Mansell, ex single-handed Atlantic race competitor and a contestant himself in this race, gave the assemblage a short talk on the Cook Strait area.

His opening comments served to put everyone at ease. "Fellow competitors, what I'm about to tell you about the Cook Strait area is no more than anyone of you can find in the relevant pages of the *New Zealand Coastal Pilot.* However, nobody here would have read that section of the *Pilot,* because if you had, there is no way you would be contemplating sailing in that area".

He continued his talk using phrases like "60 knots here at least", "75 to 80 knots there", "five to six knot tidal races and overfalls", and had little difficulty in captivating a very silent audience.

Saturday evening was spent attending the official farewell and this would be undoubtedly the most pleasant and enjoyable yachting social function I have been fortunate enough to have experienced. In a time where pettiness, politics and personal aspirations seem to dominate every quarter, half, or what-have-you contest it was refreshing to mix with people who were involved in a yacht race basically for the sheer hell of it. There is a side benefit to eccentricity.

Monday involved undocking the boats from the Devonport Naval Base dockyard, the largest sauna bath in the Southern Hemisphere. With all Air New Zealand outbound flights being fully booked, there was no alternative but home to bed with the thought-provoking realisation that it was all about to happen.

At 1130 hours on Tuesday 22 February, His Royal Highness the Duke of Edinburgh, wearing immaculately pressed whites, pulled an equally immaculately white braid lanyard triggering the naval saluting gun which signalled the start of the inaugural Two-Man Round the North Island race.

A youthful ebb tide, sunshine and 15 to 18 knots of north-easterly provided for a most picturesque spectacle as the fleet moved out of the harbour or at least, it is rumored, the Duke thought so. However, with the royal party safely returned to the *Britannia* and the regal aspects of the event over, the weather decided it could afford to take a more informal attitude to the day and the race fleet soon found itself assembled off Rangitoto lighthouse in no wind, an unpleasant joggly sea and grey drizzly rain.

While many of the crews endeavoured to row their boats with sweep oars, (permitted under the rules of the race), a light nor-westerly made gestures at establishing itself and *Gerontius, Warchild* and *Result,* (John and Heather Lidgard's new one-tonner) worked hard, using this breeze to make a break from the rest of the fleet. By nightfall when the wind had swung into the west, these three boats had established a 12 to 15 mile lead and settled into a pleasant evening of reaching up the coast.

Dawn saw *Gerontius* and *Warchild* becalmed together off Tutukaka some 15 miles ahead of the next boat. The ensuing fickle day *Gerontius* and *Warchild* alternately shared the lead while spinnakers, genoas and sweep oars were used to coax a passage north.

At dusk that evening the crew of *Warchild* were, with the aid of the odd can of beer, celebrating their skill and cunning when, like hemlock bursting into flower, the southern horizon became speckled with brightly coloured spinnakers. A mixture of panic and greed took hold, and rather than cover the fleet by sailing outside the Cavalli Islands, Peter Smith's tactician persuaded him to sail through one of the inside passages. The particular passage chosen by *Warchild* that evening can be recommended for its grandeur and great natural beauty. It can also be recommended for its complete lack of wind. Needless to say *Warchild* was fifth boat into Mangonui some 42 minutes after the leader of the fleet, *Gerontius.*

Mangonui, the first of three ports where a compulsory stop of 48 hours had to be taken, is a pleasant little town inhabited by some of the most hospitable people in New Zealand. A quiet session in the local pub, a delicious luncheon of fish and chips on the foreshore and a pleasant evening meal with our pre-arranged host quickly occupied the first 24 hours. The remaining day was spent organising the boat and tossing fitfully in the bunk as a brisk south-easterly swept down the Mangonui estuary.

By 0310 the following morning we were reaching briskly across Doubtless Bay in 25 knots of air, a lumpy sea and the occasional rain squall, with the infamous northern tip of New Zealand predominant in our minds. By dawn North Cape was well in sight and at 0830 hours we flicked on the indicaters, hung a left and flat ran down to Cape Reinga in a sizable following sea.

Those readers intimately knowledgeable of the New Zealand coastline will be aware of the Columbine Bank which extends a couple of miles seaward of Cape Reinga. Although a small quarter-mile passage exists inside the bank, this is shallow and as stated in the *New Zealand Pilot* should not be attempted without local knowledge and only in settled weather. Qualifying on neither count and in the interests of good seamanship, *Warchild* decided to circumnavigate the bank accepting the additional three-four miles that would have to be sailed.

However as we approached the point of no return it became apparent that other yachts (*Sirius, Jasmine* and *Trauma*) sailing in close proximity to ourselves, had elected to take the inside passage. The hallmark of any respectable New Zealander is conformity, and being no exception to the rule we quickly gybed and followed suit. Those readers who are students of marine biology will be interested to learn that the sand crabs dwelling on the sea bed between Cape Reinga and Columbine Bank live in colonies of up to four or five in number and when approached at eight to nine knots by large keel yachts, cover their stalk-like eyes with two large reddish nippers.

As we swept through the passage, the thunderous noise of surf breaking on the adjacent Columbine Reef became interrupted with the sound of adrenaline rushing through the blood stream. We successfully negotiated the channel, and while we were still smarting at our immense masculinity and courage, Mark Williams in *Trauma* upstaged us all by sailing between Maria Island and Cape Maria Van Diemen. There are, however, two levels of insanity, and Peter and I definitely fall into category B. Along with *Sirius* and *Jasmine* we conceded defeat and sailed outside the Island.

The slide down the west coast of the island to New Plymouth was uneventful if not frustrating due to the frequent loss of wind. Anxious hours were spent off Raglan searching for a large turning mark displaying the word invisible, but numerous sun shots served to ascertain that we had in fact passed well inside. After passing Cape Egmont we threaded our way through the first of numerous disorganised Japanese squid boat fleets that tend to be quite prolific in this region. Operating in groups of 15 or so they appear to have little knowledge of navigation and are equally ignorant regarding the rules of the road. They also completely dominate the 2090 radio frequency, through which radio skeds with Devonport operated. While I make no pretense at understanding the Japanese language, it took little imagination to realise that as with most civilisations, sex plays an important role in Japanese life.

As we approached Cook Strait an accelerating north-west breeze pushed our little pea-green boat with a big yellow spinnaker along at a wobbly eight to nine knots. Poor visibility and overcast skies prevented any reliable sun shots being taken, and Peter Smith's assistant navigator added to the dilemma by taking some magnificent hand-bearing fixes off the various dark cumulo nimbus formations floating on the horizon.

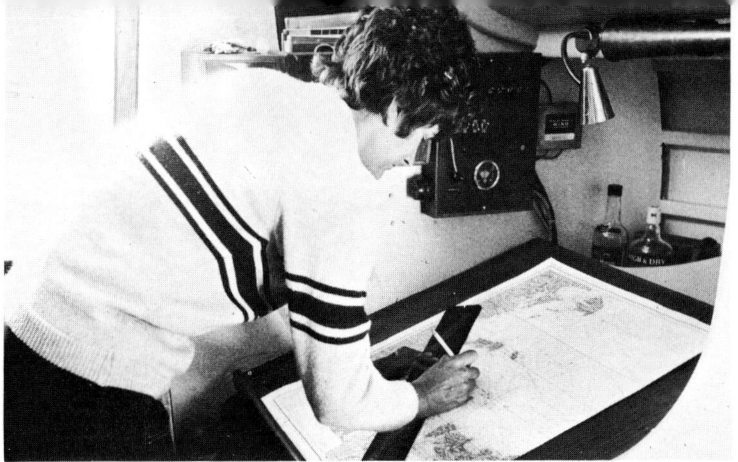

Above: **A popular figure in New Zealand ocean racing fleets. Heather Lidgard working at the chart table of** *Runaway. J. A. Gasparich*

Below: **Wellingtonian Geoff Stagg's Spencer-designed sloop** *Whispers II*, **which won the Auckland to Suva race overall in 1973. Stagg won the B-division trophy in the 1977 Suva race in his next boat** *Whispers of Wellington.*

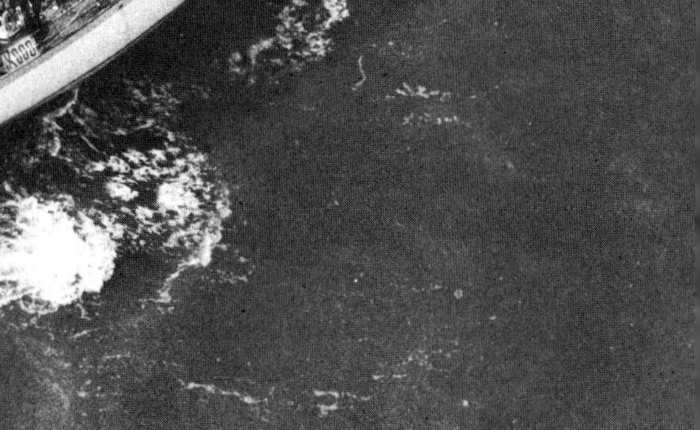

New Zealander Peter Blake crewed on the steel-hulled ketch *Windward Spirit* — renamed *Burton Cutter* for the duration of the race — in the Whitbread Round-the-World Yacht Race, which left Portsmouth, England, in September 1973. Here he stands amid the laundry as *Burton Cutter* dries out after a spell of heavy weather at sea.

Fortunately, an ancient transitorised RDF/radio was found under the chilly bin, and a bearing taken off Stephenson Island and the Brothers ensured an almost perfect landfall on Cape Jackson. Once inside the cape the decision to take off the flanker was made telepathically with the arrival of the first of many 60 knot gusts. The remaining four miles to the finish off Motuara Island was sailed in smooth but foaming water, under mainsail alone at an average speed of nine and a bit knots.

Ship Cove, the Marlborough Sounds and Picton are obviously one of the major drawcards in a race like this and in their picturesque and dramatically beautiful way certainly lived up to expectations. Most of the boats, after finishing the leg, travelled the 14 miles up to Picton in lieu of secure moorings. Owing to the presence of the inter-island ferry terminus, the locals of this little town have obviously become over-exposed to the many tourists and sundry nomads who roam its streets. While it would be grossly unfair to infer that we were treated with hostility, many of us gained the impression that we had contracted malignant bad breath.

For the majority of contestants, crossing Cook Strait was anticipated as being the hiatus of the trip. In reality it was very dull, but this tended to be a relief rather than a disappointment. We left Queen Charlotte Sound at 2070 hours on the evening of the 31st and a 20-knot south-easter saw us hard on the wind laying some 15° below Cape Terawhiti. However, a four to five-knot ebb tide under the lee bow virtually equalled the forward boat speed, and only a short slog to weather was required to clear Karori Rock before heading for Cape Palliser.

By dawn the next morning we were off Palliser, an evil sinister looking headland marking the southern extremity of the Wairarapa coast. All that day we slogged into a light five to 10-knot south-easterly, with few complaints. Despite the slow progress, we knew that the Cavalier 36s excel in these conditions.

Our confidence was reinforced after the evening sched by the realisation that we had worked ourselves into second position behind *Gerontius*.

Dawn the following morning brought a southerly change which freshened throughout the day. The 130 remaining miles to Gisborne involved a long hard run in 30 to 40 knots of breeze. This was an interesting sail because despite the prevailing fresh conditions, and the Cavalier 36 reputation for spastic downwind behaviour, we were able to maintain perfect control over the entire distance by setting the flanker on the end of a penalty pole and strapping the clew hard down.

Gisborne is always a very agreeable part of the country and our 48 hours there served only to reinforce that attitude. At 2230 hours on 6 February we began the last and by far the most arduous leg of the race. This was not necessarily because of the conditions that were incurred, more because of an accumulation of loss of sleep. During the preceding legs of the race, excluding compulsory stops, Peter and I had averaged about one and a half to two hours sleep every 24 hours. Even in port during the 48-hour compulsory stop periods, nervous anticipation of the next leg and an already established disjointed sleeping pattern precluded any sustained sleep longer than three or four hours.

Nevertheless, adrenalin can be a wonderful substitute, and up to Gisborne, the lack of any proper sleep provided no real problem. During the last leg home, however, the realisation that soft, warm beds, hot showers and endless roast dinners were all within 50 hours reach caused us to pay a little more attention to what our bodies had been trying to tell us for the past fortnight. Climbing out of the bunk to do yet another headsail change required ridiculous effort, muscles and hands began to ache, and tying a simple bowline, an automatic exercise under normal circumstances, took one or two minutes of intense concentration.

The leg itself was reasonably straight-forward. An agonisingly slow drift up to East Cape was augmented by 40 to 50 knots of north-westerly on the other side. Three or four very wet sail changes were undertaken before the boat felt comfortable after which, there being little else to do, we both had a couple of rum-cokes-and-saltwaters, the later ingredient being an involuntary addition.

By dawn White Island was abeam on the horizon, the wind had moderated and from here to the Devonport wharf we slogged into a lightish breeze and slight sea, finishing at 1542 hours on Wednesday 9 March.

Having completed this little jaunt the question is inevitably asked, "Would you do it again?" While I am keen that participating in such an exercise does not develop into a habit I also feel that the occasional fling of madness does a lot to restore one's sanity.

The first yacht to finish was Gerontius, *sailed by Graham Eder and Peter Blake.* Warchild *came in second. However the overall handicap winner, also taking handicap honours for Division II, was the smallest yacht in the race, the 7.2 m* Marimba, *sailed by Eric Wing and Dave Anderson. Handicap winner for Division I was a stock Cavalier 32,* Galant *(John Carruthers and Ian McDonald).*

A staggering win

by J. A. GASPARICH

From the *New Zealand Herald*

No doubt there were some eyebrows raised when the Wellington yacht Whispers II, *a home-made product, triumphed over some of the big names in the yachting world to win the Auckland to Suva race in 1973. Yet, as this story by an Auckland journalist relates, even before the big Suva win* Whisper's *skipper Geoff Stagg was already considered one of the country's most highly-rated offshore yachtsmen.*

SO often foiled by sailing conditions which did not suit his charge, Stagg had waited a long time to step in for the big kill. There had been the frustrations of the 1971 Whangarei to Noumea race. It was a race with a reputation to be a downwind ride all the way. But alas, that race was to be a drifter and *Whispers II* was rarely worked up to planing speed.

Then there was the 1972 Hobart to Auckland race when Stagg and his crew were left to wiggle their fingers in the light airs under a big high pressure zone, while the big boats, *Kialoa II, Buccaneer* and *American Eagle* enjoyed the fresher breezes ahead of the high.

But in 1973 it all came right. *Whispers II* had the conditions she liked.

Whispers II is a hard-chined plywood keeler designed by the Aucklander John Spencer. Stagg built her himself. In pre-race calculations she was simply not mentioned in the same breath as the Sparkman and Stephens designs like *Ta'Aroa, Salacia II, Barnacle Bill* or for that matter any number of other proven offshore designs.

But then *Whispers II* is the 13.7 m little sister of *Infidel,* who, before being sold to America was the top dog on the Waitemata. And as *Infidel* had so often shown her speed with the wind on the beam in the harbour, *Whispers* did just the same thing all the way to Suva. When the breeze freshened she started to plane and was off like a rocket. The harder it blew the faster she went. And that was the secret of the 1973 Suva race.

For while the specialist designs rely on a fair share of windward sailing, they were far from equal to the occasion of sailing a long distance with the sheets eased.

In light airs they picked up maximum speed quickly. As the breeze freshened they held their speed. But when it blew hard there was little rise in the basic speed.

But for *Whispers II,* when it blew fresh, she was up away, surfing, and making the winning break to get her to Suva only 11 hours behind *Ta'Aroa* despite a deficit, of some 4.5 m in overall length.

It was not only luck with the weather that resulted in the splendid win.

For since her launching *Whispers II* had been sailed over 30,000 miles, and Stagg and his crew applied the same dedication to their sailing as Chris Bouzaid going after the One Ton Cup.

Whispers II was launched in 1970 and sailed in the 1971 Whangarei to Noumea race. The same year she was taken to Sydney to contest the Sydney-Hobart race and then was raced back across the Tasman in the race from Hobart to Auckland.

Not content with the length of the cruise, Stagg immediately quit Auckland for his home port. He arrived in Wellington one and a half hours after the start of the Wellington to Akaroa race. Unperturbed by the headstart, *Whispers* was in the race and gave chase.

At Christmas, 1972, Stagg raced the yacht from Wellington to Gisborne and gave a hint of what was to come in the Suva race when he put *Whispers II* through her paces in the harbour race at Gisborne.

Then it was back to Wellington to tune the yacht for Suva. And it wasn't only *Whispers II* that got the treatment with Stagg insisting every man in the crew attain a standard of fitness to play his part in getting the yacht to Suva in the shortest possible time.

Geoff Stagg and John Spencer had first teamed up when Spencer designed a centreboarder for Stagg, christened Whispers. *This combination proved so successful that the emergence of* Whispers II *was a logical conclusion. The crew of centreboard sailers became the keeler crew. The boat was built and maintained on a shoestring, and the crew trained long and hard. For a month before the Suva race they drank no alcohol.*

In spite of her success in the Suva race, Geoff Stagg sold Whispers II *because she did not rate under the I.O.R. rule and he wanted to campaign for the New Zealand Southern Cross team. Accordingly, John Spencer designed* Whispers of Wellington, *which did rate and was eligible later to race in the Admiral's Cup selection trials.* Whispers of Wellington *took both line and handicap honours in the B division of the 1977 Auckland to Suva race.*

Round Three Kings to end at Cowes

by J. A. GASPARICH

From the *New Zealand Herald*

Following the launching of Corinthian *in April 1973, and the earlier appearance of* Barnacle Bill *and* Inca, *Admiral's Cup fever started to get a grip on Auckland. 1974 was the year for big boats. These large, gleaming beauties, which made such a fine sight on the Auckland Harbour, must be given a chance to compete in England's glamour event. A committee was formed, a sponsor was found, and a pre-race trial series was arranged with the co-operation of R.N.Z.Y.S. and R.A.Y.C., old hands at this type of organisation.*

The final line-up of contestants included: Aggressor *(V. Colson), from Whangarei;* Corinthian *(Russ Hooper),* Gerontius *(Graham Eder),* Inca *(Evan Julian),* Lisa *(Ron Wilkie),* Natelle *(Keith Wright),* Quando *(Jim Edmonds) and* Snow White *(Bob Graham), all of Auckland;* Barnacle Bill *(newly acquired by Ron Jarden),* Koamaru *(Brian Millar),* Whispers of Wellington *(Geoff Stagg) and* Vulcan *(Les Evans) of Wellington.*

New Zealand Herald *journalist J. A. Gasparich reports on the ninth and final trial in the Admiral's Cup series, the 550-mile Three Kings race, which began on the evening of Wednesday 5 February 1975.*

FOR the first time in the trials there was a good breeze – a solid westerly blowing a steady 20 knots – and it must have had the effect of a heady wine for the crews to feel at last their charges heel over with the bit between teeth.

With the wind on the beam for the run out through the Rangitoto Channel, there was a slight hesitation and then up went the reaching spinnakers.

At the leeward end of the line, *Inca* was the first to show out and when the spinnaker went aloft the yacht threw out a stern wave that must have gladdened the hearts of the co-helmsmen, Evan Julian and Roy Dickson.

Further up to windward, Russ Hooper's *Corinthian* also looked good value even if there was initial hesitation in the crew chancing their arms with a spinnaker.

But not too far astern the wisdom of having a good look at prevailing conditions first was proven when *Quando* (Jim Edmonds), getting a puff too much, went into a mighty roundup into the wind. They were anxious moments for the crew and a solemn warning that the first night at sea in this long ocean race would bring little rest.

Soon after the start, *Natelle* (Keith Wright), in another pulsating manoeuvre, lost a spinnaker halyard to cause her crew some concern.

And while there was action aplenty there was no better-looking yacht in the fleet than *Gerontius* (Graham Eder). Third-placed on points in the Dunhill-sponsored trials and still an unknown quantity sailing in a blow, *Gerontius,* – a new Farr design, snuggled down with a small rig and, using maximum waterline length, was right up there with the leaders.

And as the yachts rounded North Head and *Gerontius* tried a spinnaker she simply started to fly. In the gathering dusk as the yachts cleared the East Coast Bays and headed out toward the Noisies group on the first leg of the race to Channel Island, *Gerontius* was out in front.

After an hour and a half sailing time, the leading yachts were reported two miles clear of the Noisies and well on their way to the Channel Island mark.

With the prospect of the westerly holding throughout the night the fleet was getting the best start of the series, this time a splendid test of sailing with a reach up the back of the Great Barrier Island, some windward work back into Sail Rock off the Whangarei Heads and then perhaps more eased-sheet sailing on the long haul up the Northland coast.

The wind continued to freshen. This blow, the aftermath of Hurricane Val, played havoc with the yachts. Two boats had to retire with broken masts and off Great Barrier Island an injured crewsman from race leader *Corinthian* was transferred to the escort vessel *Sirdar* with a broken ankle.

The incident temporarily cost *Corinthian* her lead, but she was back level with the pacemakers, *Gerontius* and *Inca,* the following night as the fleet headed north on the long leg to the Three Kings Islands.

The injured man was the *Corinthian* crew member F. Robinson, who was admitted to Brightside Hospital, Auckland, with a broken ankle. The 53-year-old yachtsman was caught in a wire rope from a spinnaker.

The two major casualties were *Aggressor* and *Quando,* both of which broke their masts during 45-knot squalls as they were rounding Channel Island, off Cape Colville.

Aggressor was the first to be hit. The yacht lost her spinnaker pole and in the resulting confusion a wave filled the cockpit. At almost the same moment the mast snapped. Owner-skipper V. Colson and his six-man crew had to work for an hour to lash down the mast and sails before being able to put back for Auckland under motor.

Meanwhile, the 14.6 m *Quando* had suffered a similar misfortune. Struck by the same 45-knot south-westerly squall, a shackle on *Quando's* forestay snapped, and the alloy mast buckled 1.2 m above the deck.

The jagged edge of the broken shackle tore one of the yacht's sails, and according to owner-skipper Jim Edmonds it was only this that prevented the entire mast from going over the side. At the time of the mishap *Quando,* was leading the fleet in winds gusting up to 48 knots. Just before the mast broke *Quando* had been doing a steady 15 or 16 knots.

The Admiral's Cup boats continued to plough their way up the coast in winds that continued strong, then down past the Poor Knights and around the Moko Hinau Islands as the weather moderated. Finally, in a mere whisper of wind and over calm seas, the first boats glided past the finishing line off Orakei Wharf in the early hours of a starry Sunday morning. Corinthian *took line honours and a second place on corrected time.*

However, she could not match the consistency of *Inca, Gerontius* or *Barnacle Bill* who finished first, third and fourth respectively in the big race to retain their top rankings in the series.

The *Inca* skipper, Evan Julian, put the yacht's splendid performance down to crew work. "You know," said Julian after the race, "without the job Alan Bell did on our steering gear we would never have come through. There was nothing madly dramatic about the race after the first night. It was just consistent hard sailing.

"But, that first night, in the storm, we blew out two spinnakers, ripped a batten pocket out of the mainsail and ripped out the leech cord. Our biggest calamity was when we broke our steering gear and ran out of control.

"Young Alan did a magnificent job to keep us in the race. From midnight until about 4 a.m. he was working under the cockpit floor in all of that pitching and heaving. Then he was back at it from 7 a.m. until about two in the afternoon. He had to file a stainless steel shackle down to make a pin for the steering but he got it working again. It was sheer murder steering with the emergency tiller."

By virtue of her performance, *Inca* climbed to top spot on the chart with 127 points, one ahead of *Barnacle Bill,* with *Gerontius* on 120.

There was a big drop back to *Corinthian* on 105 points.

The three Admiral's Cup entries had been chosen. Inca, Barnacle Bill *and* Gerontius *were on their way to Cowes to represent New Zealand in the 1975 Admiral's Cup.*

Racing round the world

by PETER BLAKE

Peter Blake is one of a band of New Zealand yachtsmen liable to be found anywhere around the globe on the international yacht racing and delivery circuit. In 1976, at the age of 28, he had accumulated 70,000 miles in this way. When at home he lives on Auckland's North Shore, and works at Yachtspar. Here he writes of the first leg of the Whitbread Round-the-World Yacht Race, which left from Portsmouth, England, in September 1973. His steed, Burton Cutter, *was a brand new 24.4 m aluminimum cutter-rigged ketch, built at speed to take part in the race and still uncompleted inside when the starting gun went.*

SATURDAY, 8 September. A beautiful day with blue skies, blue seas, a light south-east breeze and a reasonably warm temperature. We woke early as there were still many things to attend to – navigation lights, mounting the compasses, making storm window coverings. With these done, the shore lines were slipped at approx. 1030 hours and we were towed from our berth (at H.M.S. *Vernon,* Portsmouth) towards the starting line by a large naval launch. (Although we have twin 60 h.p. diesels, neither of these was connected up to the prop units due to lack of time.) The compass was swung on the way to the start and the sails were then hoisted, properly, for the first time since the launching approximately three weeks before.

Les made a terrific start, right at the windward end of the line just as the gun went and we were away. The spectator craft were everywhere and I don't think I have ever seen so many interested in the start of a yacht race before. This is saying something when you consider what the start of the last Suva race was like. However a 35-ton aluminium ketch charging around a crowded starting line tends to command a fair bit of respect, whatever tack she is on. As we were doing a good 10 knots at times, the smaller non-racing boats soon skittled out of the way. (One nearly had his Hasler self-steering gear up on our bows.)

The first mark of the course was the Bembridge Ledge Buoy in the Solent near the north-east corner of the Isle of Wight, Tabarly rounding first, closely followed by Chay Blyth with *Great Britain II. Burton Cutter* was next and, with the number of pleasure craft slowly dwindling to a handful only, we made our way down channel under light ghosting spinnaker, staysail, main, mizzen and mizzen staysail.

The next few days were spent under spinnaker, alternating between the ghoster and worker as the wind varied in strength and direction.

On about the fifth day out we had a gust of about 15 knots from the port beam and the ghoster blew out. We changed to worker and sat down to repair the lightweight job. What a marathon exercise this turned out to be. It had torn both luffs out and had also gone right across the sail in the middle. The sewing machine was used on the luff tapes but would not handle the very light material across the sail. Yours truly did this by hand with the aid of vast quantities of special sticky tape. I think I could probably sew in my sleep from now on, as an 80 ft (24 m) ketch's spinnaker is not too small. After about a week of patching and mending, we rehoisted. The sail set pretty well for a couple of hours and then blew out again in completely different places. We just about cried as we gathered the remains in and then sat down and repeated the performance. Luckily it held and has continued to do so this far.

About halfway across the Bay of Biscay the weather turned all funny with the weather patterns becoming the exact opposite to those which should normally be experienced in this area at this time of the year. We ended up tacking into fresh headwinds for a week, before being freed a couple of hundred miles north of the Canary Islands. With working spinnaker up we really made good time with runs over 200 miles every day. The time lost in sorting all the problems out during the first week told heavily at this stage. *G.B. II* and *Pen Duick* were about 150 miles in front.

The island of Gran Canary was sighted early one morning and Las Palmas came abreast at breakfast time as we ran at 12 knots under all canvas. The wind became light for a day and then came back with a vengeance. Our speed slowly rose and rose. I was on watch one morning as we passed a row of six large Russian fishing trawlers. *Burton Cutter* dashed past the first five, all going the same way, and then came upon the sixth. This was a mother ship which we passed at 12 to 14 knots under spinnaker. I don't think they could believe their eyes because we were only about 50 yards away. Searchlights were trained on us, but these soon faded out astern. The wind continued to increase and a run at 20 knots was experienced, followed soon after by a 23, lasting for 30 seconds down the face of a wave. Half an hour later the working spinnaker just exploded, dropped in the water and tore beyond repair by us. Still, $2400 worth of kite in tatters didn't bother the owners too much. We have since bought some more from Ratsey's and had them flown from England to Cape Town.

Halfway between the Canary and Cape Verde Islands we encountered a very large fleet of fishing boats, again Russian, and spent the whole day passing trawler after trawler. No fewer than 20 large mother ships were seen during the day. No wonder the fishing grounds in this part of the world are becoming depleted.

The wind stayed astern (north to north-east) for several days until 8° north. It then died to nearly zero for three days before coming back in from the south-west, at latitude 5° north. This period was classed as the doldrums, but we had no rain squalls, no lightning, no violent wind changes, so all in all it was quite pleasant and very hot.

When the south-wester arrived, we had two days of still-sunny conditions before the effects of the Benguela Current became noticeable. Temperatures then dropped, skies became grey and the sea became very confused and lumpy. We stayed on the starboard tack, heading into the Gulf of Guinea, until the wind went south and then south-east. Then on to the port tack and away down the eastern sector of the Atlantic, on a similar route to that which we did in *Ocean Spirit,* only slightly further west this time. You would think we would have had enough of slogging to windward on that trip, but it was decided that the discomfort was worth it as the distance to Cape Town was over a 1000 miles less than by the conventional sailing ship route near Brazil.

The equator was crossed at midday on 1 October, weather conditions being perfect at the time. Just south of the equator we had our first really heavy downpour, and our first and last really decent freshwater wash. The rest of the time it was saltwater rinses, which are OK when the weather is warm, but become a little less enjoyable as the sea and air temperature decrease.

For 12 days we stayed on the port tack, plugging into mainly moderate south-east winds with completely overcast skies. We did have three days during this period when the wind increased beyond even a fresh trade wind strength and we were down to two headsails only – no main or mizzen. Under the two-headsail rig, only occasionally managing a reefed mizzen as well, the noon to noon run was 212 miles, which isn't too bad for hard on the wind. However, *Burton Cutter* is so big that she doesn't seem to fit in between the waves of the South Atlantic very well and she slammed very hard at times, so much so that we have buckled several plates up forward on the starboard side below the waterline. When out of the water in Cape Town she looked just like a destroyer. The strength appears to be alright, which is the main thing.

Very few dolphins were noticed until about 1000 miles from Cape Town, after which there was hardly a time when they left us.

One morning, very early, when we were in the main shipping lane between Europe and South Africa, the Persian Gulf and India, a large freighter came up from astern on approximately the same course as ourselves. As she drew closer and closer we became a little concerned, but not unduly worried, as several ships had done the same thing previously and had veered away at the last moment. (In very heavy fog in the Bay of Biscay we had several ships very close at one time but could not see them, only hear the sounds of the engines and the propellors thrashing the water.) This ship, however, kept on coming, so the watch on the deck shone the aldis lamp on her bridge. After five minutes and still no course alteration we fired off a red flare (Very type). Still no course change. We couldn't alter our course safely at this stage, or we would have done so. She was coming directly from astern and it wasn't obvious which side she would pass. Another red flare and no reply. By this time she was right on top of us and Len made an emergency tack and just cleared her. She missed by a couple of yards. We were looking up at the bows and could read the name quite clearly even without our aldis. Les was so angry he fired another flare straight through the windows of her bridge and this had the desired effect of waking up the watch. She was a Polish freighter. Apparently they are quite lax at times, but as soon as she had passed she slowed right down and turned in a wide circle before coming back to sit near us until dawn, just to make sure everything was ok. I bet the guy on watch (asleep) had a good talking to by the captain. If we had been another ship, with a lookout also asleep, the result would have been quite interesting.

The crew all fitted in very well together, especially considering that most of us hadn't sailed together before. One of the problems was that only Les, John and myself had ever done any serious sailing before (John Tanner was on *Ocean Spirit* in the Rio race with us). This meant that any alterations to sail trim, in fact any decisions at all, had to be made by one of us. It gets a little tiring at times telling the crew to either pull in or let out a sheet when a sail is either too tight or flapping. Some of them are at last starting to get the hang of things, which is just as well. Having crew who can afford to pay, rather than having the best experienced yachtsmen, is all very well, but it loads the work on to those who are reasonably sure of what is going on.

With approx 1000 miles to go to Cape Town, the weather went very light. At this point we were about 1200 miles ahead of *G.B. II* and 400 ahead of *Adventure,* the Royal Navy entry. Over the next three days both these yachts caught right up with us, and *Adventure* even reported sighting us on the third morning. While we had been drifting around at one or two knots, she had been steaming at seven or eight, but that is sailing for you. At this point, she tacked south and we went north, which turned out to be by far the best tactical manoeuvre we had made to date. *Adventure* stayed in calms and we sailed into a fresh southerly breeze.

With 200 miles left to go, we were really starting to get going, averaging 10 knots at 45° relative to the wind, under yankee, staysail, main, mizzen and mizzen genoa. We stayed like this all the way to a point five miles from the finish line, when we came under the shadow of Table Mountain. We sighted the mountain mid-morning on Saturday, six weeks to the day after leaving Portsmouth, and soon had a fleet of small craft escorting us to the line. Cameras were everywhere. What a perfect day it was. The weather couldn't have been better if we had ordered it. At 1317 we crossed and were towed into the yacht club basin, where we were surrounded by hundreds of spectators. As we entered the Duncan dock, all the tugs in the harbour set off their sirens, as did several ships. Boy, what a terrific welcome after such a long period at sea.

Burton Cutter *took line honours, but came sixth on handicap. Winner of this leg on corrected time was* Adventure.

Early in the second leg Burton Cutter's *damaged frames collapsed further and the crew were obliged to put her about and return to Port Elizabeth for repairs, so they missed the second and third legs. On 12 December 1973, with Peter Blake as skipper, the yacht left Cape Town for Buenos Aires to join a race from there to Rio de Janeiro, where they joined the fourth and final leg of the round-the-world race. They left Rio on 11 March 1974 and on Easter Saturday 13 April they crossed the finish line, back at Portsmouth.*

Single-handed to Mooloolaba

From New Zeatand Press Association reports

One woman and nine men left Port Taranaki on 27 April 1974 on the start of a lonely 1200 miles battle with the elements in the second trans-Tasman single-handed yacht race organised by the New Plymouth Yacht Club. The finish line was at Mooloolaba, 40 miles north of Brisbane.

ALL the competitors had first had to complete a solo voyage of 800 km to prove their ability to sail alone. Annette Wilde performed hers on the way from her home town, Christchurch, to the start line in New Plymouth. She had helped to build her yacht, the 10 m ferro-cement *Valya,* a modified Hartley Queenslander; she was the first woman to undertake a solo voyage across the Tasman. Another first went to John Jury, believed to be the first one-legged man to undertake a single-handed race. A 50-year-old Auckland block-layer who had lost the lower half of his left leg, he was extremely agile around his 9 m yacht, *Easterly I.*

A likely winner of the race was considered to be Aucklander Pony More, professional yacht skipper, at that time master of the youth training vessel *Spirit of Adventure.* Illness had forced him from the inaugural race in 1970.

His strongest competition was thought likely to come from Tony Allen, of Christchurch, sailing an 11.5 m trimaran, *Rebel II,* sister ship of the 1970 winner, which had been sailed by the American, M. Glenn. On that occasion Glenn made the crossing in nine and a half days.

Also pushing Pony More was the other professional sailor in the race, the inter-island ferry master John Mansell of Wellington, taking a busman's holiday to sail his 8.5 m cutter, *Innovator.*

The only entrant to come from overseas was an Australian, Charles Ure, of Gosford, in his trim 8.5 m Clansman sloop, *Mirrool.*

Pony More, in his sloop *Carmita,* was believed to be leading the race after the third day. In a radio report to New Plymouth he placed himself 350 miles from the start line. He also reported that his only real rival, Tony Allen in *Rebel II,* was "20 miles distant", without indicating whether ahead or behind. More was considered by race officials to be the likely leader.

Only two other contestants contacted race officials at that time – Annette Wilde and John Jury. Annette Wilde pinpointed *Valya's* position as 200 miles from New Zealand and reported having overcome her problem with storm-damaged rigging and sails. John Jury gave his position as 140 miles from the start line.

But in the end a man who had given himself "no chance" quietly slipped across the finish line to take line honours, 90 minutes ahead of his nearest rival, on the afternoon of 9 May.

Bill Belcher, aged 62, retired engineer of Waiheke Island, oldest entrant in the race and a man who entered only to have "a pleasant sail across", crossed the line at 2.10 p.m. in his 7.3 m sloop *Raha.*

His time of 11 days, three hours and 10 minutes was a remarkable one for the size of the boat, especially since he trounced the two race favourites, *Carmita* and *Rebel II,* which arrived later in the afternoon and were placed second and third respectively.

Sighted on the Monday night a bare 240 miles off the Queensland coast, one of these two was expected to be the winner. At that stage no one had seen or heard of *Raha* since the beginning of the race at New Plymouth. She was not sighted, in fact, until 10.40 a.m. on her arrival day, when two Mooloolaba-based trawlers spotted her an estimated two hours' sailing time from the harbour.

When club officials reached him, Bill Belcher was sitting in the cockpit happily cruising towards his destination, close to the shoreline. As he neared the finish line, the "old man" of the race waved triumphantly to the large crowd that had gathered.

Bill Belcher built *Raha* himself and sailed her to New Zealand via Panama in 1970-72. A popular member of the Royal Akarana Yacht Club — he used to sail *Raha* from Waiheke to race in the Sunday winter races — Bill Belcher would later receive that club's Blue Water medal for his single-handed exploit.

Second over the line was Pony More in *Carmita.* When he crossed the line he was surprised to see his wife, who had unexpectedly gone to Australia to meet him. He was even more astonished to see Bill Belcher standing on the shore holding a can of New Zealand beer.

One other trophy remained to be decided, the John Burns prize of a ship's bell for the first yacht on handicap. There was one other yacht that could win this trophy — the tiny 5.8 m ferro-cement sloop *Roc,* sailed by Roger Taylor of Hamilton. If he made Mooloolaba by 2.18 p.m., the trophy would be his. *Roc* had not been sighted since the race had started and carried no radio.

Roc had still not been sighted on 27 May, when the 30-day race period had expired, and a wide search was organised. Eventually the little yacht was seen from the air, sailing manfully on, with inoperable self-steering gear. The yacht made slow progress in bad weather and was eventually towed into Mooloolaba by the pilot boat.

John Mansell, in *Innovator,* finished fourth. Annette Wilde, in *Valya,* and Ian McBride, in *Ubique,* finished fifth and sixth, coming in on the same day from their long journey, which had taken 15 days.

For five days of his journey, Ian McBride was suffering from appendicitis. A veterinarian, he diagnosed the malady himself. He took some antibiotics and, to his relief, the pains went away. He was also met by his wife and daughter. Originally from Brisbane, he had been living at Inglewood for the previous two years. He had never sailed before going to New Zealand.

Annette Wilde, who had preceded him, arriving at 3 a.m. that Sunday morning to finish fifth, said that it had been a worthwhile experience.

"There is a very fine dividing line between being scared and going on – and being scared and turning back," she said after the race. "I was scared – frequently. Once I did not have the safety harness on and if I had not been hanging on I would have been washed over the side. I came out of it with a few bruises but none the worse for wear.

"It has been a worthwhile experience. It has taught me a lot about myself and developed my personality."

John Jury brought *Easterly I* in seventh. It was a week before the eighth contestant, Joe Davidson, arrived in his 6.7 m Giles-designed sloop *White Heron.*

Australian Charles Ure and *Mirrool* were the centre of a search and rescue operation after the yacht was dismasted. The night of 3 May was calm and he was flying a trysail in place of the mainsail, the slides of which had ripped out earlier on the voyage.

"At about 11 o'clock a terrific gust snapped the mast just above the spreaders," he said. "It fell along the length of the boat and I was able to lash it on deck."

He calculated he was 200 miles west of New Zealand. Deciding to run back to New Plymouth, he rigged the storm jib and broke the seals on his motor.

By 9 May, with his fuel almost finished, Ure calculated he was close to the air route between Auckland and Brisbane. He turned on a distress beacon. The signal was picked up almost immediately. He did not know this and kept sending the signals every half hour.

At 11 a.m. the next day an RNZAF Orion was overhead, much to his joy. This turned to dismay when the aircraft dropped a float with medical supplies.

"All I wanted was enough fuel to continue on my way," he said. "I stood on the deck waving a plastic fuel can and my largest funnel in the hope that the message would get across."

He thought an RNZAF helicopter would bring fuel, but he learned from his transistor radio that a tanker had been diverted.

The *Aluca* arrived soon after 8 p.m. and Ure's greeting: "You're a tanker – it's your job to fill up little boats like me," provoked mixed reactions. After Ure assured the Shell tanker that he always used their product, the transfer of fuel, enough to fill the tanks, went smoothly. He was also given several sandwiches, two bananas and a flash of hot tea.

Then, with a wave and a word of encouragement from the crew, the tanker left. Ure motored back to New Plymouth.

Twenty-one days adrift

New Zealand Press Association

The trimaran Rebel II *and its owner, solo sailor Tony Allen, were to be engaged in further adventures together and their parting was dramatic. On 20 December 1975, two days out from Brisbane on a voyage home to Lyttleton, the 11.6 m trimaran overturned while the solo sailor was asleep.*

Twenty-one days adrift in a rubber raft and the loss of his trimaran did not shake Tony Allen's faith in multi-hulled craft, reported the New Zealand Press Association from Christchurch.

"I HAVEN'T a clue how it happened," said Mr Allen. "I had been up a couple of hours before. There was nothing untoward, and she was rolling down the waves nicely. She was averaging about seven knots then – she wasn't pushed. Then she rolled right over while I was asleep below.

"I woke up as the boat was halfway over. Everything was falling around my head. I knew that to get out I would have to do everything upside down, so I worked my way to the back of the boat, then dived down into the sea and up again alongside it.

"I grabbed an axe which was on the back of the boat and cut a hole into the side of the hull so that I could get some gear out. I then dived back underneath the boat to cut the rubber raft free." For two days he stayed by his upturned yacht before deciding to cut free.

He spent 21 days adrift in the raft, but he was never disheartened and always felt that things would turn out satisfactorily.

He lived on several tins of food and about 45 litres of water. He finished the last of the food on 13 January, two days before his rescue.

At one stage a shark swam around the raft for several minutes and rubbed against it.

"I could only have lasted another four or five days – but I never gave up hope," he said. Finally his faith was rewarded by the appearance of the Greek freighter, *Khian Star.* His flares were seen and he was picked up – 180 miles off the Australian coast, between Newcastle and Sydney.

Mr Allen kept a log of his trip by scratching notes on the top of his sextant box with a can opener. Those and the clothes he was wearing were all he had left. All his radio equipment was washed out through the hatchway of the trimaran. His biggest discomfort was losing the boat. Uninsured, it cost him $15,000 to $20,000.

But in spite of his loss, the solo yachtsman retained his faith in multihulled craft. At least it had not broken up when it rolled over!

In 1974 Waiheke Island retired engineer Bill Belcher won the single-handed race from New Plymouth to Mooloolaba in Queensland in his sloop *Raha*. These photographs were taken as he sailed up the Queensland coast to take first place.
Sunshine Coast Newspaper Co

Above: **A study in concentration. Twice-winner of the One Ton Cup, Chris Bouzaid works on the job at hand during a training session out on the harbour.**
Alan Sefton

Below: **A yacht which caught the imagination of the New Zealand public: the mighty** ***Rainbow II*****, winner of the One Ton Cup for New Zealand at Heligoland in 1969.**
John Mallitte

A new captain takes command

by W. R. M. BELCHER

The winner of the 1974 single-handed race from New Plymouth to Mooloolaba, Bill Belcher, reflects on the mental pressures of solo sailing.

THIS solo sailing is an odd form of amusement and those doing it are inclined in their turn to become a little bit queer, or it may possibly be the other way around.

One of the oddities which are confessed to by the truthful, but only hinted at by those who are trying to live down the public's idea of normality, is the presence on board of a companion. Slocum, who did not care what the world thought, and even tried to convince President Kruger of the Transvaal that the world was round, had as his companion the pilot of the *Pinta.* Others have had talking dolls, invisible voices. On *Raha,* the self-steering used to talk, but mostly to itself.

It fell to my lot not so much to have a companion as actually to be the other presence which for a few short moments took over my boat.

The '74 trans-Tasman race for single-handers started off in New Plymouth with a sullen, oppressive atmosphere and catspaws of wind crossing the harbour in all directions. Outside, we could see through the gap between the two arms of the harbour walls that the whole skyline was a mass of white horses chasing each other in a wild stampede.

It was obvious as soon as we cleared the shelter of land that we were in for trouble. Under such conditions prudence dictated that we should shorten sail. At the start of the race, with a large crowd looking on, it is, however, a brave man who is the first to reef. Fortunately Pony More, a seaman first and a racing addict only in second place, realised what we were in for and reefed down. He was quickly followed by most of the competitors. I personally left *Raha* with only the minimum of sail up. Annette Wilde, through bravado or insufficient experience, hoisted her twin running sails.

The start, by none other than the Australian High Commissioner, was a shambles, with guns going off at the oddest intervals. Presumably affairs of state were being discussed and could not always be interrupted by the need to fire a gun in time. After the third gun, away we went, most of us bobbing up and down on the swell with insufficient sail up to give us much forward motion. Annette, however, swept past us with her red running sails drawing nicely and proving by their shape that not only the skipper but also the boat was female.

Then the wind hit us and we all started to move except Annette, whose beautiful whisker poles folded up under the strain and the wildly flogging canvas gave her an indication of what was to come.

Suffice it to say that for the next six days we had nothing but storm conditions which, whether we wanted it or not, were driving us to Australia. This was very nice, but for six days we had the shrieking of the rigging, seas which more often than not seemed to crash on deck rather than pass in the more orthodox manner underneath the keel; and the continual lurching, heeling and twisting of the boat, which made it impossible for anything to stay put unless it was held down or fixed in a locker. All this takes a toll on anyone. The process is gradual and maybe unnoticed, but slowly physically and mentally it wears you down.

On the morning of the sixth day, at first light, I struggled into oilskins and safety harness, slid back the hatch and took a quick look around. Spend too long doing this, and one of the large waves may hit you in the face, resulting in sore eyes and a wet shirt front. This is uncomfortable and needs a change of clothes which, if the storm has persisted, may not be available as, once wet, nothing dries out until fine weather returns.

The sea was still a mass of whitecaps. A small jib and reefed mainsail was as much as the boat could take and so far there did not seem to be any damage to the boat or rigging. *Raha* is a little tubby in her lines, but with the wind aft of the beam was behaving like a horse with the prospect of a warm stable and a feed of oats in front of it.

As there was nothing else I could do to further the progress, I closed the hatch, shed my oilskins and ducked down in the comparative peace and warmth of the cabin.

When single-handed it is advisable to get as much sleep as possible. The usual routine is to sleep one or two hours, wake and check the compass by the bunk. If on course and the boat does not feel over or under canvassed, back to sleep. If off course, get up, adjust the self steering and if necessary the sails and back to the bunk.

This routine is varied by the need to eat, write up the log, do a bit of navigation, check the position by sun or star sights or, in cloudy weather, by radio beacons and do the household chores. The basic idea is that, should an emergency arise, you always start off quite fresh and capable of going a long time without further sleep.

Fairly obviously, however, if the emergency does not arise, this system results in the sailor being completely slept up. I had arrived at this point and further sleep was impossible, so I had some food, did a radio D/F check on Norfolk and Lord Howe islands, wrote up the log and then looked for a book to read.

While I was getting ready for the race at New Plymouth, my wife had collected a supply of paperbacks which would be suitable reading for someone with his brain in neutral. A few detectives, some cowboys and a mixed bag which could entertain without mental effort. It was from this section of the library that I picked out a rather tattered volume contributed, as I saw by the flyleaf, by our hosts in New Plymouth.

The story was not particularly well-written but was simple and did not require much effort to follow. It concerned the adventures of a rum-soaked derelict who had been burning around the bars of Suva ever since he had lost his boat and all his possessions while engaged in a dubious enterprise apparently concerning someone else's pearl.

The inevitable oily entrepreneur turned up, proposing a voyage to be undertaken by the derelict. No-one else apparently would take the job. This involved taking the oily one's boat, itself nothing to write home about, and sailing to a small atoll, well-known to our rum-soaked hero due to his previous nefarious activities. There he was to pick up an individual and cargo (unspecified) and deliver them both to a destination of which he would be informed by the individual in question.

There were several flies in the ointment. This being Suva, it was impossible to visualise one solitary fly. The boat was unsound and had only been taken over by the owner on a debt. There was a crew to be collected, a month-long hangover to be dissipated and his lodgings to be paid for. It was also just after New Year and hurricanes can be expected at this time of year.

The oily one paid only for the minimum of boat repairs in spite of a last ditch ultimatum from the new skipper. The crew were recruited in Suva and were a pretty motley collection who for one reason or another were prepared to sail on a leaky boat with a sodden skipper. There were only two to be trusted and they were members of his old crew – remnants of the days when his reputation was still untarnished, all he could find in the time available.

The work gave him a new direction in life and slowly the drunken object began to take on the bearing and authority that he had once worn so effortlessly. New lodgings were paid for (charts apparently he did not require, was the writer perhaps slipping?). Everything was ready or as ready as it was ever likely to be, but it was still the hurricane season when they finally cast off.

It was now that the writer showed that he had really done his homework. Whether he had read the proper books, or if he had actually sailed on a pearler does not matter. He got the feel of the sea and the boat and of these he could write.

There were the first easy sun-soaked days and calm nights with the phosphorescent wake and the kanaka crew lying or sitting on the cargo hatch softly singing.

The change to dull, listless calm had the crew upset and apprehensive. The barometer started to fall and the wind, at first blowing in fits and starts, then settled in and started to blow. Hurriedly extra lashings were tied on anything which might carry away, the sails were lowered and then the storm really hit.

The cook was the first to go. He had been boiling up some water when the storm started. The water upset over him and screeching he leapt out of the galley only to be carried overboard by a wave which swept the length of the ship. There was no chance of saving him as the boat had no way on her and, even if it had been possible, to turn in such a sea would have almost certainly been disastrous.

Part of the lashing of the boom broke loose. The cordage was old and had been too many seasons in the tropical sun. This required all the efforts of the skipper and crew to control and finally secure. During this, one of his two former crew ended up with what appeared to be a busted arm, but under the conditions nothing could be done for him. The deckhouse ports were the next to go and the terrified kanakas refused to leave the crew quarters where they had fled after the tussle with the boom, taking the injured man with them.

Things were getting worse and worse. The crashing of the sea, the howl of the wind seemed to blot out all thought. The crew were useless, everything devolved on one man. Could the ship be kept afloat? Would we miss the chain of atolls which lay across the boat's path? What could be done to ride out the storm? The jobs and priorities would have to be decided and the kanakas bluffed into at least keeping the water level down. There were leaks in the wheelhouse and decks which had opened up by the pounding of the sea and these would have to be plugged if we were to have a chance. Could I get the kanakas out of their frightened stupor and onto the pumps? The course of the boat must be worked out to see if we would miss the reef and if necessary a small sail hoisted to give just that little control which might save the ship. Meantime my brain is tired from the noise and the movement and it seems as if those months in Suva have paralysed my will. I just don't seem able to start anything. The burden is too much for me. I couldn't do it. It was no good. Oh hell.

The book slid off the bunk and landed on the cabin sole. It didn't make much noise compared to the wind and sea, but it was a different noise and it was that which brought me to my senses.

I was not on a decrepit pearler in a South Seas gale and I had no mutinous crew. I was in a nice gale force wind in the Tasman and had only myself to worry about. Although the movement, the crashes of the waves and the whine of the rigging were all there, I had a nice warm dry bunk. And *Raha,* all 24 ft (7.3 m) of her, was, so the log informed me, putting up a very decent time for the trip to Australia.

New Zealand and the One Ton Cup

by LORIS CHILWELL

THE first international series to compete for the One Ton Cup – an ornate trophy originally presented by the Cercle de la Voile de Paris for 6 m boats in 1898 – was held in European waters in 1965, to become an annual event.

It did not take long for New Zealand to get into the act.

Following the launching and immediate outstanding success of Chris Bouzaid's *Rainbow II* and the discovery that its measurements fitted the then one-ton rule, the Royal New Zealand Yacht Squadron was persuaded by interested members to enter *Rainbow* in the one-ton contest to be held in 1968 at Heligoland.

Rainbow had been launched in Auckland in late summer of 1967 and the day after her launching had sailed and won her first race. A few weeks later she had left Whangarei in the Onerahi Yacht Club's race to Noumea – which she won. In fact Chris Bouzaid and *Rainbow II* had won consistently, had been to Sydney with the R.A.Y.C's Southern Cross team and had won the Sydney-Hobart race.

The crew that left for this first tilt at the One Ton Cup with Chris Bouzaid consisted of Alan Warwick, Roy Dickson, Gil Littler, Peter Shaw and Sticky Armitage.

Their training had been rigorous. Bouzaid, whose sailmaker father, Leo, had also been a champion yachtsman, had learned or inherited a professional approach to yachting contests. A daredevil sailor himself, with the ability to push his boat to the limit and beyond, he was a martinet and perfectionist in crew training. The crew had to keep fit with a daily run and gym training, as well as practising every sail change and manoeuvre over and over again, daily, in all weathers, cutting down the seconds with every practice. *Rainbow's* crew work became impeccable.

Rainbow did not win that year at Heligoland, but came second to Germany's *Optimist B* putting up an outstanding performance with a boat that, they realised, was just a poor relation to others in the contest.

In 1969 a vastly improved *Rainbow* returned to Heligoland and won the cup. Chris Bouzaid became a national hero and won the Yachtsman of the Year award that year. The next contest would take place in 18 months instead of a year to take advantage of New Zealand's summer.

In 1970 the R.N.Z.Y.S. started a campaign to attract overseas yachtsmen to the contest to take place in Auckland in February 1971.

The campaign was eminently successful and yachts and crew arrived from Australia *(Maria, Stormy Petrel; Warri)*, Germany *(Apecist, Optimist B)*; Hong Kong *(Ceil)*; Italy *(Kerkyra IV)*; Sweden *(Victoria)*; and Switzerland *(Joran)*. New Zealand yachts chartered by other visiting yachtsmen were *Mustang* (Canada); *Runaway* (Germany), *Concord* and *Outrage* (Great Britain) and *Kishmul* (Sweden). These were boats left out after the squadron picked the three winners from pre-race trials to represent New Zealand. *Runaway,* fourth boat in the trials, had been unlucky not to be chosen and proved her worth for Germany in the contest.

The three boats chosen to represent New Zealand were *Escapade* (Gil Hedges), *Wai-aniwa* (Chris Bouzaid) and *Young Nick* (Alan Warwick).

From the start of the selection trials on the Hauraki Gulf to the end of the contest itself, the event was a spellbinder and drew unprecedented crowds to the waterfront. Many spectators found an interest in yachting for the first time.

The contest was thrilling indeed. Watchers on hundreds of spectator craft groaned in despair as *Wai-aniwa,* after leading for the whole of the long second race, fell into a "hole" off Rangitoto Beacon, within metres of the finish line, Chris Bouzaid watching impotently as his rivals ghosted through on tiny puffs to eat up the rich points. Worse was to come however, when a protest from *Young Nick* disqualified *Wai-aniwa* from that race completely.

Syd Fisher in his Sparkman and Stephens design *Stormy Petrel,* sailing the whole series with finesse, took the cup home to the Cruising Yacht Club of Australia.

The following year, 1972, Chris Bouzaid and *Wai-aniwa* reversed the process and brought the cup back to New Zealand and the R.N.Z.Y.S.

According to the rules of the series, the cup had to return to Europe after two years away, and the 1973 series was sailed out of Sardinia. Chris raced for New Zealand in a chartered boat, *Hann,* and came third, vowing never again to charter an unknown, untried yacht. However he relented and campaigned *Hati* off Torquay in 1974, while Ian Gibbs also tried for New Zealand in *Offwego V,* both without success.

In 1976, following the magnificent performance of Noel Angus in the Bruce Farr one-tonner *Prospect of Ponsonby* in the winning New Zealand team at the Southern Cross series in Sydney (and the successful appearance of sister ships in local races), the squadron once more girded to contest the One Ton Cup. Trials were held and two Farr models, Graeme Woodroffe's *The Number* and Stuart Brentnall's *Jiminy Cricket,* were neck and neck. In the end it was decided that both would go to the contest at Marseilles.

The Number was rechristened *45 South II,* after her winning quarter-ton sister. Her crew included sailmaker Ross Guinevan, Joe Macky and Tim Gurr.

Two champion yachtsmen, Chris Bouzaid and Roy Dickson, joined Stuart Brentnall to campaign *Jiminy Cricket.*

The boats, although of the same design, were not identical. *Jiminy Cricket* was a timber edition, built by Kerry Alexander of Brown's Bay of ultra-light but strong construction, three skins of ply, cold-moulded and sheathed in fibreglass cloth. *The Number* was a very light glass hull, fitted with a custom-built deck and cockpit "lid".

"Fantastique! or Sacre Bleu!" The French said it all as they crowded the marina, as *45 South* and *Jiminy Cricket* berthed after taking the gold and the silver in the first race of the One Ton Cup. So cabled Graeme Douglas, *New Zealand Herald* staff reporter, from Marseilles on 7 August 1976.

It looked as if New Zealand might win the cup again.

But it was not to be.

There was a comedy of errors, protests and foul-ups, but America sailed superbly throughout and took the cup for the second year running. *Jiminy Cricket* (who took the gun in the 225 nautical mile last race) and *45 South* finished fourth and fifth on the points table. Between them they had won three of the five races and taken two second places. *45 South* was fourth overall, fewer than 10 points behind the winner, and *Jiminy Cricket* fifth, only half a point behind *45 South.*

By prior arrangement the next one-ton contest would take place in late 1977 from Auckland, to be hosted for the second time by the Royal New Zealand Yacht Squadron.

Highlights of one-ton contests

by CHRIS BOUZAID

Chris Bouzaid is champion of champions among keeler yachtsmen and a household name among the general public. He has now twice won the World One Ton Cup.

Once elusive because he was so often racing or training for international competitions, Bouzaid is now hard to find because he is often out of the country on business for his sailmaking firm.

Pinned down to a tape recorder during a lull in his almost ceaseless activity, Chris recalls the highlights of his one-ton contests.

THE first One Ton Cup series that I became involved in was in 1968 when we took *Rainbow II* to a little island called Heligoland in the North Sea. We were sent by the Royal New Zealand Yacht Squadron, and the idea was really to find out whether we were anywhere near world-class in keel boat yachting. This was New Zealand's first-ever major effort overseas in this type of racing.

That first series was very exciting. Right from the first race we realised we were in with a fighting chance, although the new German boat, *Optimist,* seemed to be very fast indeed. The most exciting race in that series was undoubtedly the ocean race. In those days the One Ton Cup series was comprised of only three races, two short ones and an ocean race. The ocean race in 1968 was sailed in strong winds and I'll always remember the last leg – in fact as we go through some of the one-tons that I have been in you will find that it is always the last leg in which the excitement occurs.

In this particular race we were running for the finishing line with the wind straight behind us. The leading boat was *Optimist,* followed by *Morning Town, Kerkyra* and then *Rainbow II.* We knew that if we wanted to finish up in the top placings we had to finish at least second in this race. The wind was blowing about 30 knots and all of the boats ahead of us put on their small spinnakers. However we came around the last light ship and put on our full size 1½ oz (42 g) spinnaker and had the ride of our lives all the way down. With about 10 miles to go we passed *Kerkyra.* Now we were getting closer and closer to *Morningtown;* however the closer we got to *Morningtown* the closer we also got to the finishing line.

With about a mile to go, all seemed lost. We were still about the best part of a boat length behind *Morningtown.* Then suddenly we got a strong gust of wind. My crew, handling the sails perfectly, managed to get the boat through a squall. *Morningtown's* crew did not and she went into a wild broach. We managed to go surging past her and finished almost half a minute ahead of her. This put us in second place and second overall in the series.

After the 1967 series we decided that the boat was definitely too slow in light airs. When it was suggested that we go back again in 1969 we revamped the boat considerably and increased the sail area.

One of the most memorable occasions in 1968 was arriving in Heligoland, having been first to Keil to race in Keil Week, in which we had four wins. We were greeted by the same people we had stayed with the previous year and I will always remember the mayor of the town saying to us: "Last time we told you *Optimist* would win, and she did. This time we tell you *Rainbow* will win". And she did.

Once again the ocean race was the most exciting race in the series. With 30 miles to go we were 10 minutes behind *Optimist,* and although we had won all previous races we still had to beat *Optimist* to be in a commanding position in the series. The year before it had been a fresh downwind run; this time it was a light downward run and *Rainbow II* with her bigger sails slowly but surely caught up to *Optimist.*

With about six miles to go, we caught her and became engaged in one of the most fierce gybing and luffing battles I have ever been involved in. We gybed and luffed for about an hour and a half until we finally broke clear and moved away from *Optimist* to win the race. All of this had taken place just after dawn and I will remember to this day being met at the dock by Norm Beetson, who has since passed away. Norm was in Heligoland to watch the series and he was standing right on top of the island, watching the whole battle going on. He had got so excited that a ballpoint pen he was holding in his pocket must have broken and the ink spread all over his hands. By the time he got down to the dock to meet us, he was so excited he did not realise that he had ballpoint ink all over his face and hands; however he did not really care.

So now the One Ton Cup contest was to be held in New Zealand. In 1970 we built a new boat called *Wai-aniwa.* That year *Wai-aniwa* was just like a fuse that kept going out. She always went in fits and starts but never performed all that well to windward.

The memorable race in that series was undoubtedly the 150-mile race, when we were coming in for the finish with only two miles to go. We had virtually the whole fleet out of sight behind us, but we became becalmed. All of the fleet sailed up to us with the new breeze and became becalmed with us. Then the wind slowly but surely started to come in again. But it came from the opposite direction, which left us completely on the wrong side. By the time we got the wind and started moving again we were back in eighth position – which was where we finished. This was probably one of the most demoralising things that has ever happened to me in a One Ton Cup series.

We decided that *Wai-aniwa* could be revamped. With more sail on we went back to Sydney in 1972, and this is where we won our second One

Ton Cups series. Undoubtedly the fastest boat in Sydney that year was *Ydra*, sailed by Hans Beilken, of Germany. However a rigging failure in the ocean race put her out of the series, which left us to do battle with *Pilgrim.* We ran neck and neck with *Pilgrim* all the way in the ocean race and finally lead her through Sydney heads by seven minutes after 80 hours of racing to win the long race and also the series.

The 1973 one-ton series was sailed in Sardinia, and this was the first time we chartered a boat for the One Ton Cup. The boat concerned was the 37 footer (11 m) *Hann,* Dick Carter-designed. Unfortunately it was not as good a boat as we had hoped for. However this series is memorable to me because I did something that I never wish to repeat. During the middle of the night in the long ocean race, when we were running before a 20 knot wind, I was leaning against the life lines. Suddenly they broke and I fell overboard. This was really quite a shock to the system. The thoughts that go through your mind when you are floundering around in the water trying to tell everyone where you are, trying to get your wet weather gear off and trying to swim to the boat, is just amazing. I can still remember vividly to this day the thousands and thousands of thoughts that went through my mind at that time.

However I finally got back to the boat. I'll always remember Bevan Woolley's comments to me. He said: "Don't worry Chris, you never really lost command of the ship – we could hear you the whole time!"

The 1973 series in Sardinia was a difficult series and we could never figure out what was wrong with our boat. But with sheer drive and determination by the crew we finished third overall in the series.

The following year in Torquay we chartered a boat again – this time a new Doug Peterson-designed boat called *Hati.* Going into the final race we had every chance of winning the series. The three boats with a chance of winning were *Gumboots, Hati* and *High Tension.* As we walked across *High Tension* to get on board our own boat for the start, we saw they had big signs posted all over her: "Beat Bouzaid".

This was a very interesting race because if we were to win the series we had to beat *Gumboots* home. For *High Tension* to win the series, she had to beat *Gumboots* home – and ourselves. *Gumboots* had to be in at least third place. To win the series *Gumboots,* had to beat us home – or be one place behind *High Tension.* So the stage was set.

During the first leg of this race we were in the lead. Right through the second leg we maintained our lead until we got back to Owers Light, which we rounded about three minutes ahead of the other boats. We then had a long windward leg all the way back to Torquay. In the early stages we held out into the tide, dragging *Gumboots* out with us, hoping the smaller boats could get through inside and past us. Then we could finish up going into the fleet, working our way through and hopefully leaving *Gumboots* behind. However it was not to be. *High Tension* went into the shore and got a tremendous lead on the fleet. When *Gumboots* and ourselves finally went in there, we were a long way back.

At this stage our plan of attack was to start sailing away from *Gumboots*. But we had committed a cardinal sin of ocean racing. We had all stayed up all through the previous night and got very little sleep; consequently when the heat was really on during the second night we were all too tired to really get the best out of the boat. Having watched other people commit the same crime so many times we should never have fallen into the same trap. Finally *High Tension* finished first. *Gumboots* second. We were in fourth place, leaving us third overall in the series.

The 1975 series was in Newport, Rhode Island and this is the only recent series that I have missed. But in 1976 I was once again fronting up, this time crewing on the New Zealand boat *Jiminy Cricket*.

The memorable race on *Jiminy Cricket* was undoubtedly once again the ocean race. In this race, navigation was of prime importance; Dicky Jones, our navigator, did a magnificent job. We finished up getting way ahead of all the other boats. However once again, just before the finish, we got completely becalmed; in sight of the finishing line we had six boats sail up to us. The morning breeze finally filled in very lightly and we slowly got *Jiminy Cricket* moving with our ½ oz (14 g) genoa barely setting. We started to move very slowly away from the other boats. We managed to get first into the new breeze this time and moved ahead to win the ocean race by 10 minutes from the next boat.

The amazing thing about this race was that all of the top boats had sagged off to leeward on the long windward leg out to the mark in the middle of the Mediterranean and in the misty conditions they did not find it. They all finished some five and six hours behind us, which was staggering for one-ton boats of this calibre in a 300 mile race.

Deadpan

by NOEL HOLMES

From the *Auckland Star*

Chris Bouzaid had every reason to be pleased with his success during the 1969 Kiel regatta held shortly before the one-ton contest that year. But when he is old and grey the thing he will probably remember most vividly as the highlight of that hectic week was the morning he gave what has become known as his "exhibition of toiletry". From Kiel, Noel Holmes filed this report to the Auckland Star.

UNBEKNOWN to the crew, the Kiel newspaper that day had devoted a full page to *Rainbow* and had hailed the yacht as prime favourite for the One Ton Cup.

Naturally, strolling crowds decided to take a look at this distinguished vessel. Nobody could object to that. But the timing was unfortunate in that Bouzaid chose the same morning to lose all patience with the ship's toilet.

Muttering to himself, he unbolted the thing and carted it ashore bodily on to the marina, with the intention of pulling it to bits and freeing up sticking valves, stop-cocks, taps, and all the other mysterious bits and pieces that go with these marine installations.

As he worked away the mob gathered. "Ah!" they exclaimed, and paused to look at the famous yacht. Having looked at the yacht they paused to look again at the plumbing operation. And the longer they looked the more fascinated they became.

Eventually, the sweating Bouzaid found himself crowded for room on the marina. Grumbling, he shifted the toilet onto the deck of the boat and resumed operations. That made a grand stage. The growing crowd edged forward. Those behind stood on tip-toe.

Finally, Bouzaid, till then absorbed in his work and only vaguely conscious that there were more passersby than usual, glanced up and found himself the cynosure of hundreds of pairs of eyes.

He was flabbergasted. "What's the matter with everybody?" he demanded. "Haven't they seen a simple toilet before?"

"Maybe they're waiting for you to do some sort of a trick with it," suggested a helpful crew member. "Why don't you make it disappear or something?"

Embarrassed, Bouzaid tried to work on. But his fingers became thumbs. The spanner kept slipping. The sticking valves remained stuck. In the end he accepted the advice offered. He made the toilet disappear.

He took his pan under one arm and assorted pieces of plumbing under the other and retreated down into the cabin, where he was cramped and got in everybody's way, but could at least work in privacy.

Later when the crew ran across the newspaper they discovered their skipper had been described as what they laboriously translated as "24-year-old gaff-rigged Auckland sailmaker, Christ Bouzaid".

Cross-questioned, Bouzaid sheepishly admitted he did recall somebody asking him his age.

But why claim to be 24?

"Well," said Bouzaid defensively, "I've been claiming to be 23 for the last six years, but I reckon I'm looking a bit older these days."

And gaff-rigged?

Bouzaid denied he was gaff-rigged. He claimed he had been misreported. As for the misspelt Christian name it was left for a crew member of the German champion one-tonner *Optimist,* to make the inevitable remark.

"Now I know how you go so well in the flat calms," he said accusingly. "Your skipper jumps overboard and pushes you along."

Success in France

by C. S. COOPER

From New Zealand Associated Press in the *New Zealand Herald*

During the early summer of 1975 a really remarkable boat kept showing up as winner among the Royal Akarana Yacht Club's smallest offshore division. Genie *was the first off the production line of Bruce Farr's new quarter-ton design. Later she was eclipsed by her sister, Bruce Farr's own boat, co-owned with Murray Crockett, called merely* 727, *the prototype name of the design.* Genie's *performance had caused R.A.Y.C. officials to think seriously about sponsoring a New Zealand challenge for the world quarter-ton title. Now they were sure that in* 727 *they would have a winner.*

The decision to challenge was not made until mid-March, after the conclusion of the national contest — and the world contest was to be sailed at Deauville, France, in July. 727, *properly christened* 45° South, *was chosen to go. Wilson Distillers Ltd came to the aid of the party as a major sponsor. Donations were also forthcoming from banks, business firms and individuals.*

Bruce Eady decided that he too would join the challenge with Genie. *Meanwhile an American boat,* Bof, *already in Europe, was co-opted to make up a team to contest the Coupe de France.*

In despatches from London to the New Zealand Herald *C. S. Cooper told the story of the contest for the world title.*

45° South and *Genie* made a splendid start with first and second placings respectively in the first heat of the five-race series. From almost disastrous positions at the last mark the two New Zealand yachts roared through the fleet in Seine Bay, off Le Havre, for the one-two triumph.

45° South led after the first 20 minutes sailing and maintained the lead through to the last mark of the 35-mile race. And that is where all the excitement started. Approaching the mark, the wind dropped away and the New Zealander was passed by two other competitors. Then all three yachts were becalmed.

But worse was to follow as the main body of the fleet carried up the new breeze and the leading trio were left in their wake. *45° South* rounded the mark in 25th place, with *Genie* ahead in 12th.

"I really thought we both had had it at that point," said Murray Crockett, the *45° South* builder and co-owner. "But the wind continued to increase up to 18 knots. We both dropped our spinnakers and started to whittle them back."

Strangely enough the other yachts in the fleet did not follow the New Zealand example and continued with their spinnakers.

While *45° South* sailed a leeward course on the vital 6-mile last leg,

Genie sailed over the top of the fleet up to windward. Both yachts revealed how incredibly fast they were reaching across the wind and put the whole fleet behind them for first and second at the finish. The French boat *Arabelle* was third.

The second race was over a 30- mile Olympic course. With the former world OK Dinghy star, Graham Woodroffe, of Auckland, at the helm, *45° South* had a tough fight to defeat the Swedish candidate *Go,* with the famous Paul Elvstrom, designer and skipper, in command.

In rough conditions with unpredictable winds punching between 12 and 20 knots, *45° South* led to the first mark, slipped to third slot at the third, trailing *Go* (Sweden) and *Fred Jnr* (Canada) – and was elbowed out to sixth at the last turn. But with a brilliant comeback on the pattern of the first race the day before, *45° South's* crew hauled back the leaders to present them with another depressing view of a winning stern.

The Swedes had started the race acknowledging that *45° South* was the boat to beat and, although they used every tactic in the book, they were reduced to a dejected runner-up role. The Canadians in *Fred Jnr,* third home, had to concede that *45° South* had a basic boat speed little short of astounding.

Genie, a brilliant second to *45° South* in the first race, was a disappointment in the second. Skipper Bruce Eady said that they had started badly and after that nothing went right for them as they struggled to a final 26th at the line.

With two wins and a huge psychological advantage, the *45° South* men now had a strong grip on the cup. One reason was the perfect understanding among the yacht's crew. There could be no doubting that among the bigger keel boats there could be no finer tactician than Roy Dickson, who had sailed the One Ton Cup and Southern Cross series. The remainder of the yacht's crew were small-boat men and it was this small-boat experience that paid off in the second race.

The builder and co-owner of *45° South,* Murray Crockett, was well-known in the unrestricted Q class in Auckland. R. Martin was among the best-known New Zealand Cherub class helmsmen. Woodroffe, among the best-known OK Dinghy helmsmen in the world, had been placed second in the class world championship, sailed in Sweden in 1972, and fourth in the 1974 championship sailed in Brisbane.

After the 100 mile third race, *45° South* still had a share of the lead. She finished 11th in this short ocean race; *Genie* was 14th. *45° South* now shared the points lead with *Charliepapa* of Italy.

45° South also retained favouritism to win the overall contest – the other competing crews were still bemused by her remarkable speed. With truer wind they maintained that *45° South* would also have won the 100 mile third race, even after a very bad start which had her about five minutes late over the line.

The course itself off the coast of France was difficult enough, for it ran over 12 legs, none of them more than nine miles long; the breeze varied greatly, and sometimes died completely away. There were a few thunderstorms for variety and the race would not rank as one of the truer tests of ocean racing.

According to *Genie's* skipper, Bruce Eady, the total unpredictability of the wind was the greatest burden. *45° South* and *Genie* were together and well-placed early in the race, when the wind collapsed on them completely; they watched 20 of the opposition go through just a little to windward.

During the night there were long reaches and the two New Zealand yachts hauled in much of the fleet.

"These boats fly on reaches and we knocked them off one after the other," said Eady. "But in the morning, switching and expiring winds destroyed the New Zealanders' chances and one wind change pulled *45° South* from fifth down to 13th. Our boats are not designed for these light conditions, but we are learning all the time and beginning to get shrewd about the conditions."

There was widespread interest in the New Zealand designs and the yachts were repeatedly photographed and examined. Buyers were beginning to show firm interest and two prospective French owners were continuing negotiations.

The fourth race was reduced to a total shambles. For two days irate local fishermen kept the international sailing fleet bottled up in the basin with a task force of eight trawlers blockading the exit of the lock to Seine Bay. The fishermen were protesting against the increasing pollution of the bay which they said was killing the fish. They chose the quarter-ton series as a target to embarrass local authorities and gain international publicity.

Their blockade forced the postponement of the fourth race, over an inshore triangular course, and the start of the fifth race, the long ocean haul.

Murray Crockett commented that he didn't disagree with the protest – only the timing. "Seine Bay is the filthiest water I have ever seen," he said. "It is murky brown, covered in oil, littered with junk and full of floating plastic. I don't blame them, but I wish they were not getting at the mayors around here through us."

However, he criticised the yachting officials for being caught without plans to combat the siege. "The trawlers' patrol was well organised and perfectly executed and everything points to the fact that officials must have known about the cooperation in advance," Crockett said.

Finally the French trawler men went back to fishing and let the yachting series off the hook. But they battered the programme enough to force the abandonment of the fourth race and the cutting of the major ocean race from 200 to 180 miles. There was no argument from crews over the dropping of the short race and it was readily accepted that the long race was the fairest test of finding a worthy victor.

The New Zealand camp, on reflection, was far from unkind in its

Top: **Chris Bouzaid won the One Ton Cup for the second time in 1972 in** ***Wai Aniwa.***
J. A. Gasparich

Above: **Success in France. Bruce Farr's prototype 727 design** ***45 South*****, co-owned by Murray Crockett, racing in France for the 1975 World Quarter-Ton Championship. The boat was a brilliant success, bringing the trophy home to New Zealand.**
Murray Crockett

Left: **In 1976** ***Jiminy Cricket*****, here pictured at Marseilles, and** ***45 South II*** **narrowly missed winning the One Ton Cup for New Zealand for a third time. Although between them they won three of the five races, they just failed to take the series and the cup.**
Lex Kempton

Graham Eder's 12.8 m Bruce Farr-designed *Gerontius*, a fine ocean racer and one of New Zealand's team for the Admiral's Cup series at Cowes in 1975. *New Zealand Herald*

Paul Whiting's sensational *Magic Bus*, here once again showing her unusual stern to all competitors. In 1976 she won the World Quarter-Ton Cup for New Zealand at Corpus Christi, Texas.

In "Navigator's First Landfall" Auckland yachting personality Jack Allen tells of a pre-war voyage in the 13.7 m yacht *Inyala*. This is *Inyala* as she looked in 1953. *Auckland Star*

thoughts toward the fishermen. Over the two days of cancellation there had been only light and faltering winds, conditions in which the twins *45° South* and *Genie* did not revel.

The ocean race was starting in brisker weather – and with the promise of a channel blow that would exploit the quite dramatic speed of the Auckland-designed boats.

The English Channel certainly provided the brisk and consistent winds that the New Zealanders relished. When the shrunken fleet, down to 34 boats from the original 43, left the startline *45° South* surged away from a perfect position and began weaving into a leadership role that she firmly established three hours later as the boats emerged from Seine Bay into the vigour of the Channel.

As contact for the night was lost, *45° South* was confidently showing the way up the Channel with *Genie* lying a comfortable seventh or eighth. The Italian *Charliepapa* was again the main threat.

From her early showing it was expected that *45° South* would further increase her lead. In fact Dickson and Woodroffe brought *45° South* home 26 minutes ahead of the 34-yacht fleet to clinch a magnificent win for New Zealand designing and sailing skill.

An outstanding feature of the World Quarter-Ton Cup win (and of the team win in the Coupe de France) was that the whole operation took place on a very limited budget. To get *45° South* to Europe the Royal Akarana Yacht Club, the name of which appears on the international trophy as the challenging club, worked to a budget of only $8000.

To small-boat men, the $8000 challenge to win a world championship appeared a more feasible proposition than the $120,000 target set to get a three-boat team away to the Admiral's Cup, for which New Zealand was competing almost currently.

There could be no denying that *45° South,* a yacht designed, built and sailed by New Zealanders, had a vast impact on international design trends. Bruce Farr had come up with a low cost offshore racing yacht that could hold its own anywhere. The winning of this quarter-ton championship opened up new horizons for the average yachtsman – the man with the desire to compete in international competition while keeping the cost within his personal means.

Magic Bus **ride**

by ALAN SEFTON and MAX LAMBERT

Condensed from reports in the *Auckland Star,* and the *New Zealand Herald,* and by the New Zealand Press Association

In February 1976 Paul Whiting quietly telephoned the Royal Akarana Yacht Club to enter a new boat, Magic Bus, *in the club's classic the Balokovic Cup race. When that race was over* Magic Bus *was the new sensation on the yachting scene. In one dramatic swoop, Farr boats were no longer champions on the quarter-ton circuit.*

Within a few weeks, Magic Bus *had won the Lynn-PGH National Quarter-ton Contest, beating boats taken from the Farr 727 mould in four out of five races. The Panmure Yacht and Boating Club (organisers of the contest) and the Royal Akarana Yacht Club (holders of the World Quarter-ton Cup) combined to send the* Bus *to contest the cup at Corpus Christi in Texas in September.*

Part-owner and skipper of the Bus, *sailmaker Murray Ross, already had a distinguished record in centreboarders behind him. Describing the new boat to a* New Zealand Herald *interviewer, he said:*

"PAUL designed and built the boat with my assistance. I rigged it and made the sails, with his assistance. I had asked Bruce Farr to design me a new quarter-ton yacht but he was too busy, so I got together with Paul.

"*Magic Bus* went into the water as a concept and hardly had to be altered. She cost $10,000 in materials alone, much of this being spent on sophisticated electronic sailing and navigation equipment. The log gives a digital read-out that can be set to give the average speed for periods of from three to 90 seconds. In steady going it can be highly sensitive to small changes. But in rough conditions where the boat speed surges according to wind and wave changes it automatically computes the average.

"*Magic Bus* also carries a depth sounder with digital print-out which can be used as a major navigational aid, to prove useful in the waters off Corpus Christi where the bottom shapes are distinctive."

Another New Zealand yacht, *Fun* designed and sailed by L. K. Davidson, was a private entry in the cup contest, which was to start on 13 September.

The first race in the series was a triumph for the New Zealanders, reported Alan Sefton in the *Auckland Star.* Murray Ross sailed a brilliant final leg to ensure victory for *Magic Bus* and paved the way for *Fun* to make it one-two for New Zealand. The *Bus* was only five seconds ahead of the crack American yacht *Business Machine,* skippered by Bob Chilton from Dallas, at the last mark, with *Fun* another 46 seconds astern third.

The aggressive Chilton had attacked immediately going for the windward burst, while Ross was in trouble with a jammed tiller extension. But the *Bus* recovered quickly and forced *Business Machine* to tack away for clear air. Once in the box seat Ross slowly but surely ground *Business Machine* down until Chilton was forced into a flyer out to the left hand side of the track to the finishing line.

Fun took her chance and sailed for the more-favoured right side of the course where the lifts had been on the previous two windward legs, while the *Bus* let *Business Machine* go and worked up the middle with a loose cover on both *Fun* and *Business Machine.* At the line the *Bus* was one minute 25 seconds clear.

Business Machine came in from the left, *Fun* from the right and all of a sudden it was obvious that the New Zealand boat was ahead. *Fun* sneaked home with just seven seconds on *Business Machine* and New Zealand was away to the perfect start of the series.

There was no team racing about what Ross did – it isn't allowed anyway. "I just slammed down on top of *Business Machine* every time he came at us on port tack and gradually forced him off to the left of the course," said Ross. "In the finish it caused us problems, as we then had to get back to cover *Fun.*"

The second race was another triumph, the New Zealand Press Association reported. Ross sailed *Magic Bus* across the finish line of the 20-mile Olympic course one minute 43 seconds ahead of the American boat *Potent Star* to increase her overall lead. The yachts were first and second for much of the race, and staged an exciting duel, with the American leading *Magic Bus* at the end of two of the six legs. No other boat ever threatened these two.

Fun, which had chased the *Bus* home for second in the first race, was sixth. But *Fun* was not sailed well, and it was not really until the final stages that she settled down to show any pace. On the final slog against the wind to the line she pulled up three places and dramatically edged *Business Machine* into seventh place.

"It was a good race," Ross told the New Zealand Press Association. "We had a few problems on the second beat, where *Potent Star* was going well, but I guess everything couldn't have been much better today."

Later *Fun* came sixth in the race and was still provisionally second on the points Table. *Fun* was effectively knocked out of the series when she was judged to have breached start rules in the second event, New Zealand Press Association correspondent Max Lambert reported in the *New Zealand Herald.* The international jury allowed a protest against *Fun* by the Canadian boat *Squeeze Box.* The points lost dropped *Fun* to tenth place overall, too far behind to have any chance of winning the title in the remaining races.

The third race saw *Magic Bus* retain her overall lead. The race, over a 100-mile course, was an intermediate offshore event, sailed in a moderate south-easterly. The American *Potent Star* reversed the placings of the second race, beating *Magic Bus.* A combination of fierce squalls, holes and wind shifts cost *Magic Bus* the win. The Auckland yacht rounded the last mark of the triangular course with a comfortable lead but the margin evaporated about daylight.

The fleet of 36 yachts, witness to a night of lightning and rolling thunder all round the horizon, was hit by a violent squall with winds of 40 knots around dawn. When the wind died, *Magic Bus* was left becalmed, while yachts on either side of her sailed with sufficient wind to fill their sails. When *Magic Bus* finally got wind she caught everyone but *Potent Star.*

The fourth race was a disaster. Starved for wind on the final leg of the short Corpus Christi Bay race, *Magic Bus* and *Fun* crashed to 18th and 21st. They picked the wrong side of the course of the four-mile run to the finish line and, with sails flapping uselessly, watched more than half the fleet sail by.

Fun had been a close second and *Magic Bus* fifth rounding the buoy marking the end of the second-to-last leg of the 22-mile race. The 35 competitors then scattered to left and right with some in the middle, searching for a breeze under a scorching sun.

The wind had been about eight knots from the north when the race started at 10 a.m., but changed to the east and dropped and then died away at the start of the last leg. When it freshened slightly from the south-east the boat farthest from the New Zealanders got it and set up an unbeatable break.

Potent Star finished among the last half dozen and slipped down the points table. They too were victims of the light and shifting wind.

The race upset results all round. The winner was *Look-After-Me* (United States), whose previous effort was ninth. Second was the consistent American yacht *Business Machine* with *Dollar Two* (France) a narrow third over Britain's entry, *Tom Cat.* The French yacht's best until now was 18th and *Tom Cat* had been unable to do better than twelfth.

The race elevated *Business Machine* into an unofficial tie on the points table with *Magic Bus,* which had led going into the race with two wins and a second. The American yachts *Espresso* and *Star-Eyed Stella* were now very close in third and fourth places.

The outcome of the championship now depended on the final race, the 225-mile offshore event. *Magic Bus's* handy points lead had now evaporated and her 18th ensured she would have to win or at least defeat the leading American yachts to retain the championship won by New Zealand the previous year.

Forty-eight hours later, *Magic Bus* was triumphant. New Zealand won the World Quarter-Ton Championship for the second successive year when *Magic Bus* beat *Business Machine* at the finish by an unbelievably close margin. In a yachting "photo finish" *Magic Bus* crossed the finish line and one minute 11 seconds ahead of *Business Machine.*

The Canadian yacht *Fred Again* won the race by more than 40 minutes, but *Magic Bus's* second place was enough to win her the Quarter-Ton Cup.

The *Bus* sailed into the Aransas Pass shipping channel late on Saturday morning with a quarter-mile lead over *Business Machine.* But the American yacht, coming in from the south, struck a better patch of wind and remorselessly chopped back the New Zealand boat's margin.

She also had a bigger spinnaker and was less affected by the outgoing tide than *Magic Bus,* which had chosen the north side of the narrow channel formed by two massive concrete and granite block moles.

New Zealanders watching the finish were stunned as the American overhauled *Magic Bus.* Desperately the crew on *Magic Bus* threw everything into the effort to win, and even sliced their boat across the tide to the south side of the channel. They had just enough left at the finish line to win. It was a toss-up that Ross described in an understatement as "bloody close".

"As he came down on us in the channel we thought we'd blown it," Ross added. "We were pretty worried. But we beat him and that's what counts. It doesn't matter in level rating yachting like this whether you win by 50 yards or a mile. All you've got to do is win."

The 225-mile race, sailed twice around a triangular course, didn't particularly suit *Magic Bus,* for the wind never blew above 10 knots. But the conditions were ideal for *Fred Again,* which set up a big break on the field and crossed the line 41 minutes ahead of *Magic Bus.* However, she was only 11th on the points table after the fourth race and could not threaten the leaders. In the end she came seventh.

The consistent American yachts, *Espresso* and *Star-Eyed Stella,* took third and fourth places in overall rankings, and *Fun* hoisted herself into fifth when she finished a creditable fourth in the final race.

Magic Bus, with two seconds and an 18th, proved the outstanding boat of the series and there was not much doubt her crew was one of the best of the fleet. The two New Zealand yachts were easily the best of the non-North American entries and prevented a clear sweep by American and Canadian yachts. The Europeans and Japanese were outclassed.

Murray Ross returned home without Magic Bus. *Transport costs made it uneconomic to bring the yacht back to New Zealand, and as early as the second Corpus Christi race the crew had been hanging out "For Sale" signs each day after cleaning up* Magic Bus *after racing. The nibbles came early, and* Magic Bus *was sold "for a reasonable price to some chap from Dallas". She now races under American flags.*

Even as he returned home, Murray was working with Paul Whiting on plans for a one-tonner for the world contest late in 1977 — "probably a lightish boat, but she might not look anything like the Bus*". See "Reactors and Racing Machines" later in this book.*

Delivery trips

OVER the years, hundreds of pleasure boats have been delivered from New Zealand ports to buyers around the coast and overseas. In *Little Ships* Ronald Carter mentions the earliest recorded overseas deliveries: "Three notable cutters were built in Auckland for Australian owners. These were *Secret,* 1875; *Waitangi,* 1878; and *Taniwha,* 1880. Within a few weeks of being launched, *Waitangi* was sailed across to Australia by Captain Hardy . . . *Taniwha* sailed from Auckland on 4 December, 1880, and reached Melbourne 10 days later . . . ." *Secret's* voyage is not recorded.

Today shipbuilders, marine brokers, amateur yachtsmen and professional sailors constantly make these delivery trips. To some staff members of yacht brokerage firms, delivery trips are a commonplace part of their duties. Never mind the weather or time of year, they are liable to be off the coast on their way to deliver a purchase to an impatient buyer. Even the most experienced of these sailors have been known to get into strife as faults develop which have not been apparent on survey, boats intended for use in sheltered waters meet conditions for which they were not designed and foul weather comes up when there is no safe anchorage within reach.

Most of the voyages go off without incident or with problems solved without gaining publicity, but a few have hit the headlines as they came to grief around New Zealand's often boisterous coastline.

Navigator's first landfall

by J. E. ALLEN

One of Auckland's most sought-after navigators and best-loved yachting personalities, Jack Allen is a past commodore of the Royal Akarana Yacht Club and owner of the John Lidgard-designed half-tonner Demijohn. *A former school teacher with school holidays free for sailing and connected activities, he has made many yacht delivery trips, has taught navigation at night school and is an I.O.R. measurer.*

IN the years before World War II, I read all the books I could find on long-distance yacht cruising – Slocum, Voss, Gerbault and similar classics. One of these was about a boat called *Inyala,* built in Cornwall in 1898. With plumb stem and long, flat counter, she was 45 ft (13.7 m) on the water and 54 ft (16.4 m) overall.

The boat was sailed to the Pacific and stayed in Suva for some years and I was interested to see her when I was on my way by ship between Auckland and Samoa. Eventually she was sold to an Auckland man, who went to Suva to fetch her. On the way she was damaged in heavy weather and went to Noumea. The owner, whom I shall refer to as "Mac", put her in the hands of a local shipwright – an Australian by birth, but New Caledonian by adoption and married to a Frenchwoman. This was Monsieur Frank Hubbard, "charpentier de marine demeurant a Noumea", (and father of Bibi, whom dozens of New Zealand yachtsmen have since met). Mac stayed there some months while the job was done and then returned to Auckland to look for a navigator; this turned out to be me.

My crew consisted of two New Caledonians – Alfred Ménzières, a baker, aged 25, who had worked in Australia and could speak English and René Bierge, aged 21, a welder, who could speak only French. Neither had been to sea, but both seemed intelligent enough to steer a compass course.

And so at 10.45 a.m. on 24 May we made sail, weighed and set off in a fresh easterly. At 15.10 we sailed out through Bulavi Pass, near the Isle Amédée. About four hours later sea sickness was taking its toll and we hove-to under staysail. The next day we hoisted the mizzen and tried to set the trysail, but were still too sick and weak, and gave up and lay hove-to, in sunny weather, but with a heavy swell.

The next day we set sail and were on our way – making good a course something west of south. In three days, with the wind very light and mostly southeast, we made good about 200 miles. The next three, by contrast, brought winds rising to gale force, still from the easterly quarter. In the early stages we took in the jib. This was an easy job, as it was set flying, with the tack on a ring which could be hauled out the 10 ft (3 m) to the end of the bowsprit without the crew leaving the foredeck. Work on the mizzen was not so good – part of it meant getting out on the bumpkin and I had an uncomfortable moment when I slipped off. But I had a tight hold of the gasket and René gave me a hand back aboard. Eventually we lay-to under staysail only, but rolled heavily for the rest of the night.

In the morning we tried the mizzen on her again and it was much steadier, but by that time the stove had been thrown upside down and everywhere inside was wet. With the wind a steady 40 knots and gusts heavier, the lacing along the foot of the mizzen had to be replaced – a nasty job – and also the servings to the mast hoops. The long counter stern pounded very badly while we were hove-to and I was afraid of structural damage being done, but none occurred and that night the wind moderated.

On 2 June, our ninth day out, we had a light, fair breeze. This was the day we set the squaresail. With the wind aft (north-west), we rolled uncomfortably. In that respect squaresails seem to be every bit as bad as spinnakers can be. With the wind rising that evening, the mizzen gooseneck carried away. A further wind shift, to west, and a gybe at 2 a.m., a bight of the mainsheet caught the binnacle, which stood up on the open flush deck, and tore its fastenings out. We stowed all sail except the staysail and turned in. At daylight we set the binnacle up again and hoisted the squaresail. When it blew out at 8.30 p.m., we hove-to again under staysail.

The following day dawned with a strong cold south-westerly and we set the trysail until evening when, cold, wet and miserable, we hove-to again. I estimated the seas at about 30 ft (9 m) high. Another day of the same conditions and we sailed under trysail and staysail by day heaving-to again at nightfall.

That was the last of our cold, wet weather. June 6 was a day for airing the ship and drying clothing. On the 7th and 8th we slowly made our way onwards, with a prediction on the evening of the 8th that we should make our landfall about noon next day. In fact I was below writing up the log at 12.15 on the 9th when René sighted Great Island of the Three Kings ahead. It was 03.45 the next morning before we rounded North Cape and by then we had the beginnings of a north-east gale. This gave us a great ride down the coast until one of the mainsheet blocks began to fall apart. (This was one of the old type – iron, with wooden checks.) With mainsail stowed, we ran on, intending to run into the Bay of Islands, but with visibility down to barely a mile, and with no previous knowledge of the bay, this became less inviting. Next we saw a Union Steamship Company ship heading out from the bay at very slow speed, virtually hove-to, and decided to do likewise.

We shackled on an anchor and hove-to under staysail and mizzen, with the main, gaff and boom lashed together and rove down on a crutch of the old scissors type. Land was in sight on our starboard beam and at nightfall the flash of Cape Brett light told us what land it was. We were drifting slowly south-south-east and cleared the land safely.

Then the mainsail and its spars came adrift. An eyebolt in the deck, to which one of the mainsheet blocks was shackled, had been weakened by rusting and had given way – the mainboom had come out of the crutch but, supported by the topping-lift, had swung round and hit a backstay with enough force to break both spars. With some of the cabin floorboards, we "fished" the gaff, i.e. put it in splints, as it were, and lowered the broken parts of the main boom to the deck. From then on we set the mainsail loose-footed, with just a block at the clew. This was all right for running or reaching, but not very weatherly.

Between the Hen and Chickens and the Moko Hinau group to the north, and Little Barrier to the south, there was marked on the charts a minefield (the one laid by the German radier *Orion* and in which the *Niagara* was sunk). The safe passage was between the Hen and the mainland, but as the wind had gone south-westerly and there seemed no way of getting to windward, I decided to chance a passage south through this dangerous area – after all, mines were set to catch bigger ships than ours. With a draft of only 7 ft (2.1 m), it seemed a reasonable chance.

Another day and we were past Flat Rock. At 1.30 a.m. on 13 June we passed Tiri, but not being able to enter before daylight, as the port was closed, we hove-to again until 6 a.m. During the slow three weeks our voyage had taken, snippets of news heard as we turned on the radio briefly for time signals had included the sinking of the battleship *Hood* and the fall of Crete.

That was my first ocean trip, my first paid ($10) delivery trip, my first "command", my first landfall.

Inyala's *story ended sadly. In the early 1970s she lay vandalised, stripped of all her gear, abandoned and rotting in St Mary's Bay boat harbour.*

Ordeal off Cape Kidnappers

by LORIS CHILWELL

THE experience of a yacht rolling over completely in a storm is rare, but as more and more yachts venture out on ocean voyages the stories of this disaster are becoming a little less extraordinary.

New Zealanders who have lived to bring back the story include Graham Eder, who gave us his account in "Suddenly It Was Very Quiet" earlier in this book.

Others in this mounting list include Tony Armit and "Tig" Loe, who survived when *Marco Polo* was caught in high cross seas and thrown down, then upside-down, in winds of 100 to 130 km.p.h. an hour on their passage from Durban to Port Elizabeth in 1955. The glass portholes were all broken and "Tig" Loe was thrown against the jagged edge of one, cutting his leg so badly that it is a wonder he survived.

Johnny Wray gives a vivid description in *South Sea Vagabonds* of how he and his crew suffered and overcame this ordeal off the Northland coast in March 1936.

In March 1959 George Dibbern and his crew in *Te Rapunga* were dismasted and rolled over twice in a storm 30 miles east of Whangaroa. The adventurous German, who had adopted New Zealand as his home, was then 70 years old.

Captain Voss and two companions endured a terrible pasting on another of his venturesome voyages – in a typhoon in September 1911, 250 miles from Japan. Like Johnny Wray and Tom Brightwell, he was washed overboard, saw his ship with its keel in the air, and clambered aboard as she was righting herself.

This disaster struck for four Auckland yachtsmen as they were tearing along under bare poles in stormy seas off the Poverty Bay coast in September 1972 on a delivery trip from Auckland to Christchurch. They were taking the $12,000, 8.4 m Tarrabochia-designed half-tonner *Diablo* to a new owner when their capsize took place in high winds and heavy seas off Cape Kidnappers.

Browns Bay boatbuilder Kerry Alexander was at the helm. With him were his three crew – David Braniff, Peter Jarvie and John Maunsell.

After running all day under bare poles, the yacht had been driven about 80 miles out to sea. She was several times rolled on to her side, the mast dipping in the water. The skipper estimated that the waves were 25-30 ft (7.5-9 m) high. Finally, one bigger than the rest hit *Diablo* and turned her over.

"I was lashed in at the helm," he recalled, "but the others in the cabin were thrown about quite a bit. The after end of the cockpit was sprung at the corners where the sides meet the bottom. This structural failure took place when the huge wave burst inside the cockpit."

The mast was broken in three pieces, the yacht being left with a stub about a metre high. The capsize took place about 11 p.m. When the boat righted itself, the cabin was awash above the floorboards. The crew bailed all night. They would open the hatch to fire out a bucket of water, then close it as another huge wave approached and engulfed the boat. From 2 a.m. until 7 a.m. they lashed the tiller and left the boat to look after herself while they bailed and bailed.

At 7 a.m. they started to organise a jury rig. They lashed the spinnaker pole to the stub of the mast, securing it to the mast collar, and stayed it with four ropes tied to stanchions. The jury mast was about 3.6 m high. A towel plugged the leaking cockpit.

By 9 a.m. the wind had moderated to about 25 knots, although the sea was still choppy. By midday conditions had lightened still further and they got going under storm jib at about two or three knots. They took four-hourly shifts at the helm.

All afternon the crew worked at getting the motor going. They took the carburettor apart, removing the magneto and drying all the parts on the stove and then putting it all together again.

By late evening their efforts were rewarded. They got the motor started. Conditions had lightened to a moderate swell. There was water in the petrol tank, but each time the motor faded out they emptied the filter and started it again. Motoring and sailing they limped over 50 miles.

At 6 a.m. the following morning they reached a long beach just north of Gisborne. They were just about out of fuel. They hailed a passing trawler which was on its way out. The trawler turned around and towed them the remaining five miles to Gisborne. Their ordeal had lasted over 30 hours.

Thankfully they handed over their charge to insurance assessors in Gisborne for eventual repairs and delivery to Christchurch by a different crew. Then they returned to Auckland, tired and shaken by their ordeal.

Ten dollars' worth of safety

From New Zealand Press Association reports

Sending a liferaft from Dunedin to Auckland at a cost of only $10 before setting out on a voyage saved the lives of four people in the 7.5 m yacht Sombrero, *which sank in rough seas south of Timaru in June 1974. On board were Mr Gordon Caley, aged 40, of Dunedin, his two sons, Grant, aged 11, and Ross, aged 13, and a friend, 26-year-old Mr Alan Partridge. They were delivering* Sombrero *from Auckland to Dunedin for the new owner, Mr Graham Dawson.*

They abandoned Sombrero *at about 11.30 a.m. on Tuesday 3 June when the yacht began breaking up in mountainous seas. Their liferaft was spotted by an Air Force Devon after Mr Caley had sent out a Mayday call, and the crew were lifted from the liferaft by two RNZAF helicopters and taken to Timaru.*

MR DAWSON had travelled to Auckland in search of a bilge keeler or other shallow draft boat to use in the shoal waters near his home. However he was so charmed by *Sombrero,* a Primrose and Illingworth "Top Hat" design fin keeler, that he decided to purchase her.

To comply with recommendations in the survey report made prior to the purchase, he left her in Auckland to have the rudder and port side of the hull strengthened. As soon as the repairs were completed, Mr Caley and his Dunedin crew started on the journey south.

A teacher at Logan Park High School in Dunedin, Mr Caley had sailed up and down the east coast on many occasions, often accompanied by his sons. This time they were taking the opportunity to deliver the yacht during the May holidays.

Before leaving Dunedin, Mr Caley decided to send the liferaft and radio transmitter from his own boat to Auckland to use on the journey.

They made the trip from Auckland to Lyttelton without incident and left Lyttelton on Friday 31 May on their final leg to Dunedin. They had already sailed 800 miles of their journey. All went well until Sunday when they encountered a gale which whipped up 6 m waves.

The little craft continued into the teeth of the storm until 9 p.m. when Mr Caley decided to take in the sails and ride it out. When the weather showed signs of moderating on the Tuesday morning Mr Caley decided to set sail and continue to Dunedin.

"At about 9.45 a.m. my sons said there was water in the bilges and it was coming from the bow," he reported later.

Earlier, he had called Taiaroa Heads to indicate his position and to ask that his wife be told that all was well. After checking the situation below decks, he decided to tell Taiaroa Heads that he was changing course and making for Timaru. But a quarter of an hour later water was pouring over the small front bulkhead.

"It was like a little waterfall and I decided to make the Mayday call because it was coming in so fast," he said. "In fact, in the few minutes I was sending the message the water rose right up to the bunks. I told Taiaroa station that I didn't think we could cope with it, even with a pump going, and that we intended to abandon the *Sombrero.*"

Mr Caley spent a few anxious moments wondering whether the liferaft would inflate when its 36 kg canister was "fired". However, the raft worked according to instructions and they were quickly on to it.

"We had a few minutes before the yacht went down and I stepped back on to her to rescue some more gear, such as clothing, life-jackets and lifebuoys," said Mr Caley. "There was only a little freeboard and by the time I had got the gear the water was over the cockpit. She seemed to hang there for a long time and I cut away the jib sheet and part of the mainsail.

"She went down by the bow with the stern sticking up high out of the water, and then she slid under with only about 2 m of the mast showing for a short time. Then she disappeared. It was a sad sight."

Sombrero had logged at that stage, about 930 miles. Without the liferaft and radio the four would have had little hope of surviving long in the cold, rough seas.

"It cost me $10 to send the raft to Auckland, but it was worth every penny of it," Mr Caley said when rescued. "It is an inflatable, covered raft and was equipped with smoke flares and food.

"We had enough food to last us for many hours, but I am also pleased I took my radio transmitter from my own boat, the *Red Gurnet.* Without the radio we could have been at sea for hours without anyone knowing about our trouble, and without the raft we could have been in real strife trying to survive in the cold water. Officially I was not supposed to have taken the radio on to the *Sombrero* because of regulations about the changing of call signs, but it certainly proved its worth."

The search for *Veronica*

From *New Zealand Herald* and New Zealand Press Association reports

A MYSTERY which may never be solved is the fate of *Veronica.* A sound ship with an experienced crew, the H28 ketch disappeared without trace on a voyage from Gisborne to Lyttelton. She left Gisborne on Saturday 16 August 1975 and gave an expected time of arrival in Lyttelton for the following Saturday.

When she did not arrive as expected on 23 August Mrs Hay, the owner's wife, notified the search and rescue organisation. But the search did not get underway until 2 September and the affair sparked off a series of complaints and accusations which reached the highest levels of government. One of the most expensive and extensive searches ever undertaken for a yacht, it continued with private vessels after the official search had ended, and continued into October.

Criticism by yachtsmen of the way in which the search was planned led to an agreement by the Government that, in future, yachtsmen would be rostered to help the Search and Rescue Organisation in planning yacht searches at the Auckland, Wellington and Christchurch headquarters. It also led to tighter controls over proposed yacht voyages.

The three men on board were the owner, Mr R. W. Hay, of Dunedin, and two Aucklanders, Commander R. A. Hoskyn, of Takapuna, an experienced sailor, and Mr W. G. Cornthwaite, of Orakei, popular owner of the yacht, *Spray II.* The two Aucklanders were friends and business acquaintances who had worked together before, delivering boats.

Finally the search was authorised and at 7.30 p.m. on the first day, a Tuesday, an RNZAF Orion commanded by Flight Lieut. B. L. O'Neill took off from Whenuapai. He used a special night search technique which involved the firing of flares every few minutes. *Veronica* was known to be carrying red flares and it was hoped that her crew would see the flares from the aircraft and respond with her own.

A radar search was carried out by the aircraft at the same time. The Orion was directed to search an area of 7000 square miles up to 50 miles from the coast between Cape Palliser and Banks Peninsula.

In estimating the search area, the officials considered the following facts: three days after *Veronica* left Gisborne there was a southerly gale and they considered this could have blown the ketch north. After that there had been little wind. On Friday 29 August the Gisborne Harbour

Board radio station heard a faint signal which seemed to be *Veronica* calling Wellington Radio. It was not an emergency call. Nothing else had been heard from the yacht since her departure.

Nothing was found.

On Thursday 4 September the search was resumed by ministerial order amid mounting criticism that Search and Rescue had been lax and haphazard in their approach. It was started at first light by Orion and Hercules aircraft from Whenuapai. The total area to be covered was 70,000 square miles compared to the 45,000 square miles covered previously.

Hampered by bad visibility, the two planes searched their area on Thursday and continued on Friday 5 September without result. On Saturday 6 September the aerial search was suspended once more, although a surface search continued and all shipping and aircraft were kept on alert for the missing yacht. The air search had covered nearly 125,000 square miles.

Friends and relatives of the crew renewed their efforts over the weekend to get still another search made. They claimed that searchers may have been looking in the wrong place for the ketch, which was then a fortnight overdue. They felt that another air search should be made north and east of the Banks Peninsula to East Cape area already covered. Conditions during the voyage would put *Veronica* right in the north-east corner of the area already searched, they claimed on their drift calculations.

Harry Pope, well known yacht surveyor and yachtsman, who spends much of his time delivering yachts said, "She could have drifted 700 miles off course without any trouble at all and considerably further than the area searched."

Discontinuing the search and asking aircraft and ships to keep a lookout was paramount to saying: "You've had it, mate."

Late on the night of Monday 8 September Dr Finlay, the Minister of Civil Aviation, decided that Orion would make a one-day search in the areas of highest probability, but would not cover any new ground. Persistent agitation by relatives of the crew had caused this change of heart and the Opposition spokesman on transport, Mr C. C. MacLachlan, asked Sir Basil Arthur to widen the search.

There was a general feeling among yachtsmen that the Search and Rescue Organisation had searched the wrong area. Members of the public telephoned and telegraphed their support for the moves being made to get another search further out to sea. Many thought the search should have been to the north and east of East Cape.

On Tuesday morning 9 September an Orion covered 43,500 square miles in an area centered 250 miles north of the Chatham Islands. The weather was good, but the Orion returned in the afternoon, having failed to find any sign of the ketch or her three-man crew.

The RNZAF also made available two Dakotas which were on exercise duty for the afternoon. Both planes were re-routed over the search area for their exercises but were also unsuccessful.

Late in the afternoon Search and Rescue co-ordinators decided to continue into the night. A spokesman said they had had to take into account changed weather patterns during the past few days which had extended the "area of probability".

The search for *Veronica* now ranked as one of the most intensive ever conducted by Search and Rescue. By the end of the morning's flight it had covered 175,000 square miles. Of this area, 80 percent was covered three times and a considerable area four times. Relatives were still not satisfied and said the operation should be repeated in daylight.

But early on the morning of Wednesday 10 September with one Orion still in the air, no sign had been found of the missing yacht. The official search came to an end.

On 15 September Gisborne signal operator, Mr W. Edwards, a former fisherman with 27 years experience in small boats, repeated that he was absolutely certain a call he had received on 29 August, at 12.10 p.m., had come from the missing ketch.

The exact message he heard was: "ZM 5459 *Veronica* calling ZLW Wellington Radio." This message was repeated, but he did not hear the sender sign off.

If this had actually been *Veronica* calling, the crew must have still been aboard an intact hull and within reasonable distance of land.

On 16 September commodores of three leading Auckland yacht clubs requested the Minister of Civil Aviation to take up the search again. Rejecting the request, the Minister said there was no question of the search for the missing ketch being resumed.

On 17 September the Prime Minister, Mr Rowling, rejected a request from the New Zealand Yachting Federation for a further search. This brought a strong reaction from the federation president, Mr Harry Julian: "I do not want to embarrass the Prime Minister, but I think the advice he has been given is not valid and we are not going to accept it."

The following day, in response to an invitation by the Prime Minister, representatives of the federation and yacht clubs met Search and Rescue officials in Wellington to discuss the issue. They learned that over the six days of the air search RNZAF Orion, Dakota, Skyhawk and Hercules aircraft flew 13 sorties, making both visual, flare and radar searches, and covering a total area of 210,000 square miles.

The ketch had been sound and fairly well equipped, with good lifesaving equipment, including a six-man rubber liferaft equipped with enough food for 72 man-days and flares.

The weather in the area had generally been good during the search and, although there had been a storm three days after the ketch had sailed from Gisborne, it was unlikely to have been bad enough to do anything other than put the ketch, with its experienced crew, off its course.

Above: Midnight Mover, **the luxurious Hong Kong junk which disappeared without trace on a voyage from Auckland to Rarotonga in 1970.** *New Zealand Herald*

Left: **"One of the most ill-prepared sea trips ever to leave New Zealand shores." Geraldine York (holding bucket) and Christine Braham, standing at low tide by the** *Sospan Fach* **as she lay stranded on Middleton Reef, 640 km from the Brisbane coast.** *The Sun, Sydney*

Above: **The Reactor format of brilliant young Auckland designer Paul Whiting has become a popular one-design class. Here highly competitive Reactors start together off Orakei Wharf, Auckland.** *Neil MacKinnon*

Left: **"A designer who has gone far." Bruce Farr's** ***The Number*****, well reefed, sailing to victory in the first race of the 1976 one-ton trials on Auckland Harbour. Renamed** ***45 South II*****, she competed for New Zealand in the One Ton Cup series off Marseilles later that year.** *Auckland Star*

Squadron Leader B. N. Tunley said that parts of the search area had been covered three, four, even five times. There had been a total of 120 hours flying time. Radar conditions had been good and many boats, including fishing boats, had been spotted and checked, both visually and by radar.

Asked about the delay between Mrs Hay reporting the Veronica being overdue on 23 August, and the launching of the air search on 2 September, Captain Henry of Search and Rescue said that because of the weather and the slow speed of the ketch, the authorities had estimated that the *Veronica* could not possibly have arrived in Lyttelton by that date.

Still not satisfied, Mr Julian implored the Prime Minister by telegram to reinstate the search. When Government turned a deaf ear to these pleas, yachtsmen organised their own operation.

Many well-known yachting personalities rallied to the cause. The 17 m motor-sailer *Nereides,* owned by the Mayor of Tauranga, Mr R. A. Owens, left on the night of Tuesday 23 September from Westhaven, Auckland, farewelled by a large crowd, just one calendar month since *Veronica* had failed to meet her ETA. Among the crew of volunteers was the American veterinarian Dr Bob Griffiths, veteran of three circum-navigation voyages in his New Zealand-built ferro-cement yacht *Awahnee. Nereides* was to search the area north of East Cape to east of East Cape, an area not covered in earlier searches.

The following evening, at 5.30 p.m., the 13.7 m ketch *Aderyn Mor* left Lyttelton to sail north and then cover an area north-east of the Chatham Islands. *Aderyn Mor,* then owned by Christchurch yachtsman Graeme Kendall, had been fitted with a $3000 radar set by a Christchurch electronics firm for the trip.

Bad weather delayed the departure of the third search vessel. The 18.3 m luxury cruiser, *Parimer,* owned by the chairman of the Otago Harbour Board, Mr C. G. Skegg, and skippered by Captain K. Middleton, head of the Southern Friends of *Veronica,* left Dunedin on 26 September. It headed for the Antipodes Islands, where the crew would make a ground search.

On behalf of the Government, the Prime Minister announced that a routine Orion patrol in southern waters, originally scheduled for the following week, had been rescheduled to assist the searchers and would devote special attention to the general area between the Chathams and the South Island.

From the beginning this phase of the search was plagued with bad weather. On 24 September, the night after she left Westhaven, *Nereides* was 120 miles east of Cuvier Island in rain, with winds 20 to 25 knots, sometimes gusting to 45 knots. The conditions did not make searching easy, and at times visibility was down to one and a half miles. But the planned search area had not yet been reached. By the night of 25 September East Cape had been reached, but the weather was still bad. It was not until 28 September that the weather cleared and a full search was able to be made.

But good conditions did not last. Twelve-metre seas and 60-knot winds off East Cape cracked a frame in the hull of the motor sailer as she crashed down after broaching. A frayed backstay endangered the mast. The skipper, Mr D. Gulliver, decided to head for port. The seas off East Cape were the worst he had encountered since he began sailing the boat, reported the skipper. Off Hicks Bay one of the crew members, S. Hudson, was suffering so badly from seasickness that he had to be put ashore.

On only one day of the eight spent at sea was a sextant reading possible, the rest of the navigation being "by guess and by God". Sailing conditions deteriorated 18 hours out of Auckland and it was only on Monday 29 September after the decision to abandon the search had been made, that the seas calmed.

At the height of the storm, *Nereides* began to ship water through the water-cooler and took in a lot over her deck. It was almost impossible to cross the deck, and sleep was a catch-as-can affair.

Meanwhile the luxury cruiser *Parimer* was returning after a hazardous, storm-tossed unsuccessful search of the desolate Antipodes and Bounty Islands. The Antipodes search was the first one for shipwreck survivors this century.

No sign of *Veronica* was found. *Parimer* made a cautious patrol around the Bounty Islands, but spotted nothing. Rough seas prevented getting in close to the islands, but all on board were on the spray-lashed deck with binoculars, making a visual search.

"There is no possibility of anyone surviving on the Bountys, which are just rocks jutting out of the sea, the slick sides as slippery as glass from thousands of years of seals slithering over them," said a crew member.

Earlier *Parimer* made an extensive search of the Antipodes, about 100 miles to the south of the Bountys. Nine men spent a full day on the island, scaling a near-vertical 30 m cliff to gain access to the interior.

The first place the searchers checked was a hut, the sole indication that the island had ever had human habitation. The hut was erected early last century to aid shipwreck survivors. But the only signs of life on the islands away from the cliffs were seaweed, seals and albatrosses.

Experienced yachtsman Graeme Kendall and his crew sailed the *Aderyn Mor* to the Chatham Islands and back, with no success. He believes *Veronica* may have foundered quite quickly.

"It is possible that *Veronica* went down on the first or second night out and any evidence would long have disappeared by the time the search took place. I believe weather conditions were very bad about this time and a harbour board tug boat had to turn back at Gisborne. It must have been very rough offshore (50 miles plus). The current runs south and then east towards South America and I believe this is the way any flotsam would travel."

On 15 June 1976 an official finish was written to the story of the Veronica *when the Gisborne Coroner, Mr D. R. Kohn, found that the three men on board had died at sea. The Ministry of Transport reported the following September that the search for the* Veronica *had cost $57,021.*

Farewell *Midnight Mover*

From the *New Zealand Herald*

On 17 April 1970 an unusual piece of cargo was offloaded from the Straat Singapore *at Auckland. It was a Chinese junk, built in Kowloon for an American owner. It was all fine teak and luxurious appointments, but Auckland visitors who were shown over it were not impressed with its ocean-worthiness.*

The junk, named the Midnight Mover, *departed on 6 May for Rarotonga and Tahiti. The crew of five included the owner and two young New Zealanders, Stuart William White, aged 23, of Papakura, and Charles Frederick Winterbottom, aged 18, of Herne Bay.*

On 14 May the Midnight Mover *made her last contact with Auckland Radio. On 26 May a worried Mrs Winterbottom made contact with the police. But no details of sailing had been given to the Search and Rescue Organisation before the junk left New Zealand.*

On 14 May an Orion aircraft had seen the junk, becalmed about 400 miles east of Auckland. For eight days after that a series of depressions, varying in intensity, crossed the South Pacific. After 14 May there was no further sign of the ship, nor any sign of wreckage or bodies.

On the last day of September 1971 the scanty picture was filled in at the Coroner's Court in Auckland.

IVAN DESMOND ARMSTRONG said he had been on board the junk during a trial sail at Auckland. Although he was not an experienced sailor, he had serious misgivings about the ability of the crew.

On this trip, said Mr Armstrong, it was quite obvious that the crew did not know how to handle the junk. It took them two hours to raise the sails and one and a-half hours to lower them.

Ian Peter Dunn, then general manager of a Howick marine company, said he had visited the ship a day before it sailed and found that the stores on board were barely adequate. Because of prevailing winds from Rarotonga to Tahiti, the diesel fuel stocks on board were not sufficient.

Jack Edward Hargraves said he was in Honolulu when he was approached by the owner, Mr R. G. Riviere, who asked him to skipper the junk on an ocean cruise. As an experienced ocean sailor, Mr Hargraves said he accepted the offer and flew to Hongkong on 14 January to meet up with Mr Riviere.

He remained there for five weeks and discovered that the two men with a local cook, were to be his crew members. Mr Riviere refused to take on an experienced crew member, unless Mr Hargraves "sponsored" one himself.

Mr Hargraves said he then refused to sail the junk. There were steering difficulties on the *Midnight Mover,* but his main reason for withdrawing was the lack of an experienced seaman. He told the court that another man had been taken on as captain, but he, too, had resigned when he found the limitations.

Mr Thornton Keals-Smith, co-ordinator of Search and Rescue, said that before 27 May he had no knowledge of the junk. No details of the junk, or its intended passage, were forwarded to the organisation.

He had learned that the *Midnight Mover* hoped to reach Rarotonga on 14 May. This was a grossly inaccurate time of arrival. It had been estimated that the junk was travelling at a speed of 50 miles a day. If it had maintained this speed, it could not have reached Rarotonga before 5 or 6 June. Mr Keals-Smith said a full-scale search was decided against because the area was too great. But shipping and aircraft were briefed and asked to keep a look out.

Giving his verdict, the coroner, Mr A. D. Copeland, said: "The evidence shows that the crew was inexperienced and untrained in ocean sailings, particularly in such an unusual vessel as a junk. It also showed that the junk had rudder trouble which would reduce its manoeuvrability and increase its liability to broach in heavy seas."

Mr Copeland found that the five men died in the Pacific Ocean, about 400 miles east of Auckland, on or about 15 May 1970, death being due to misadventure by drowning when the *Midnight Mover* foundered in a storm.

The jinx

From New Zealand Press Association reports

Do jinx ships exist? After a series of misfortunes which seemed never-ending, those close to the ketch Ariana *had cause to wonder.*

It began in August 1971, when four months after arriving from Canada to settle in Nelson Mr Jack Davis arrived in Christchurch to buy the Ariana. *The ketch was surveyed and found seaworthy, and the sale went through. She left one Saturday soon after for her new home in Nelson. The crew consisted of her new owner; Mr James Harper, aged 56, a meteorologist, also of Nelson; a 26-year-old American, Mr Randy Hansen; and 20-year-old Mr Dick Taylor, a navigation instructor at the Outward Bound School at Anakiwa. Mr Taylor had already sailed a yacht single-handed from Panama to Tauranga earlier in the year.*

THE ketch left Lyttelton on Saturday, 14 August 1971 and met stormy weather and winds gusting to more than 100 miles an hour in the Cook Strait area on 16 August.

She was thought to have taken shelter in the Marlborough Sounds but on Thursday 19 August Nelson police notified search and rescue headquarters in Wellington that the *Ariana* was missing. An extensive air search was begun. It covered the Marlborough Sounds, Tasman and Golden Bays, the Wairarapa and South Taranaki coasts. No trace of the ketch was found.

The only person not really worried was the skipper's wife, Mrs Diana Davis. She was sure they would turn up, and she proved to be right.

On 25 August crew members on the *Ariana* waved delightedly as a Nelson Aero Club aircraft circled the ketch after she was sighted by a fishing boat. She was almost becalmed two miles due east of Farewell Spit, about 60 miles north of Nelson.

The ketch had been sighted by the Nelson fishing trawler *Sealord II* at a distance of about 12 miles the previous afternoon. The *Sealord* radioed to shore that it had sighted a two-masted vessel with a schooner-shaped bow. She went alongside the ketch and passed provisions. The men on the *Ariana* declined a tow. The fishing boat then left the *Ariana* to continue into Nelson. The *Ariana* reported to the fishing boat that it kept well out to sea during the storm. The crew had food and water but both radios had ceased to function.

As the fishing boat left there was no wind and the ketch was barely making headway. However, even with the auxiliary motor not working, her men were confident of reaching Nelson. When the Nelson aircraft left the *Ariana* near dusk she was under jib, mainsail and mizzen. The sails were flat and the ketch was making little progress. She then had about 75 miles to reach Nelson. From the air the ketch gave little evidence of not having weathered the storm which struck the area, although paint was missing from her starboard side. The life raft was firmly secured and the *Ariana* was riding high in the water.

Ariana finally came into Nelson under tow, pulled by the Nelson trawler *Marine Maid.* There had been further misfortune. She had run aground in fog the previous day in Golden Bay.

Skipper Jack Davis was near tears of relief as he described the voyage: "We didn't know when death might come – it could have come at any time," he said. "We didn't know when we would see land again.

"Floorboards were ripped up from the cabin and nailed to the skylight above the bunk area. If we hadn't had that protection those waves would have just smashed through and we would have been dead. During the three days of the storm the crew could only stand one hour at the tiller before they had to go below."

At the height of the storm the crew decided they would go as far as Australia if it meant escaping the teeth of the gale and having the winds behind them. But by Thursday morning all four men were able to get on deck, rig sail and head for home.

Jack Davis suffered the only major injury. His chest was badly bruised. "The wind was terrifying. It seemed to be singing," he said, describing the storm. Two things went wrong when the ketch was well out of Lyttelton and in the storm. The bilge pump would not function and the sea-cock to the engine would not close. The engine then gave out.

In spite of the fierce gales Mr Davis said one of the worst parts of the voyage came the previous morning when the *Ariana* ran aground. "That was the last straw after getting so far".

There was little damage to the ketch. "She looks dirty now but she'll be a beautiful ship," declared Mr Davis.

Unfortunately his beautiful ship was to cause him further anguish.

In May 1972 he set off again, this time for Sydney, with a crew consisting of G. Eichmann, S. Griffin and W. Vanduyn, none of whom had had any sailing experience.

First inkling of trouble came to those on shore when the ketch was sighted on the north coast of Tasman Bay at a time it was expected she should have been well clear of the bay and heading out across the Tasman Sea.

Ariana eventually limped back to port after six days at sea in two violent storms. When strong winds and seas 5 m high had the ketch almost on the rocks off Opunake, the decision was made to return to Nelson. The crew of three were nearly prostrate with sea sickness and Mr Davis was prepared to abandon ship. "I got mad and took a chance on using the engine while broadside to waves and wind," he said. "We inched out to deeper water and decided we had had enough."

Mr Eichmann said that when the ketch was almost on the coast he knew they had barely a 50-50 chance of survival. "I would have paid anything to have got off the boat," he said. "But now I would not sell the experience for anything." Mr Vanduyn said: "I thought I was going to die at one stage, I was so sick."

Gaunt and near exhaustion, Jack Davis said: "The sea had beaten me again, but I'm not finished." He planned to sell *Ariana* and buy a craft which could be sailed by two people. His attempt to sail to Australia had been in order to conquer the fear engendered by his maiden trip in *Ariana.* "I've just got to prove to myself that the sea doesn't blow up a gale every time you get out of sight of land," he said. "I got the life scared out of me the last time and I want to get that fear out of my system.

"There are some times you can't run and you must just turn and face things."

Jack Davis did sell *Ariana,* but the reputation she had built up as a jinx ship continued. Just 24 hours after the new owner and crew declared they would "bust the jinx myth about the boat wide open", the yacht ran aground – twice.

The *Ariana* was leaving the Nelson boat harbour under motor for compass testing when she struck the submarine bank of the channel and stuck fast. The crew put the 25 h.p. diesel engine into reverse and, with the aid of the incoming tide, managed to free the boat. But further down the channel the *Ariana* grounded again.

There was more to come. A week later, *Ariana* was forced to put in at Napier after the mainsail was shredded in a gale 140 miles south of that port.

"We were about a mile from the shore when the gale suddenly hit us with full force," said Mr John Hamilton, the new owner. "It struck within 30 seconds without warning, with winds up to 50 or 60 knots. One of these squalls took the mainsail." The main was repaired at Napier and one of the crew left her there, having been sick all the way from Nelson.

Still the new owner stoutly refuted the suggestion that she was a "jinx" ship. "There is nothing wrong with her that can't be fixed," he said. "I admit we had to throw a few rocks in the front to balance the ballast and she is still a bit topheavy, but we are certain this can be fixed."

But Jack Davis had the last word. He said that he would never sail her again. Asked if he believed her to be jinxed, Mr Davis said: "Well, every time I got her out of port I got blown to hell and now these guys go out and they get blown to hell. What's a man to think?"

Lifeboat to the rescue

From the New Zealand Press Association

"It was like going through hell."

That's how Mr L. G. White described the rescue in huge seas of his yacht Aderyn Mor *on 20 December 1972. The 13.7 m steel-hulled ketch, with six persons on board, had just been towed to safety at Kaikoura by the rescue lifeboat* Rescue II *after she had called for assistance in heavy seas.*

The inter-island ferry Rangatira *took part in the rescue, lowering a lifeboat to assist the ketch in winds gusting up to 40 knots. During the rescue a crew member fell from the lifeboat. He was taken back on board after spending 10 minutes in the rough seas.*

THE first calls for assistance from the *Aderyn Mor* were received by Wellington Radio just before midday. The message said: "We don't think we can last much longer."

An RNZAF Orion from Whenuapai spotted the *Aderyn Mor* about 1 p.m. and *Rescue II* put to sea at 1.30 p.m. The ketch was about 40 miles off Kaikoura.

The *Rangatira,* which had been making a daylight sailing to Lyttelton, launched a lifeboat to go to the aid of the ketch just after 3 p.m. The lifeboat was unable to take anyone off the ketch and was low on fuel. *Rescue II* reached the yacht about 3.45 p.m.

In the meantime a fishing boat from Kaikoura, the *Virgo,* skippered by Mr P. Baxter, also reached the scene and took the *Rangatira's* lifeboat in tow. The lifeboat could not be taken back on board the ferry because of rough seas. The Union Steam Ship Company's roll-on, roll-off ferry *Wanaka,* on a trip to Lyttelton, reached the scene about 7.35 p.m. and relieved the *Rangatira* until the ketch and lifeboat got to shelter. The *Virgo,* with the *Rangatira's* lifeboat, reached harbour about 9 p.m.

The *Aderyn Mor* was skippered by Mr White and crewed by his wife, son Simon, daughter Penelope, and Messrs J. Farrant and R. J. Marshall. They had left Christchurch on Tuesday, headed for Picton. The difficulties began when Mr White became seasick.

Mr White, holder of a second mate's ticket, had served in the British Merchant Navy from 1942 to 1952. But he said he had never before been through a sea such as that which swept the Kaikoura coast. "I have seen big seas before, but not from a small boat such as mine. It is quite a different experience," he said.

With other members of his family and Mr Marshall, he spent most of

Wednesday lying down or being sick. Mr Farrant, who also had his share of being sick, was at the helm from 8 a.m. until the rescue several hours later.

Mrs White, who attempted to comfort her two children during the battering, was thrown around the inside of the yacht. "It was difficult to move. We were all sick – all we could do was crawl into our bunks and just lie there," she remembered.

The worst part of the voyage was when Mr Gordon Briggs was swept away after being flung over the side of the lifeboat from the *Rangatira*. "The motor of the boat was swamped, and the crew tried frantically to row after him. I was glad to see him picked up again," Mrs White said. She also feared a mishap when the lifeboat came alongside the yacht to take them off. There was little she could have done if the men had collapsed – and they had nearly reached that stage. One of them had been so weak that he could not have tied a knot.

Rescued, they all spent the night in Kaikoura Hospital. Interviewed at that safe haven, the Christchurch family did not seem enthusiastic about going on board the yacht again after their brush with the seas.

Simon said that he had been sick and afraid. "I will not be going back on the yacht again, not even in calm water," he vowed. His sister, Penelope, said that she was frightened throughout. Their mother said that she and the children would never tackle a long trip again.

Mr White had taken five years to build Aderyn Mor. *She was designed for long-range cruising and equipped with a 30 h.p. engine. She was launched only two years earlier, in December 1970. In 1975, skippered by a new owner,* Aderyn Mor *reversed roles when she joined in a search for the missing* Veronica.

The voyage of the *Sospan Fach*

by GAVIN ELLIS

From the *New Zealand Herald*

On 7 April 1974 an 11.5 m ferro-cement sloop named Sospan Fach *left Auckland on what was later described by search and rescue co-ordinators as one of the most ill-prepared sea trips ever to leave New Zealand shores.*

Police discovered after it was reported missing that the Sospan Fach *had no engine, no radio, only one set of sails and only a one-person liferaft. No attempt was made to obtain Customs clearance, an omission which could have led to prosecution, and the yacht could never have met safety requirements.*

The Sospan Fach *was built in Auckland by a Welshman, Irfon Nicholas, who intended to sail it round the world. He advertised for crew and planned a Tasman crossing as a shakedown cruise. Naturally those who signed on were inexperienced — no experienced yachtsman would have left New Zealand under such conditions.*

The crew consisted of a young Auckland nurse, 19-year-old Geraldine York, on four weeks leave from Middlemore Hospital, Christine Braham, 25, of Adelaide, who was working as a medical research assistant in Auckland, and 18-year-old Peter Lindenmayer, of Melbourne. The 35-year-old skipper was a mystery man, although he said he had spent three years in the British merchant marine in the 1960s.

A MAN who befriended the crew of the *Sospan Fach* some weeks before they sailed for Australia tried several times to persuade the skipper to install an engine in the yacht.

Mr E. C. Schollum, of Ostend, Waiheke Island, even found an engine and made arrangements for it to be put in the boat. However, the skipper said he could not afford the $400 it would cost. Mr Schollum also suggested that the crew spend some time sailing around Waiheke Island to gain experience.

He was concerned about the lack of communication and rescue equipment in the yacht, but he assumed it had been cleared by the New Zealand authorities.

The *Sospan Fach* had taken about two years to build and was professionally plastered. However, it did not have a cockpit, just two park-bench seats on the deck near the stern. It was steered by tiller, but without a cockpit there was nowhere for the helmsman to shelter. "I wanted them to put a cockpit in," said Mr Schollum. "Park benches do not provide much shelter."

There was only one set of sails, and the crew had only a scant knowledge of navigation. There was a sextant on board and one of the crew had a book explaining how to use it. Mr Schollum said the night before the *Sospan Fach* left the two girls in the crew seemed nervous. They had never been in blue water and friends had pointed out the shortage of equipment.

Nine weeks after the sloop left New Zealand, with no word from any of the crew, all had been given up as dead. Then came the electrifying news that they had all been discovered alive, on Middleton Reef, 140 miles north of Lord Howe Island and 400 miles east of Brisbane. The reef is a graveyard of ships covered by the high tide twice every 24 hours. There the crew had lived for seven weeks, eking out their existence on a wrecked Japanese fishing boat, the *Fuku Maru,* whose wheelhouse they used for shelter during high tide.

The miracle of their rescue was compounded by marvellous coincidences. Their rescuers were the Tongan crew of a Sydney-owned fishing boat, *Ata.* About seven years earlier many of the *Ata's* crew had been castaways themselves, shipwrecked on a deserted island south-west of Tonga. They were rescued by Sydney businessman Peter Warner, who was cruising in the area, and he took them to their home island. In gratitude they told him of some secret lobster grounds. He returned to Sydney, built the *Ata,* sailed back to Tonga and took on the former castaways as crew.

It so happened that two salvage experts had been marooned on Middleton Reef for four days about 18 months earlier when foul weather prevented them from returning to their base on Elizabeth Reef, 30 miles to the south. The crew of the *Fuku Maru* left large stocks of non-perishable food when they abandoned the ship after she ran aground on the reef and the salvage crew had restocked the wreck for future use.

"The Japanese just walk off these trawlers when they run aground," said one of the salvagers. "There were thousands of tins of rice and packets of egg noodles with sachets of soya sauce in the *Fuku Maru.* We threw tons of it over the side after the rats got to it, but there was still plenty there when we left."

The salvagers restocked the trawler with tinned and preserved food and even cans of beer – and left poisoned bait to kill the rats.

"On our first trip out there we suffered terribly from coral ulcers," said the salvager, Mr Hanigan. "After a few weeks we had big sores all over us so when we went back to the reef we put full medical supplies on board the *Fuku Maru,* including antibiotics." But somehow there was a fire on board after they left and the stores were all destroyed.

The crew of the *Sospan Fach* were discovered on 11 June.

The oceanic search centre in Canberra was flashed news of the discovery late in the afternoon and immediately an RAAF Hercules aircraft was put on stand by. That night, with south-westerly winds gusting up to 30 knots on the reef, conditions were too rough for the castaways to be taken off. But the *Ata* managed to get one sailor ashore with a transistor walkie-talkie and some supplies. While the fishing boat

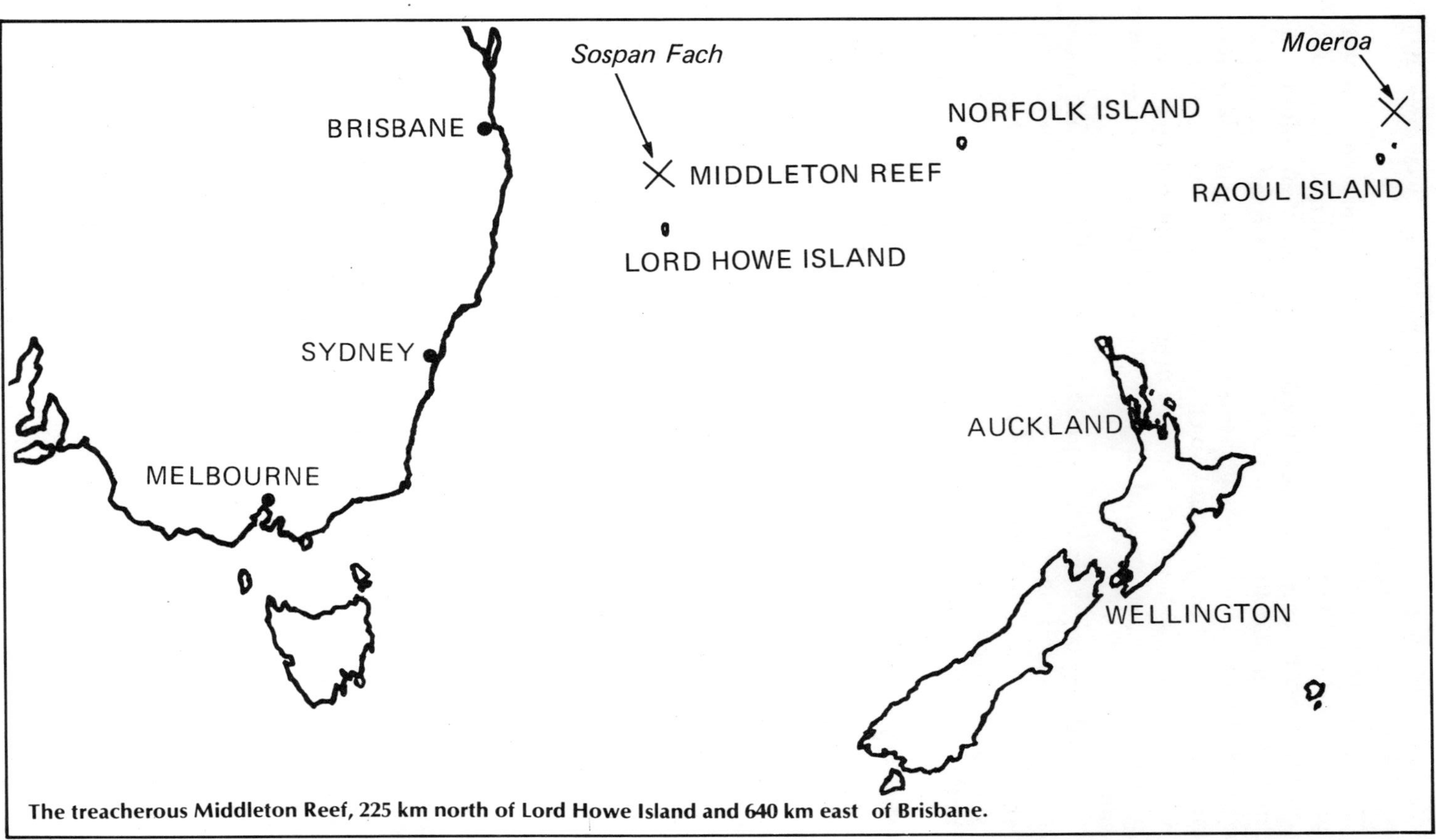

The treacherous Middleton Reef, 225 km north of Lord Howe Island and 640 km east of Brisbane.

stood off the reef in the rough seas, the sailor reported to his skipper that the castaways were in good health.

The race to snatch the four from the reef in the face of rising seas and an increasing wind began at 9.30 a.m. the following day. It took about two hours for the girls and two of the *Ata* crew to edge an aluminium dinghy through the sharp coral and out to the trawler, anchored three miles off the reef. Then the rescuers set out again for the wreck in which the castaways had been living to pick up Peter Lindemeyer and Irfon Nicholas. While the survivors, wearing brightly coloured jackets, were being taken off, the kidney-shaped reef was washed with over a metre of water.

The ill-fated *Sospan Fach* ran aground on the reef on 28 April. Soon after the crew had scrambled on to the reef the ferro-cement yacht capsized and sank. The castaways lived on rations and water they had managed to save before the *Sospan Fach* went down. Twice a day they retreated from the tide into the wheelhouse of the Japanese trawler.

Mr Mano Totau, the Tongan seaman on board the *Ata* who first sighted the flashing signals from the *Fuku Maru*, said of being described as a rescuer: "I feel very powerful to rescue somebody because I am looking for it in my sea responsibility. I been rescued myself. We were trolling along the edge of the reef. I saw the paint on boat (*Sospan*) and I think it is still new. We went into the cove of the reef and I still had my mind on the yacht and I keep looking around the reef. I was fishing for about an hour when I saw the signal from the wreck. Then I rushed inside to tell everybody to get the glasses.

"The rescue – I really feel good about it. I would say they would have lasted only another three weeks, even if it had rained. They were very depressed. I had the opinion they had given up. And, of course, they were delighted to see us. The youngest ones responded quicker, but I think the skipper is still suffering from delayed shock because he was under considerable strain.

"There were a few basic survival operations they could have carried out that they didn't. For example, they were not keeping a lookout 24 hours a day, and we found pots of white paint on the ship with which they could have painted SOS to attract ships and aircraft. Middleton Reef is an area avoided by all except crazy fishermen like ourselves. I suspect that if we had not come along there would not have been a vessel for some time."

Once the crew were aboard the Tongan trawler, there were still problems to endure. Fifty-knot winds and heavy swells sent the trawler back to the reef to shelter from the storm. Constant vigilance had to be maintained if the vessel was not to become another victim of the reef.

But finally, on 17 June, the *Ata* steamed into Ballina harbour on the coast of Australia, 300 miles from Middleton Reef. There the castaways were tearfully and joyfully reunited with the families who had once feared they would never see them again.

Reef-dweller remembers

by GERALDINE YORK as told to Gavin Ellis in Ballina

From the *New Zealand Herald*

"We were wearing shorts and very little else — squeezed together in a three-by-three box afloat in the cabin. We cuddled each other for half the night to keep warm. It was freezing — the worst night I have ever spent in my life."

Geraldine York was a crew member on the Sospan Fach *when she went aground on Middleton Reef. At Ballina in Australia she told* New Zealand Herald *reporter Gavin Ellis about that extraordinary voyage.*

RIGHT from the beginning of the voyage I was seasick. The first week is rather vague. The *Sospan Fach* was towed out of Auckland at 9.05 a.m. on Sunday 7 April and I started to feel seasick right away.

We were just towed out from the wharf and left in the harbour. Then we struggled all day against a head wind, and I could hear things banging and crashing. In the afternoon we gave up and anchored off Rangitoto Island for the night.

The yacht was okay. But I can't say the same for the crew, Irfon Nicholas (35), of Wales, Christine Braham (25), Peter Lindenmayer (18), of Melbourne, and myself.

We left the next day, and it was pretty hard going because the wind was wrong. On the third day out we struck a force five gale and the hatches started to leak water over our food in the stern. It didn't damage anything, but later the sun shining through the perspex hatch cover quickly sent our bananas and tomatoes rotten.

It was not until 10 April that I was able to get up top. After that I was improving a little after vomiting all the time. What I felt most of the time was that I wanted to die. We lost sight of the coast on 9 April and caught sight of it again on 13 April. We presumed it was the coast. I was feeling so rotten that Christine and I asked Irfon Nicholas if we could get off.

He had taken a reading, thought we were near the Bay of Islands and said he would go into there and let us ashore. He was afraid of bumping into the land, so all night we tacked for two hours to the east and then for two hours to the west. The next morning we were just to go west and reach land. We did so but we never did hit land.

We had charts of the east coast of New Zealand and the east coast of Australia. I think we also had one general chart. I can remember seeing that just Lord Howe Island was marked. It did not have Middleton Reef marked and we didn't even know there were reefs in the area.

We had been told that the only thing we could possibly have banged into was Lord Howe. And Irfon said we couldn't possibly bump into that.

We had some pretty rough weather and had to reef the sails every night. The tiller was also affected. The steering was not very positive and it was difficult for one person to hold it. We were having quite a struggle.

Irfon was pretty vague. He never used to tell us anything unless we asked him a question. Christine and Peter were trying to teach themselves navigation. Irfon is a very quiet sort of person. He kept very much to himself. Sometimes he was very hard to understand because he is Welsh.

We had been pretty upset when we found we had passed North Cape. But . . . well, we just accepted it.

We had a few problems with sails – we only had one set – but generally things went pretty smoothly. The boat was going pretty well.

We were doing two-hour watches. I had come off at about 2.45 a.m. on 28 April and Chris had been on watch for three-quarters of an hour. She said she saw this white foam ahead, and before she knew what it was we were on the reef. It sounded like gravel on concrete, a grating noise. The boat went sort of bumpity-bump and Chris screamed – of course. This is what alerted us.

The boat went over on its starboard side. I was thrown against the wall, and I think Irfon was thrown out of his bunk.

I ran up on deck because I thought Chris had fallen overboard. I said: "What's happening?"

She said, "We've hit some thing, it's land, it must be Australia." But it couldn't be because Irfon said on the previous day that he estimated that we were approximately 480 miles east of the Australian coast.

We had hit something, but we weren't sure what it was. In fact, we didn't know.

We let all the sails down. We were afraid the yacht would topple over. Waves were crashing against the hull and moving the boat up and down. Peter went down to see what the bottom was and saw it was coral. We thought it couldn't be a reef because we didn't think we were so far north as to be in the Coral Sea.

I wasn't frightened. The only thing I was worried about was that the yacht was going to topple over. It was lying at a 45-degree angle from vertical, possibly a little more. We realised we were on a murky-brown coral reef . . . it had a very particular smell, very fishy and "corally".

When the tide went out we were able to walk on it in ankle-deep water. I saw two vague shadows further over the reef and I guessed, "that's a boat". Then we watched the dawn come, thought the shapes were boats and as it got lighter, realised they were. We realised that they, too, were wrecked on the reef.

We looked the yacht over and from what we could see it wasn't holed. Seeing the draught of the boat was only 1.4 m, we hoped it would float

Above: **Reactor 25s being assembled in Paul Whiting's factory at Onehunga, Auckland.** *Creative Photography Ltd*

Right: Spartacus, **the first production line Whiting Reactor 45.** *Paul Whiting*

Above: **A design from the man with the "golden" touch. The Ron Holland-created** *Measure for Measure*, **built for Ian Gibbs, racing on Auckland Harbour.** *Neil MacKinnon*

Below: **She met with a sad end. Kem Cox's Wellington sloop** *Matuku*, **which was sunk by a whale in mid-Tasman in 1968. Miraculously, the crew were picked up by a tanker way off her planned course.**
Evening Post

off at high tide. But it wasn't a very big tide. And by that time we had discovered a hole on the starboard side under my bunk. It wasn't a big hole at that stage – only about the size of an orange. But that orange-sized hole got bigger and bigger as the tide moved and battered the boat just where it was leaking. The cabin was filling with water and we used the bilge pump.

But after a while the flooding became too much. We gave up. Now we knew we could not possibly sail away. But all the time we had been waiting for the tide to come in I had the funny feeling that we were not going to float off – that we were going to be there a bit longer.

It was getting late in the afternoon. We realised we could not sleep inside the boat because the tide had risen so high, so we got all our packs out and all the food. We had quite a few cans of food, and we reckoned we could get another month out of it if we were careful. We also had a tank of water. I think there may have been about 70 litres left.

We put all of our gear on the highest part of the boat. Then we made our beds outside and rigged a canopy over them. That night was bad. It was windy, really windy, and when the tide came in, the breakers were breaking on to the hull of the boat, smashing on top of it. We were soaked. The canopy was absolutely useless. It was just blown out. We lashed all our gear down. Irfon was sleeping in his bunk, which had not been flooded out. But he had to come on deck after water rose further in the cabin.

We realised we would have to go to one of the wrecks. At the time we could pick out two of them distinctly (the *Fuku Maru* and the freighter *Runik*) and the vague outline of a third.

We decided on the *Fuku Maru* because it was closest, and the next morning Peter took a pack and went over to it. It took him about three-quarters of an hour and when we saw he had reached the ship, we too, set off. We used our packs to take all our own gear, plus the tinned food. Then on the next day we went back to the *Sospan Fach* for more gear. Chris, Peter and I made the trip. Irfon stayed on the *Fuku Maru* to take a sun reading at midday.

When we got to the *Sospan Fach* we realised we were trapped by the tide, so we had to stay on the yacht that night. We had waited until 6 p.m. for the tide to fall. Then we set off in water that was up to our knees, but it was up to our waist soon after. We were trying to pull an inflatable dinghy full of supplies. We just had to turn back.

Spending that night on the *Sospan Fach* was really bad. We all had shorts on and very little else. At night we went into the cabin and it was freezing, the worst night I have ever spent. There was this little three-by-three table in the cabin. We turned it upside down, and Christine and I huddled into it, cuddled together for warmth. We used the plans of the *Sospan Fach* as blankets, wrapped all round us. At about high tide, the box was afloat with us in it, but it wasn't waterproof and we had to get out and perch on the bunks. Still the water kept rising, and we had to move from there. The only place not under water was the toilet, so we crammed in there.

We left the next morning, again towing the inflatable dinghy. We had to wait for the tide to recede, as we had seen shadows which looked very much like sharks. And there were sharks, because later I caught two and Irfon caught a big one.

We had to have enough water for the dinghy to float in, but after a while it got caught and we had to tie it to a rocky outcrop and carry the stores to the *Fuku Maru* on our backs. We were going to go back for the dinghy, but it broke loose and was lost.

Before we left the *Sospan* we discovered the fresh water tank was contaminated. It had been holed and saltwater had seeped in. Our fresh water supply was gone. This was pretty devastating as we had only a few tins for water storage. We had only been able to collect about 13 litres of rain water because we did not have sufficient containers.

The next day Irfon went over to the *Sospan*, because he did not believe that the freshwater could be contaminated. We, too, made a couple more trips to the *Sospan,* because we wanted to get tools and things.

Our first inspection of the *Maru* was pretty devastating. We had had a hard job getting on board. Peter and I climbed up ropes and found an old railing we used as a ladder. The ship had been completely burnt out, and gave us nothing but shelter. We were rationed to a third of a pint of water each day and a tin of fruit between four of us.

We started fishing straight away and caught lots of fish. There was firewood on board the boat and we made fires in the wheelhouse where we made our home. We used sails to cover the windows, cut up a conveyor belt to lay on the floor. The wheelhouse was ankle-deep in ash and we had to scrape it out. The whole place was covered in ash. You touched any part of the ship and it got all over you. In the end we just gave up.

We used to go down on the reef each day for washes. We didn't have any encounters with sharks, but we saw plenty of them.

Peter's feet were quite lacerated, and the wounds would not heal. We treated them with antiseptics, but they still haven't really healed. All of our cuts were slow to heal, and took a long time to clot.

We slept a lot. As we had no light, we would go to bed at about 5 p.m. and get up at about 6 a.m. We discovered all the resources of the reef almost as soon as we arrived.

We had to drag ourselves around half the time, depending on the tide. We would go fishing, then cook, then eat. All our time was occupied with food-gathering and sleeping. That is all it really was. That is all we did.

We found each other's moods had a lot to do with things. We were very sensitive toward each other's moods. You could tell when Christine was in a mood, I always tried to encourage her along, and vice versa.

We didn't see any other vessels before the *Ata* appeared, at 9.30 a.m.

on Tuesday of last week. It would have been about four miles away. It was anchored there.

We had built a raft. You see, all our resources were running pretty low on the *Fuku.* Our canned supplies were going; the fish weren't biting. We thought the next plan of action was obviously to move to the wreck of the *Runik,* because it looked so good from where we were. We were sort of dreaming of kitchens, of flour and things like that. Days later, when we left the reef, we looked at the *Runik* from close quarters. And it was an absolute mess.

When we saw the *Ata,* everything started to move. We quickly took orange shower curtains and an orange hammock and tied them to the highest point of our ship. We erected a clothesline with all our gear strung out along it right along the deck. We put all the gear we could find on it, including our orange packs.

Then Chris and Peter started flashing mirrors at the *Ata.* That is what actually caught their attention. We tried two flares, and they were absolutely hopeless. They were just like candles. We expected them to go like skyrockets. We had smoke canisters, but they didn't really work. There was such a strong wind that when we threw the can over the water, the smoke never rose.

The crew of the *Ata* had been watching the wrecks, keeping an eye open, because they had seen the yacht. They had been trawling from the Saturday.

When I saw them, I just couldn't believe my eyes. I screamed. I was running all around the boat. I cried. I jumped for joy. Since I have been on the reef my faith in God has increased. I think we all had come much closer to God. We just watched that boat. We didn't know at that time whether they had seen us or not. We just hoped they had been looking. So we just carried on as usual collecting food – but half-heartedly at this stage.

It was the next day before they came over. It was pretty rough, they had a real struggle. They had to abandon any attempt to get back that day. They came over on Tuesday morning, stayed Tuesday and we all left on Wednesday morning.

The first thing they said when they came over the side, I can't remember. But we said, "Boy, are we pleased to see you!" That was in a scream.

Once on board the *Ata,* I just wanted to get going. But at my first sight of the coast of Australia I was a bit frightened. I knew there was a waiting army of reporters and photographers. It frightened me, because I had been so long on board. Then I saw my parents. I was overjoyed. And I really couldn't believe I was on firm ground. Now all I want to do is get home.

Wrecked at Raoul Island

From the *New Zealand Herald*

The sea gods must have been in an angry mood one Easter day in 1974 when 24-year-old Gary Treadgold, an Auckland civil engineer, launched his 9 m yacht, Moeroa, which he had built himself. Very soon afterward she set off across the South Pacific, his young crew consisting of two secretaries, Sharon Reid (20) of Kaitaia and Debbie Lee (19) of Auckland, and two other Aucklanders, Murray Williams (23), an electrician, and Graeme Cornall (24), an industrial engineer.

Their maiden voyage was to be part of the Royal New Zealand Yacht Squadron's first Auckland-to-Rarotonga race, but Moeroa had to withdraw to make repairs at Kawau Island. Giving up the race, they completed the repairs and started on a South Pacific cruise instead, heading for Fiji. But on 29 May, after suffering storm damage, they put into Raoul Island, about 600 miles north-east of Auckland, once more for repairs.

Here disaster struck.

Moeroa was anchored securely out on the sheltered side of the island and a crew member remained on board at all times until the night of Saturday 8 June, when they all accepted lodging and hospitality at the weather station. Early on Sunday morning Murray Williams went to check that all was well. Looking down from the nearest cliff, he found the yacht smashed to matchwood below. There had been a storm overnight which caused the yacht to drag her anchors and drift onto the rocks, where she was pounded to pieces. Only a small portion of the shattered decking was recovered.

Gone were four and a half years work and an investment worth $10,000. The yacht had not been insured. Gone also were thousands of dollars worth of personal equipment belonging to the five, including transistor radios, cameras, tape recorders and binoculars, also all their cash and passports.

Raoul Island, one of the Kermadec group, covers about 2800 ha and is inhabited by the ten men who operate the weather station. It is utterly cliff-bound, with one tiny jetty. Normally a ship calls about once a year with stores and replacement staff, and passengers must be lowered down the cliffs by crane. This is only possible in calm weather, because of the difficulty of getting a boat to the jetty in rough seas. Winds there are unpredictable and liable to change in seconds.

Naturally the isolated weathermen are delighted to see a visiting yacht and are keen to offer hospitality. Doug Johnstone, original owner of the Admiral's Cup contestant *Barnacle Bill,* described his visit there when returning to New Zealand from England in his next yacht, *Running Wild:* they were sailing toward the island in a light south-east wind, toward a group of welcoming weathermen, when suddenly the wind changed to 30 knots from the north-west and they had to turn away, to the accompaniment of dejected waves from their disappointed would-be hosts.

The crew of *Moeroa* were taken off the island after a few days by the New Zealand Shipping Corporation's Pacific Island trader *Lorena,* diverted to the island after a call from the meteorological staff. They arrived in Wellington on 17 June, just nine days after the loss of the yacht that had been launched with so much happy anticipation only two months before.

Even their journey home in the *Lorena* was not without incident, for the trader arrived, as a storm gusting to 110 km an hour pounded Wellington. All Picton-Wellington ferries were cancelled and the *Lorena* was unable to enter Wellington Heads until later. By a strange coincidence, the crew of the yacht *Sospan Fach* were also delayed by gales in their rescue trawler *Ata* at the same time that the crew of *Moeroa* were steaming toward New Zealand in the *Lorena.*

Designer who has gone far

From the files of the *New Zealand Herald*

Bruce Farr's international reputation as a designer of centreboarders was well established when at the age of 23 he designed his first winning keel boat, the half-tonner Tituscanby. *Yachtsmen watched in disbelief as* Tituscanby *ran off with honours in the shorter races of the Schweppes Half-Ton contest in Auckland in 1972, but predicted his crew of centreboard sailors would never have the stamina, or the boat the ability, to withstand the rigours of the long ocean race. They were proved wrong again and* Titus *came in first in the long race and won the Schweppes Half-Ton trophy.*

From then on, his keel boats, large and small, continued to surprise, and yachtsmen who were serious contenders for racing honours in world classes began to abandon their current yachts to have Farr boats built. Excerpts from the files of the New Zealand Herald *tell the details as Farr boats carried off honours at home and abroad. In 1975 his designs raced for New Zealand for the Admiral's Cup at Cowes, England, and won the world quarter-ton title at Deauville, France, almost simultaneously; the first of his new one-ton designs won the Southern Cross Cup in Australia at the end of that year. In 1976 two models of this design,* 45° South II *and* Jiminy Cricket, *represented New Zealand at the One Ton Cup contest at Marseilles, France.*

New Zealand Herald, 13 April 1972:

PITTING personal theories against the proven principles of the experts is a gamble. But for Bruce Farr, the gamble produced a winner when *Tituscanby* won the Schweppes New Zealand and South Pacific Half-Ton Trophy. For Farr, the *Tituscanby* win was no flash in the pan, for this talented designer has turned out champion centreboarders with the regularity of clockwork.

Yacht racing started for Farr at the age of 12 in a Flying Ant. In 1964, the year International Moths were introduced to New Zealand, he designed one for his brother. The following year his first major success came at 16, when he not only won the New Zealand International Moth title, but completed the double by designing the craft (*Mammoth*) himself. He won the designers' trophy in the Moth fleet for the highest placed own-designed craft in the national contest for three years.

This was the start of a series of championship wins which came to a climax in 1970 when Farr won the interdominion 3.6 m (12 ft) unrestricted championship in one of his creations, *Miss Beazley Homes.* Farr designed the 3.6 m *Beazley Homes* and in partnership with R. Blackburn – the owner of *Tituscanby* – built the yacht and won the Silasee trophy from the Australians. It was a splendid effort for a 20-year-old. Farr, who in the meantime had designed a Cherub, Javelin, catamaran, JOG keeler and 18-footers, was starting to get a reputation.

Such was the respect of the Australians for Farr's talents that when he announced his intention of designing a one-man 12-footer, the contest rules were quickly amended, banning such a craft. When he did produce his one-man 12-footer, he not only beat the conventional two-man 12s with their big sail area but there was also the day when he beat the much bigger contenders.

Turning his attention to 18-footers (5.4 m) Farr produced *Miss UEB,* second in the 1971 world championship and winner at the Long Beach Sea Festival.

In 1972 he designed and built *Smirnoff,* the first New Zealand 18-footer to win the world title in Australian waters.

In 1968 he had made his first attempt at keeler design with an entry in the Royal Akarana Yacht Club's JOG design contest. This design did not win a prize, but then maybe if it was based on Farr's *Tituscanby* principles, it may have been "too way out".

New Zealand Herald, 4 January 1975:

The big name in Australasian waters as the designer of centreboard craft, Farr, for the time being, has his eyes set on the 12 ft (3.6 m) inter-dominion contest for the Silasec trophy, currently being sailed in Sydney. On top of this – and this is the big one – there is the world 18-foot championship to be sailed in Brisbane, starting on 16 January.

And Farr has now successfully branched out into keel-boat design. So his attentions for the present are divided between 18-footers and the tuning of the 62.8 m *Gerontius,* to be sailed by Graham Eder in the New Zealand Admiral's Cup trials. For Farr, it may well be the way the egg cracks in the early Admiral's Cup trials that dictates how long he will spend on the Brisbane River. But to Brisbane he will go.

And, of course, the centre of attention in Brisbane is how his new creations, *Travelodge* (T. McDell) and *Rank Xerox* (J. Douglas) fare against their Australian counterparts. The yacht that McDell sailed to win the world series last year has now been taken over by the parent company in Sydney and will be sailed in the series by the former world champion 18-footer skipper, R. Holmes.

There are, however, a few other Farr boats in the championship which may give the big guns a few problems.

First, there is a new design for Sydney 18-foot exponent D. Porter. "This is a bigger boat than *Travelodge* with more beam," said Farr. "Dave Porter carries a heavy crew so I drew him up a beamier boat. They can carry a bigger sail area."

Other Farr designs to sail in the world contest are the 1970 design now known as *Levi's,* sailed by E. Bland for New Zealand, and *Harold's Place,* sailing for New South Wales.

His centreboard achievements were very soon overshadowed, however, by the spectacular performance of his new quarter-tonners, which outshone other contestants in every race in which they competed, and his New Zealand Admiral's Cup team challenger, Gerontius. *So outstanding were the quarter-tonners that the Royal Akarana Yacht Club decided to send one to challenge (and to win) the World Quarter-Ton Cup.*

On 24 July 1975 New Zealand Associated Press correspondent C. S. Cooper reported to the New Zealand Herald *from London:*

The successful Auckland yacht designer Bruce Farr was wearing his world quarter-ton triumph lightly yesterday with a business-as-usual routine at Cowes, where he was helping to prepare *Gerontius* for the Admiral's Cup series.

He acknowledged modestly that he was "pretty pleased" with the runaway victory of *45° South* and the sixth placing of *Genie,* both of which boats came off his drawing board. He was sure that it was the first time that a New Zealand-designed yacht had won a world-recognised level rating event but he emphasised that *45° South* had had a superb crew — perhaps the best crew ever to come out of New Zealand. Roy Dickson and Graeme Woodroffe, as skippers, had shown splendid seamanship.

The sisters *Genie* and *45° South* were developments of an earlier Farr quarter-ton design that had shown considerable promise. *Genie* had been the first of the new style and was followed by her twin, *45° South,* produced "in a hurry" for the New Zealand quarter-ton event last March, which she won.

After *45° South's* first two wins at Deauville, sailing interest had been riveted on the boat and it had been sold to a French yachtsman before the final victory race. Farr said he had high hopes for the design known professionally as the Farr 727 (for 7.27 m in length) being built in Europe under licence. After the Admiral's Cup series he would be investigating business prospects on this side of the world.

Three Farr 727s had already been exported from New Zealand, one each to Australia, Japan and Hawaii, and it was expected that this trickle would now increase to a significant flow. The selling price of a 727 fully rigged for speed sailing was around $10,000. In Europe the designer would also be looking at the market potential for his new half-ton and one-ton styles.

Three of the one-tonners were already under construction in New Zealand. Not yet on the drawing board but due there within a year was a new quarter-tonner, a development of *45° South,* but trimmed specifically for high speed and without the cruising potential built into the current Farr 727s.

New Zealand Herald, November 1975:

Design of a quarter-ton yacht, *45° South,* a bigger boat, *Gerontius,* and a super one-tonner, *Prospect of Ponsonby,* have in a very short time elevated Bruce Farr to the top bracket of world keel-boat designers.

45° South won the world quarter-ton champion. *Gerontius* was top points scorer in the New Zealand Admiral's Cup team and *Prospect of Ponsonby,* after five races, remains unbeaten in local sailing.

While Farr may well be called a whiz-kid of design, so too is he a most remarkable helmsman. And there can be no greater praise than that of *Prospect of Ponsonby* owner-skipper Noel Angus, who says Farr is simply uncanny in anticipating wind swings and vagaries of sailing conditions long before they happen.

Success may force Farr to leave the country – but not, he hopes, before one of his designs has won the One Ton Cup on the Hauraki Gulf in 1977.

Fresh from his latest triumph – a remarkable five straight wins by the Farr-designed one-tonner *Prospect of Ponsonby* in the Southern Cross Cup team trials – the whiz-kid designer was in his workshop last night photo-copying boat plans. The workshop is the garage of his parents' home in Devonport. His design office is his mother's sewing room.

Apart from *Prospect,* all his keel designs began as cruising boats, he says. But their racing success has meant that his designs are now being built in Germany, the United States, Australia and Japan. Canada and France will soon be added to the list. He says that for economic reasons he will probably have to set up in Europe, or America.

Success may send Farr overseas, but it is unlikely to spoil him. When the *Herald* asked for an interview last night, his first reaction was: "You should be seeing Noel Angus (owner-skipper of *Prospect of Ponsonby*). He was the driver."

Prospect of Ponsonby *was soon to be lost to Auckland, for she was the most successful boat of the winning New Zealand Southern Cross team and was snapped up by an Australian buyer. Noel Angus came home without her. In the meantime, the success of* 45° South *looked as if it could lead to the establishment of a new international offshore class – as the* New Zealand Herald *reported on 6 April 1976:*

After *45° South's* exciting win in France the Farr 727 design has aroused considerable attention around the world. Fifteen yachts of the design are already sailing in Auckland waters. There are three in Japan while others are sailing in Australia, France, England and Hawaii.

There is also a Texan who plans to sail a Farr 727 at this year's quarter-ton championship at Corpus Christi, in the Gulf of Mexico.

But the big news as far as the 727 class is concerned is that the yachts are being built, under licence, in Canada and France. It is already estimated that in the next northern summer 60 Canadian-built 727s and 30 built in France will be heading for the water.

The success story continued. In July, Jenny Green reported in Sea Spray *magazine:*

Auckland designer Bruce Farr, back from a rapid jet-setting trip to the U.K., France, Germany, Switzerland, Canada and the United States, tells us a possible eight one-tonners to his design will compete in the world one-ton series in Marseilles, depending on how well they fare in selection trials.

Added to that total is one German half-tonner for Trieste and several quarter-tonners for Corpus Christi. Quarters to Farr's design will be representing Canada and Germany, and some of them, he says, could be expected to be faster than the New Zealand 727s in light weather. The Farr quarters are being produced in Canada by North Star Yachts, who apparently have a planned production of 200 boats in a year! Farr plans to be in Marseilles for the one-ton contest.

He had good reason to go to Marseilles, for the Royal New Zealand Yacht Squadron had sent two boats of his design, 45° South II *and* Jiminy Cricket, *to challenge for the One Ton Cup. As we have seen in earlier chapters, both yachts sailed brilliantly but just failed to win the contest.*

The New Zealand Herald *reported on 15 October that year that Farr was now moving into the two-ton field:*

A new Bruce Farr two-ton yacht is to be built in Auckland for a Hong Kong businessman and then entered in the Admiral's Cup in Britain next year. And the yacht will probably have a few New Zealanders on board when it makes its bid for the colony's cup team.

The designer said that the new boat was to be built in solid glass fibre by a very sophisticated and extreme development of the method used to build his highly successful one-tonners.

The new method, which is being kept secret, will enable Ocean Racing Yachts Ltd to turn out a hull that is extremely light for its size – the new two-tonner will have an all-up weight of 5580 kg, less than that of many of the one-tonners which competed at Marseilles earlier this year.

A female mould will have to be built for the Hong Kong yacht – an expensive proposition for a "oncer" – but Farr says much interest has been generated in the new design and many more hulls could be produced for New Zealand owners, both as racing and cruising yachts.

Building will start in December to take account of any changes in the I.O.R. rules made at the meeting of the Offshore Racing Council next month. By March the boat will have to be shipped to Britain, where, if necessary, it will race in the trials to select the Hong Kong team.

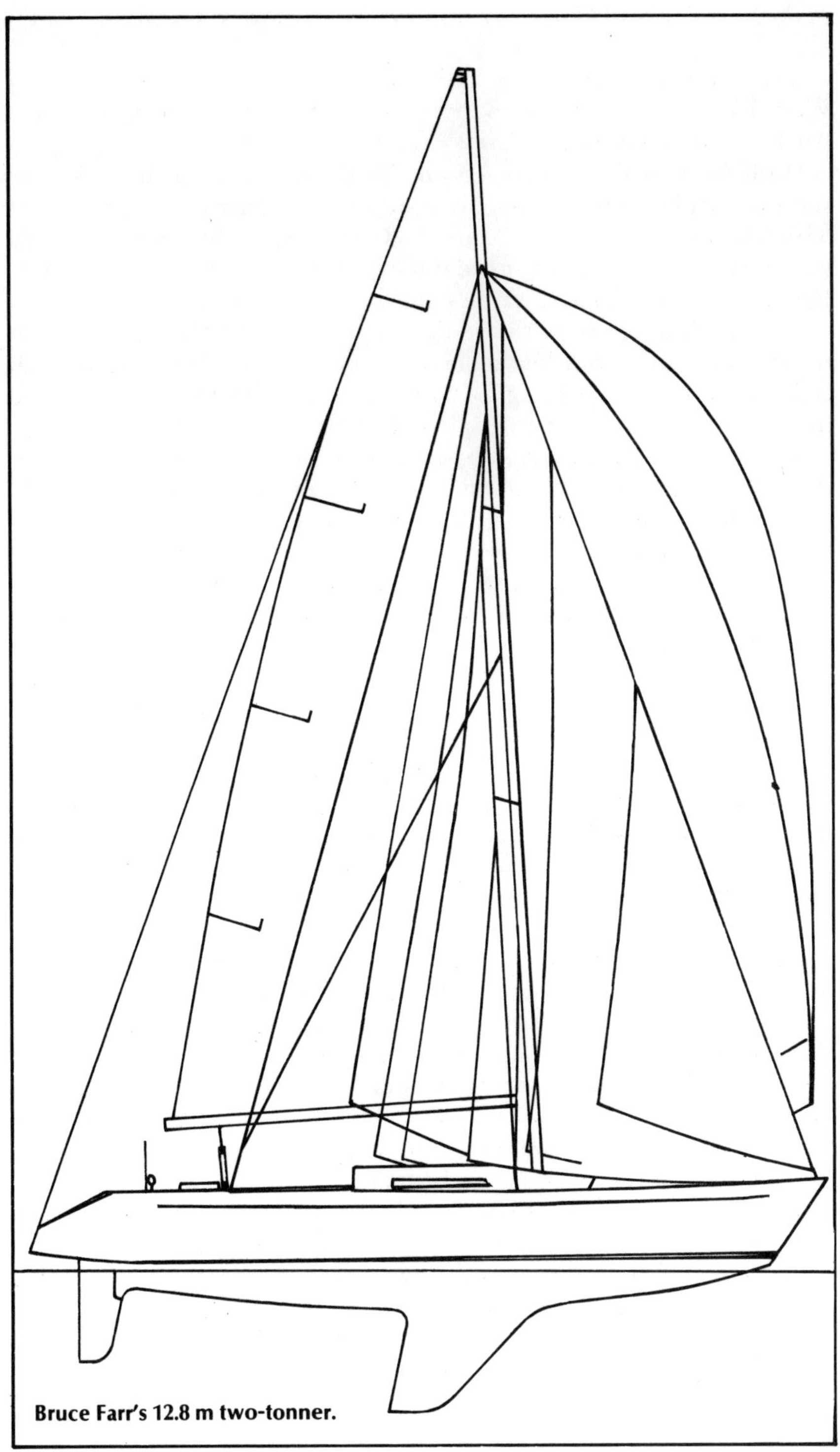

Bruce Farr's 12.8 m two-tonner.

In the New Zealand Herald *on 11 November 1976, J. A. Gasparich wrote:*

The launching of a new half-ton yacht, a Farr 920 design, at Westhaven today, will introduce a new chapter in the saga of the Auckland designer Bruce Farr.

With his foot firmly planted on the bottom rung of the ladder of success, Farr has consolidated his position as a designer of world renown with quarter, one-ton and Admiral's Cup-sized yachts. Now, with the world half-ton series to be sailed out of Sydney in December next year, Farr has returned to half-ton design.

And needless to say, with the Farr reputation, the "920 design" was not long off the drawing board before the orders started pouring in. Such is the demand for Farr-designed yachts that the first 920 to be launched in Auckland today is the 10th shell off the mould.

Two of the hulls, moulded by Alpha Marine, have been shipped to Australia and another to Canada. Even the plug from which the mould was made is being finished in the Brin Wilson shed and will be sent off to Australia. Among 14 orders still in hand is a yacht, at present under construction, for an American, A. Diamond of Los Angeles.

Farr himself is enthusiastic over the new half-tonner. "She is nearly a metre longer and 10 percent lighter than *Tituscanby,*" said Farr. "That means she can have more sail area. She will be more powerful with a higher ballast ratio, but less wetted surface – and that means she will go a whole lot faster."

While for the present Farr will not predict how fast the new 9 m yacht will go, there is the confident air that, sailing off the wind, she will give some much bigger yachts a good run for their money. Racing yachtsmen are being catered for with the "performance" version of the 920 design, and the list of prospective owners includes some well known yachtsmen. The cruising yachtsmen will be looked after with a "cruising" version, due to be produced soon after Christmas. This version will be the same hull as the racing yacht but a different deck layout.

The launching of the 920 design does not mean that Farr will have time to take a rest. Besides plans to put a trailer-sailer on the local market there is a definite order for a three-quarter ton yacht to go to Europe. Next month's work includes what Farr describes as "a new heap of one-tonners. I have orders for different design styles from three New Zealanders and two overseas yachtsmen."

This is far from the end of the Bruce Farr story; perhaps it is only the beginning. In 1977 he was 27 years old and was known internationally as a designer of fast racing yachts for world competitions. His yachts were being turned out as fast as they could come from New Zealand factories for impatient buyers and were being produced in quantity overseas. In 1977 he won the Yachtsman of the Year award. It will be interesting to watch his future progress.

Reactors and racing machines

by LORIS CHILWELL

AT Christmas 1969 *Reactor,* a 7.6 m fibreglass sloop, appeared on the waters of the Hauraki Gulf in time to race successfully with the Junior Offshore Group at their rally at Kawau Island. Her designer and builder was Paul Whiting, then aged 17. *Reactor* was an instant success, a constant winner, the attractively-designed forerunner of a proliferation of production line yachts in fibreglass.

Paul built altogether 15 Reactors in an old tin shed next door to his father's factory in Carr Road, Mt Roskill. He inherited the shed when it was vacated by the family yacht *Coruba,* which D'Arcy Whiting had been building to a John Lidgard design.

Early in 1972 Paul moved operations to a new factory in Princes Street, Onehunga, and by the end of 1976 67 Reactor 25s had been launched. By now the design was well established. Reactors had been racing in their own one-design class with the Royal Akarana Yacht Club for several years.

In the meantime Paul had designed the 13.7 m *Tequila* for his parents. *Tequila* was launched in December 1972 and in spite of having been designed as a family cruiser, won the R.A.Y.C. White Island race in January 1973. As we saw earlier in this book, part of the Whiting family took off on a world cruise in her in 1974.

Paul had already started turning out a modified version to be known as Reactor 45. First of these was *Spartacus,* built for Owen Cleave. *Neeleen,* the boat made from the wooden plug from which the mould was taken, was finished and sent to the United States. Two other fibreglass models went to Honolulu. In 1977 production rights were taken over by Cavalier Yachts.

In February 1976 a new craft took to the water. As we have seen, it electrified the yachting world. It was *Magic Bus.* It was to win almost every race it started in at home, retain the World Quarter-Ton Cup for New Zealand at Corpus Christi, in the United States, and be sold abroad, all before the end of September. Paul was 25.

He was spectacularly busy, for during this period he designed and built the first of his new half-tonners, *Candu II,* besides campaigning *Magic Bus,* preparing her for shipment to the United States and finally crewing in her in the world championships.

Magic Bus was a more radical design than Bruce Farr's, designed to improve on the less outstanding qualities of Farr's 727 design, which was at a disadvantage in light airs. It was necessary to design a light displacement boat which could carry enough canvas to excel in the light. The result was a very unusually shaped boat with an extreme dinghy-type three-quarter rig and a long, acute-angled overhung stern.

The new Paul Whiting half-tonner, *Candu II,* had a cold launching at 7 p.m. on 15 June 1976. A nine-week wonder, she had been commissioned by Ian Gibbs in a crash programme to make the World Half-Ton Cup contest in Trieste, Italy, at the same time as the quarter-tonners competed in the United States.

Ian Gibbs had already owned two half-tonners by New Zealand designers – *Measure for Measure* (Ron Holland) and *Tohe Candu* (Bruce Farr). Two days after her launching, *Candu II* was to compete against *Tohe Candu* (which Gibbs still owned) in the half-ton division of the Royal Akarana's winter race, to decide which yacht Gibbs would take to Trieste. *Candu II* was victorious and left soon after for the world contest.

While the spotlight shone on *Magic Bus* and the winning team in Corpus Christi, nothing was heard of *Candu II.* Light wind conditions had spoiled her chances and she came only eighth.

When Paul returned from Corpus Christi it was back to the drawing board. He was planning a one-tonner with Murray Ross, whose sail loft adjoins the Whiting factory, a partnership that had proved so successful at Corpus Christi. He was also making modifications to the *Candu II* design. The one-tonner was to be ready to race in October 1977 in trials for the One Ton Cup team in the world contest to be held by the Royal New Zealand Yacht Squadron on the Hauraki Gulf the following month. The result was *Smackwater Jack,* which won the trials but failed to live up to expectations in the one-ton contest.

Bad news came with the new rating rules released by the I.Y.R.U. at the end of 1976. Both Farr and Whiting designs would be heavily penalised. Consternation reigned among yacht owners whose newly-launched racing machines would not meet the rating requirements for their class after April 1977. Unruffled, Paul prepared to meet this challenge.

By the first week in February 1977 he had made the new mould for his "new *Bus*" to fit the modified rule and had arranged production rights in Germany. His new quarter-tonner, started that week, had to be in the water in 20 days time to compete in the Panmure Yacht and Boating Club's trials for the yacht they would send to the world contest in Helsinki, Finland, in July.

Four one-tonners to his new design, not then even on the drawing board, had been commissioned to be in the water by October; and he and Murray Ross planned themselves to field both a half-tonner and a one-tonner for the championships that year. The half-tonner, christened *Newspaper Taxi,* won the Schweppes Half-Ton trophy at Easter. The quarter-tonner missed the entry deadline.

The esoteric language of the I.O.R. rating rule almost defies ex-

The lines of a champion. The revolutionary *Magic Bus.*

planation to the layman, but Paul had a stab at explaining how his designs had been penalised and how he was coping with the change.

"Basically, the new rule is penalising flat runs aft, and this has affected my boats quite a bit," he explained. "I have found that by changing my buttock height on the after end, I can pick up quite a bit of rating. The buttock height is a measure of 15 percent of the boat's beam out from the centre line on each side; the vertical height measurements, which are basically to determine the slope of the run of the boat, and these are from the gunwale down.

"What I am actually doing is making my boats shorter and by doing this I can still keep the type of stern the boats have at present, which I believe is fast. It adds stability to the boat upwind and makes a very comfortable boat to sail in downwind. I'm planning on sticking to the same style of boat, even though they're changing the rule to beat this type of boat.

"I'm presently doing a boat which Murray Ross and I have got together and done. This boat features a centrebroad with an all-up weight of 104 kg. We've got internal ballast in this boat, which is lighter again than the earlier *Candu II* and I'm sure this boat is going to be competitive under the new rule.

"For the boats we are producing now, we've got two deck moulds, one for the racing man and one for the cruising-racing man. We've found that it's necessary to do that in this day and age, where an out-and-out racing boat has got to have a deck layout where the crew don't have to move out of the cockpit to make fine adjustments. There's definitely quite a performance advantage in this, and this is the reason we've gone for two deck mouldings. The larger cabin version, of course, has a lot more accommodation, which is appealing to the cruising man; and we're surprised at how many of these boats we're actually selling to cruising type people. The cruising plan has accommodation for six and we've only got accommodation for four in the racing.

"Modifications that we have to do to our older boats without reducing sail are putting bumps in the boat basically and these bumps will have to go in the forward depths and the buttock height aft. This is going to stiffen the run aft, of course, which the rule gives quite an allowance for. I think it will affect the performance of the boat slightly, but these boats are fast in a breeze anyway; its the light airs they miss out on.

"I think the authorities should draw up some sort of guideline and decide what sorts of boats they want to race. I think ocean racing yachts should be like racing cars, not like family cars and the future of ocean racing should be with racing yachts, not some sort of compromise."

The golden touch

by GRAEME KENNEDY

From *8 O'Clock*

EXPATRIATE Auckland racing yacht designer Ron Holland seems always to have been in the right place at the right time. So it was in his home town in October 1976 when, with only five days leeway, the Ireland-based creator of some of the fastest "ton" boats afloat was on hand when his American wife Laurel gave birth to their second daughter, Benna.

"I was very lucky," the tousle-haired 29-year-old said at his parents' Torbay home. "I could spare only 10 days away from the office in Cork and I have to be at a meeting in London on Saturday. I wanted to be here for the birth and hoped I'd picked the right time slot. Benna was right on time."

Weighing in on just over 4.5 kg, Benna (a North American Indian and Hebrew name) left North Shore Hospital just eight hours before her famous father flew home.

Holland is one of the world's top dozen yacht designers and the busiest in Europe after his successes in the 1976 quarter, half, three-quarter and two-ton international championships.

He specializes in designing what he terms formula one yachts – the boats built for speed instead of comfort. "Yacht racing has become very much like car racing," Holland explains. "The gap is widening between people who want a cruising boat they can race and those who want serious racing boats. These are machines and, like cars, must be very finely tuned to obtain maximum performance.

"A really good Admiral's Cup yacht – like the one I'm having built for an Italian group – can cost around $160,000. Big yacht racing has become a very curious sport – there is no prize money for the winners, transport and operating costs are devastating. It has become a sport for only a very rich elite."

That same elite is making the youngster from Torbay one of its members. Working from a converted farmhouse he and Laurel bought at Crosshaven, 14 km from Cork in Ireland, Holland had six Admiral's Cup designs under construction in 1976 – more than any other designer in Europe. All were commissioned after his triumphs that year and marked his first departure from his specialist ton designs.

His *Silver Shamrock* took the half-ton title and *Southern Shamrock* – chartered by an Australian group – came fourth in the same race.

Holland's *Business Machine* came in second behind *Magic Bus* in the quarter-ton race, while three-quarter-tonners *Machismo* and *Golden Delight* came in second and third.

His two-tonner *Iorana* finished second, three places ahead of his *Irish Mist.*

That's the record which made Holland Europe's most talked about – and wanted – racing yacht designer.

That the New Zealand Admiral's Cup team yachts did not quite live up to expectations in the Fastnet race was compensated for by the performance of *Golden Delicious,* a half-ton yacht designed by Holland. *Golden Delicious* was successful in a fleet of 255.

Holland first got himself wet as an eight-year-old, sailing P-class sailing dinghies off Browns Bay. "I was pretty successful in club races, and graduated through to the bigger classes," he says, "which really is no surprise for someone growing up in Auckland.

"This is a maritime city, perfect for sailboats – I believe the chances of a youngster becoming involved in sailing are about the same as his taking up rugby. That fact, I think, is the very basis of my success."

Holland left St Paul's school at 16 after having already crossed the Tasman as a 15-year-old crewing the Australian boat *Aloha,* and working on offshore racers in well-known New Zealand and Sydney-based boats.

"I loved the big keel boats, the feel of them and the sea," he said. "I read all I could about sailing through the Pacific and the romance of it. At school, my academic career was without note – I was too busy drawing yachts in my arithmetic book to pass exams."

Holland joined Browns Bay's Atkinson boatbuilders as an apprentice at 17 and continued to crew the best boats around in races like the Sydney-Hobart, Hobart-Auckland and to Noumea and Suva. His big break came when Auckland designer and close friend John Spencer was commissioned to build a 21 m schooner, the *New World,* for United States shipping magnate Kiskaddon.

"It was an unusual design and John, knowing my interest in traditional boats, asked me over for a chat about it," Holland explains. "We built a 7.2 m scale model of the real thing, named it *Great Hope* and Kiskaddon asked me to go to San Francisco with him to help with its trials. I was only 22 and his was the greatest offer of my life.

"We took the boat across the Pacific on one of his cargo ships – a very interesting and very alcoholic three weeks – and I sent performance data back to John in New Zealand.

"I got the opportunity there to meet and sail with some of the best yachtsmen on the West Coast – all very heady for a young Aucklander."

Holland also met United States designer Gary Mull who, impressed with his work, gave him a job. Through Mull, Holland became involved with the design and construction of the 12.8 m *Improbable,* which was being built at Atkinson's at Browns Bay.

Back home watching the boat's progress, Holland one day found himself chatting to an American visitor on Takapuna Beach during the world OK Dinghy championships. "He was interested in the new yacht and I took him over and showed it to him," Holland recalls. "We became quite friendly and he asked me to look him up if I ever visited Florida."

Holland and crew shipped *Improbable* to Miami the following year, planning to compete in several American races before sailing across the Atlantic to race in the Admiral's Cup series in England.

He looked up his old friend who suggested that his daughter Laurel, an art teacher in San Francisco, might be interested in working as a cook on the trans-Atlantic crossing. "I telephoned her with the idea," Holland said, "and although she'd never met me, she packed her bags and was in Miami within a week."

Improbable finished fourth in the cup races, sailed off Scotland, and Laurel and Ron were married at a tiny Loch Tay church. They sailed back to Miami together – "a wonderful honeymoon" – and Holland took a job with a Florida yacht design firm. There, the first Holland-design was launched – a quarter-tonner named *Eyghtene* and spelt that way in deference to his Kiwi accent.

His first effort was a winner – taking the United States championship at Florida and the world title in Europe soon afterwards.

He was also associated with the American designer Doug Petersen in the construction of the yacht *Gambare* which nearly pulled off the 1973 one-ton series.

With his name on every yachtie's lips, Holland was invited to Cork to design the quarter-ton *Golden Apple* for an Irish syndicate. *Apple* is still racing successfully and, taking advantage of his quarter-ton success, Holland set up shop at Crosshaven.

"Sparkman and Stevens were the big names then, but they were based in America," he said. "There was really no one making the scene in Europe. I decided then to specialize in fast, racing ton boats – once you've made a name you can branch out into other areas, but not before."

Holland made his name and is being sought for the design work he puts on paper in a studio he has made from a former pig-sty farmhouse. "With the international aspect of the yacht design adjacent to the old Irish business, it doesn't really matter where I live," he says. "But Crosshaven is a beautiful place and it is at the heart of the European scene."

A major U K. boatbuilder produced 60 of Holland's three-quarter ton boats in 1976, with plans to produce his half-ton designs as well.

"The future, though, will depend a lot on how my Admiral's Cup boats go next year," said Holland. "If they do well and show good potential, my career might take a different turn. I've got my fingers crossed."

Holland's designing, construction monitoring and tuning leave him little time for leisure at his "special place" in Ireland. "I haven't even got time to enjoy sailing," he said, "so I haven't bothered to get a boat of my own."

Ron Holland's design successes abroad have been somewhat overshadowed at home by the spectacular — and close — successes of his contemporaries, Bruce Farr and Paul Whiting. However two Auckland yachtsmen with their ear to the ground, Ian Gibbs and Gil Hedges, chose Holland designs for their half-tonners — Ian Gibbs with Measure for Measure, *Gil Hedges with* Golden Kiwi.

Whale stories

Over the centuries — the last few at any rate — man has inflicted untold misery on whales, bringing them near to extinction. Once in a while the whale strikes back, and it is usually the hapless yachtsman in the way who is the innocent victim. Interesting though it may be to see a whale spouting not too far away on the ocean, prudence, if not panic, suggests to the boatie that he should move away as quickly and quietly as possible.

Several New Zealanders are among those who have found whales to be their Waterloo.

In the two chapters which follow, a young Aucklander describes how he drifted in the South Atlantic for three days after hitting a whale and experienced skipper Kem Cox relives taking to a liferaft with his crew after his yacht was smashed by whales in mid-Tasman.

South Atlantic saga

From the *New Zealand Herald*

Twenty-six-year-old Aucklander Chris Cels drifted for three days in the South Atlantic after a whale smashed his 5.7 m yacht. He flew back to New Zealand at the end of March 1972, still wearing a pair of trousers borrowed from his rescuers.

HE left Panama on 23 January to sail his yacht to the Galapagos Islands, 1000 miles away. The trip should have taken 15 days.

"I was 48 days at sea. I hit a huge calm and drifted in one spot for two weeks," he related.

About 4 a.m. on 9 March he was drifting when his yacht bumped into a humpback whale floating on the surface. The whale, which was about 7.5 m, lashed out with its tail and split the underside of the hull.

"I worked the pumps for about five hours, but the hole got wider. Then the yacht went down in a matter of seconds and I jumped over the side in my lifejacket," Mr Cels said.

Before leaping overboard he grabbed a plastic case containing the yacht's log, some papers and a small container of water.

He drifted for almost three days before being rescued by an Ecuadorian crayfish trawler. His container of water floated away when he fell asleep.

"The first day I thought I was going to die, but by the beginning of the third day I just didn't care," he said. "My tongue was swollen, I was burned on the face and my lips were blistered. And cold! I was frozen from the neck down." He said he did not think much about anything while floating except about losing the yacht. He had spent months and $2000 rebuilding the yacht after someone abandoned it in Cape Town.

"I wasn't worried about sharks. In fact I didn't see a one during the whole time I was floating. The only thing I saw were large turtles."

On 11 March he heard the engines of a boat. "It was about eight o'clock. The water was like a bathtub – very still. I heard the engines and fired a pencil flare I had in the lifejacket. When I could see the trawler I fired another flare. If the water hadn't been so still, I reckon I'd have had it."

When the Ecuadorian fishermen hauled Mr Cels on board he was only wearing a pair of shorts. The fishermen thought it was a great joke. He tried to explain that he had been sunk by a whale and tried drawing a whale to demonstrate, but the fishermen thought he had drawn a porpoise.

Five days later Mr Cels was put ashore in Guayaquil in Ecuador. "I went to see the British Consul wearing my shorts and the lifejacket."

He cabled his sister, Mrs Simone McClusky, of Meadowbank, for money for his air fare home. While he was waiting, Mr Cels was locked up by police for being vagrant. Fishermen from a British trawler in port bailed him out.

A one-time Post Office employee, Chris Cels left New Zealand in 1967 to work as mate on board South African coastal ships. He decided to sail to South America after rebuilding the yacht. He spent about a year in Trinidad before sailing to Panama.

In spite of his misadventure he wanted to go back to sailing. "I'll go down to the wharves tomorrow to see what trawlers have got jobs doing," he said soon after returning to his parents' home in Sandringham.

Trouble in the Tasman

by K. L. COX

Halfway across the Tasman on their way to take part in the Sydney to Hobart race, Wellingtonian Kem Cox and his crew in his John Spencer-designed plywood sloop Matuku *came upon a school of whales.* Matuku *was going pretty fast under spinnaker, so the crew aimed for a space between two whales. But they must have sailed right over another. There was a tremendous crash and as they looked back they saw three whales where there had been two before.*

So great was the impact that the steel skeg and rudder were torn right out of the bottom, leaving a gap one and a half metres large. Bolts were torn bodily through the frame.

The crew struggled to get the sails down, but as soon as the boat stopped the stern dropped from the planing position and Matuku *started to sink. In about a couple of minutes, before they could get properly organised, she was gone.*

Kem Cox reconstructs the events from his memory and log book.

WE launched our John Spencer-designed yacht in March, 1968. She was a sister ship to John McKenzie's *Sirius.* On Monday 9 December we left Wellington bound for Sydney. The crew besides myself were Edward Borrie, Sven Satre, Ross Baxter, Peter Prendeville, Frank Johnson and Eric Williams. The wind was a fresh southerly of 25-30 knots, but dropping. Conditions in Cook Strait were fair, with a large sea running.

We had a fast passage through the straits until getting becalmed off Stephens Island. On Tuesday and until Saturday 14 December we met with varying conditions, but the yacht was proving to be very comfortable and performing excellently to weather in the large, confused seas we were beating into. Speeds of up to eight knots were being held on the wind. On Friday the wind turned to south-east. The spinnaker was hoisted, the wind strength increased up to 25-30 knots and the yacht was touching 14-15 knots as she slid down the crests of the running seas. Spirits were high, stomachs were full and thoughts of a fast trip were envisaged.

From the morning of 10 December radio contact had been established with the Auckland yacht *Sirius,* our sister ship, and later with the yacht *Jupiter.* A previously arranged schedule of 10 a.m. and 4 p.m. on 2182 kilocycles and then 2284 worked extremely well from this date. Reception was excellent at all times. A spasmodic radio schedule with the Wellington yacht *Arapawa* was attempted, but they appeared to be getting a lot of radio interference.

We carried the fresh south-east wind through the night into the morning of Saturday 14 December, still with the small spinnaker set and making excellent speed, with the yacht virtually sailing herself. On all points of sailing she proved to be extremely light on the helm and easy to control, provided she was not allowed to become heavily over-canvassed.

Several large shoals of whales had been sighted during the previous 24 hours and it was usually necessary to alter course to avoid them. Our speed and quietness of approach seemed to make them unaware of our moving toward them. We all realised that a collision between one of these monsters and a yacht of our size could do great damage, especially at the speed we were travelling.

A good lunch of salad and fresh meat, with several cups of coffee, was consumed at approximately 1 p.m. on the 14th. At 1.45 p.m. a call was put through to Wellington Radio on 2182, but we could not raise them. After the silence period, Wellington Radio was again called, then Auckland Radio, but neither station could be raised. I then decided to wait until our schedule at 8.45 p.m., when conditions would be better. I also intended to try to contact Sydney Radio on 6280, as we were just due to pass the halfway mark.

Everyone was up talking or moving about, with two men on watch on deck. At about 2.30 p.m. the helmsman, Sven Satre, called out excitedly "Whales, whales everywhere round us – all on deck!" I rushed to the companionway with the rest of the crew in time to see a tremendous tail thunder down on the water only inches from the side and showering the boat with spray. There were at least another three outside this one, and on the port side there were others just submerging. Off the bow I could make out another three about 40 ft (12 m) ahead. I held my breath, eyeing the narrow gap we must ease through to escape.

We seemed to have every chance of getting through unscathed, when suddenly there was a grinding crash which heaved and shook the whole boat and momentarily slowed her down. An unseen whale had surfaced right underneath our stern.

A startled yell came from the helmsman, "I have lost the rudder!" I glanced quickly at the rudder stock – there was none. The helmsman was holding an unsupported tiller. I looked below and it was still dry. The spinnaker and mainsail were dropped and all the crew rushed to their posts. The liferaft was unlashed and survival rations placed alongside.

I rushed below to inspect the damage. Water was pouring in rapidly. Lifebelts were thrown on deck along with warm clothing. The batteries were still operating and another attempt was made to send a Mayday signal, but the radio disappeared under water. The water was now over deck level; the radio operator was pulled from below. *Matuku* was now sinking rapidly by the stern.

The liferaft was slowly inflating, but the cord attaching it to the vessel was still made fast. One of the crew was trying to cut through it with a knife, but was being carried down with the ship. Finally he got it free.

We assembled aboard the liferaft, fending off the mast and rigging as *Matuku* slid under the sea. One crew member dislocated his shoulder as he heaved to prevent the rubber of the raft being torn by the rigging.

The time from when we struck the whale to the time of foundering could not have been more than five minutes.

We lay in the liferaft, exhausted, for some minutes, after having a check that all the crew were accounted for. Floating vegetables, notably onions and carrots, were collected from the water. We sorted out our survival gear aboard the raft. Total rations were one gallon (4.5 litres) of methylated spirits, 14 onions, four carrots and no water. In the scramble to get clear, all our other rations were lost. Spirits were high, however. Although we realised that the lack of water could be serious, we were not too concerned about the lack of food.

The raft, an eight-man size, proved to be very cramped for seven men, especially as it was not possible to stretch our legs out. It rained that night and a third of a gallon of water was collected in the meths tin. All we could do now was to wait and hope that our Mayday had been heard. Of this I was extremely doubtful, and by my calculations it could be some time around the 20th to the 23rd before fears for our safety would arise. However I was sure that *Sirius* or *Jupiter,* with whom we had been in regular contact, would raise the alarm if we were not in Sydney when they arrived, which I estimated would be on 20 December.

A constant watch was kept for ships and planes day and night. Three planes were sighted, but by the time the parachute flares were ready to fire they had disappeared into the clouds. Morale was high as the days slowly passed, everyone appearing to be in excellent spirits and, as yet, showing no signs of depression or starvation.

On Wednesday 18 December our supply of water from our tin had not been touched, but the condensation from the canopy of the raft had ceased and it was now necessary to use some of the stored water. Two ounces (55 g) was duly consumed by each man. Some were now starting to show signs of exhaustion. Still no more rain had fallen. All we needed was one good shower.

On the night of the 18th a lively discussion was held as to when we would be found. All were in good spirits, although I could see we would have to double our water ration to survive. This meant our water would last until 21 to 22 of December.

The next morning we resumed our discussion and a bet was placed that we would sight a ship in half an hour. To our amazement, in half an hour the look-out called that there was a tanker on the horizon. We could hardly believe it at first, but after our initial surprise was over, we fired off our flares. Our one parachute flare finally fired successfully and was seen by the tanker.

The ship flashed three white lights to tell us we had been sighted and altered course toward us. It took about an hour for the ship to manoeuvre close enough so that we could paddle towards it. It proved to be the BP tanker, *British Queen.* A rope was lowered and we secured it to the raft, although the swell was lifting us 10 to 12 ft (3 m) and dropping us again. Our final thought was to make sure that the liferaft which had saved us was also safely brought aboard.

We were rescued. It was a miracle!

It was indeed a miracle. The freighter, which was two days overdue on its voyage, was actually taking a short cut through a slice of ocean not on its regular course.

Kem Cox was not deterred by his narrow escape. The skipper visited John Spencer on his way home through Auckland and ordered a new yacht, to be named Savant. *He sailed her in the 1977 Auckland to Suva race.*

A sad postscript to this miraculous escape was written on 26 December 1976 when Frank Johnson, the radio operator who had survived the sinking of the Matuku, *fell overboard from the sloop* Reremai *in Cook Strait and was drowned.*

Index

Picture references in **bold**; facing page number is given.

ALSO FROM REEDS

Little Ships of New Zealand *by Paul Titchener*
The original *Little Ships* by Ronald Carter was a popular book in the 1940s. Paul Titchener has now brought the story up to date. He picks up where Carter left off, tracing the development of New Zealand yachting through the plywood revolution in 1950s to the yachting explosion in the 1960s and 1970s. New Zealand's great international racing successes are covered in full. The book includes a superb collection of yachting photographs.

Trailer-Sailers *by Jeff Toghill*
All that the yachtsman needs to know about trailer-sailers – buying a trailer-sailer, keels and stability, fittings, handling, trailering, maintenance. The book also includes a comprehensive guide to the main trailer-sailer designs that can be bought in New Zealand and Australia.

The Yachtsman's Navigation Manual *by Jeff Toghill*
A practical approach to the navigation problems faced by both cruising and racing yachtsmen. Covers every aspect of accurate navigation needed by the yachtsman and includes invaluable information on planning long ocean voyages and sailing in far-off waters. Fully illustrated.

Sailing for Beginners *by Jeff Toghill*
The young sailor will find in this book basic but comprehensive information about sailing boats of all sizes and classes. Starting with sails and rigging, the author covers how to get underway, starting positions, boat handling, balancing, spinnakers, ropes and cordage.

The Boat Owner's Maintenance Manual *by Jeff Toghill*
A comprehensive volume covering all aspects of the maintenance and repair of yachts, from sailing dinghies to keelers, and power craft from the small runabout to the large launch.

The Galley Cookbook *by Gwen Skinner*
A practical approach to cooking at sea, based on the assumption that only simple galley equipment is at hand and that food storage and water tankage are limited. Specially designed for easy reading in difficult conditions.

Away they go! Half-tonners off to a good start off Orakei Wharf with the Royal Akarana Yacht Club on a brisk winter race day. *Neil MacKinnon*